The Liquid Metal Fast Breeder Reactor

The Liquid Metal

FAST BREEDER REACTOR

An Environmental and Economic Critique

THOMAS B. COCHRAN

Published by Resources for the Future, Inc.
Distributed by The Johns Hopkins University Press
Baltimore and London

RESOURCES FOR THE FUTURE, INC.
1755 Massachusetts Avenue, N.W., Washington, D.C. 20036

Resources for the Future is a nonprofit corporation for research and education in
the development, conservation, and use of natural resources and the improvement
of the quality of the environment. It was established in 1952 with the cooperation
of the Ford Foundation. Part of the work of Resources for the Future is carried
out by its resident staff; part is supported by grants to universities and other nonprofit organizations. Unless otherwise stated, interpretations and conclusions in
RFF publications are those of the authors; the organization takes responsibility for
the selection of significant subjects for study, the competence of the researchers,
and their freedom of inquiry.

This book is one of RFF's policy studies, prepared under the auspices of the quality
of the environment program, directed by Allen V. Kneese. It was edited by Joan
R. Tron. Figures were drawn by Clare and Frank Ford.

RFF editors: Mark Reinsberg, Joan R. Tron, Ruth B. Haas, Margaret Ingram.

Preface

In this monograph Thomas Cochran takes a critical look at the economic and environmental arguments which have been made in favor of an early introduction of the liquid metal fast breeder reactor (LMFBR) as a central component of the United States electrical energy system. In general he finds that the economic arguments put forth are open to many serious questions. Furthermore, on balance, the LMFBR appears to have no environmental advantage over the presently operating light water reactors and especially not over the high temperature gas reactor, which is another developed nuclear technology.

To many, the most compelling argument in favor of introducing breeders rapidly is the limited supply of high quality uranium ore available. A breeder-based energy economy is capable of extracting vastly more energy from a given supply of uranium than are non-breeder fission reactors. However, as with many other ores, commonly used estimates of current stocks are based on explorations that have already taken place; further exploration is most likely to expand known reserves. Even so, the problem of exhaustion still would be serious if it were true, as many believe, that the uranium from which fuel for nonbreeder fission reactors has been extracted is of no further use. But this is not the case. If fusion is not developed in time, breeders could still be introduced later to extract the same overall energy from a given supply of uranium as if they had been introduced earlier. Thus, early introduction would seem to have to depend heavily on the economic and environmental arguments which Cochran questions.

v

Even though its scope is deliberately narrow, this study should be a useful addition to the national discussion of energy strategy. By implication it sheds light on some large issues of great pertinence.

Abundant low-cost energy is a matter of great importance to the continued prosperity of the American economy. It is not stretching the truth much to say that energy is *the* key resource. It permits us to extract useful materials from ores of declining quality and will, no doubt, in the future be used in large quantities for recycling operations. Declining energy costs have been one of the key factors in productivity gain for many years. A problem is that, especially in the recent past, low power costs have been bought at the expense of much environmental disruption. Private costs and social costs have become significantly out of balance.

In contemplating a future energy strategy for the United States, we must realistically face the fact that none of the sources which exist or are on the relatively near-term horizon are free of major environmental problems. Even the "natural" sources of solar heat and geothermal steam, on close examination, carry their share of environmental difficulties. In the face of this, some have advocated what to most appears to be a radical strategy—to depend heavily on better control of the environmental impacts of using fossil fuel and to push hard for the early development of fusion energy, thus bypassing fission entirely as a major energy source. As an intermediate-level alternative, efforts could be pressed to make sure the high temperature gas reactor can be safely introduced and operated as work continues on on various types of breeder designs, while still pressing hard to develop fusion.

These large strategic questions of high importance are not resolved in this report. To do so would require a much broader inquiry than is reported here. But this study does provide one important piece of the analysis needed to develop a rational overall energy policy, not only with a view to costs in the usual sense but with respect to managing environmental disruption as well. A broad program of research and development in the energy area deserves strong support as a matter of high national priority.

Allen V. Kneese
Director
Quality of the Environment
Program

Acknowledgments

The author is particularly indebted to his colleague Milton Searl, whose comments and guidance provided a basis for much of the material in this study. In addition, valuable criticism and helpful comments were obtained from Blair Bower, Charles Cicchetti, Joel Darmstadter, Edwin Haefele, the late Orris Herfindahl, Allen Kneese, Hans Landsberg, Kerry Smith, and other staff members at RFF. The secretarial services of Vera Ullrich and the editorial services of Joan Tron are greatly appreciated.

Additional help was obtained from a number of individuals not at RFF, including many who reviewed an earlier draft manuscript.

Contents

Tables

Figures

The Liquid Metal Fast Breeder Reactor

Introduction

Since 1946 the United States has acquired twenty-seven years of engineering development and over thirty plant-years of pilot plant experience with liquid metal fast breeder reactors (LMFBRs). The scientific feasibility of breeding fissile fuel has been demonstrated with two small operational LMFBRs, Experimental Breeder Reactor I and II, in the United States, and with several similar plants in the U.S.S.R., United Kingdom, and France. However, the economic benefits and safety of commercial-size LMFBRs has yet to be demonstrated.

Since 1967 the Atomic Energy Commission (AEC) has accorded the LMFBR the highest priority of the civilian reactor development program, in an effort to make this energy source a commercial reality.

In 1971 Commissioner Ramey summarized the AEC's view of the economic and environmental benefits of the LMFBR program:

By taking full advantage of the fast breeder, we can extend our use of the uranium reserves from decades to thousands of years and at the same time produce economic electric power. ... The cost of power from the fast breeder will be relatively insensitive to the cost of uranium; this will permit the economic use of low-grade as well as high-grade uranium ores.

In addition to the economic and resource conservation benefits associated with the breeder, we believe that significant environmental advantages will accrue from its use. Like the light water reactor, the breeder will not add products of combustion to the atmosphere. Since the breeder will operate at high thermal efficiencies, the amount of waste heat

1

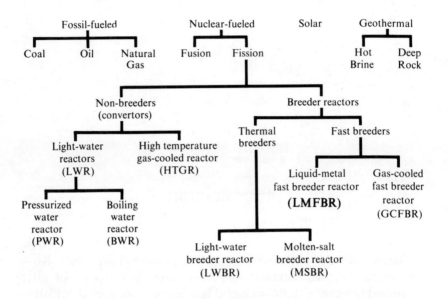

released to the environment per unit of power produced will be comparable to that from the modern fossil fueled power plant. Finally, because of its inherent characteristics, the liquid metal fast breeder can be readily designed to even improve on the already very low releases of radioactive wastes to the environment at the nuclear plant site.[1]

The liquid metal fast breeder reactor is one of several such reactor types and, of course, one of many nuclear energy sources.

In order to place this reactor in proper context, it may be useful to the reader to examine the illustration above, which shows the relationship of the LMFBR to other energy sources, particularly those discussed in this report.

According to the AEC, the LMFBR was chosen over other breeder concepts:

. . . principally because of predicted performance, industrial support, a broad base of technological experience and proven basic feasibility. These advantages offer the best prospect that this concept can be brought to commercial usefulness in a relatively short time period.[2]

[1]James T. Ramey, "The Breeder Reactor: Need for Greater Utility Participation," AEC Press Release S-44-70 (Dec. 10, 1971).

[2]U.S. Atomic Energy Commission, *Liquid Metal Fast Breeder Reactor Demonstration Plant Environmental Statement*, WASH 1509 (April 1972), p. 17.

Based on the AEC's recommendations and the belief that its position with respect to the need for an early commitment to the LMFBR is sound, the United States government has launched a national program plan in an effort to develop large, economically viable, commercial-scale LMFBRs by the mid-1980s.[3] The LMFBR program has proceeded in accordance with the plan along two complementary lines—the technology development or "base" program[4] and the LMFBR demonstration plant effort. As part of this latter effort, the government has given full support to developing the first demonstration plant, and funds have been authorized for preliminary design work on a second. The arrangements for financing, constructing, and managing the first demonstration plant were spelled out in a 1972 Memorandum of Understanding and a subsequent series of detailed contracts among the AEC, Tennessee Valley Authority (TVA), Commonwealth Edison Co., Project Management Corporation, and Breeder Reactor Corporation. The Memorandum of Understanding and the contracts have the approval of the Joint Committee on Atomic Energy. Through personnel and services provided to the Project Management Corporation, Commonwealth Edison will manage the project and TVA will construct and operate the plant, which will produce about 350 to 400 Mw of power to the TVA system.[5] Construction of the plant is due to begin in 1974 or 1975, with power generation unlikely before 1981 or 1982. A site has been selected near Oak Ridge, Tennessee, and Westinghouse Electric Corporation has been selected as the prime reactor manufacturer. According to the Memorandum, the total cost of the demonstration plant project will be about $700 million, approximately two-thirds of which will come from the AEC.

The purpose of this study is to evaluate this heavy commitment by analyzing the economic and environmental claims made for the

[3]U.S. Atomic Energy Commission, *Liquid Metal Fast Breeder Reactor Program Plan*, Vols. 1-10, WASH 1101-1110 (1968), prepared for the Division of Reactor Development and Technology by Argonne National Laboratory.

[4]The LMFBR "base" program is focused on safety research, the development and testing of components as well as the construction and operation of test facilities.

[5]One Mw is one million watts (megawatts) or 1000 kilowatts (kw), electrical. In this paper, power plant ratings are given in electrical rather than thermal units. Although the Memorandum of Understanding lists as a design parameter 350-Mw to 400-Mw net electric power, an earlier description of Westinghouse demonstration plant indicates 300 Mw. See W. M. Jacobi, "Westinghouse Liquid Metal Fast Breeder Reactor Demonstration Plant Design," *Combustion* (June 1971), pp. 49-58.

LMFBR by the AEC and others. The reader may note that the discussion is almost entirely critical. This does not mean that no part of the AEC's analysis is valid, or, indeed, that the LMFBR is a poorer choice than some alternative energy sources. It means merely that I have chosen to discuss only those parts of the AEC's analysis that I feel are sufficiently invalid (or poorly reasoned, or exaggerated) to raise serious doubts about the overall favorable results reported by the AEC. In short, the intent is to provide a more proper balance to discussions of energy alternatives in the hope of providing a better basis for ultimate policy decisions.

Today, the LMFBR is the largest single energy R&D effort in the federal government. Given the huge sums already spent on the LMFBR program and, more importantly, the even larger sums estimated for future expenditure (see Introduction to Part I), I believe it is legitimate to raise questions about the desirability of continuing this heavy commitment to the LMFBR program on a priority basis and to look in detail at the evidence offered by the AEC to support its recommendations. While much has already been spent, commercial demonstration plants have not yet been built,[6] and there is still time to rethink the problem without undue loss.

The central policy questions are the following:

1. Will safe, reliable, commercial-size LMFBRs be economical in the foreseeable future, and, if so, when?

2. Will the economic advantages (if any) outweigh the health and environmental risks from unscheduled events following large-scale commercial utilization?

While the basic question of what the optimal energy R&D program should be is beyond the scope of this analysis, my thesis is that, given what we know or can best estimate about the cost and environmental consequences of each type of energy source, an allocation far less heavily weighted toward early commercial introduction of the LMFBR would constitute a better R&D strategy, and my discussion is in part directed toward this view.

In the chapters that follow, I make a detailed analysis of the AEC's latest (1970) cost-benefit analysis of the program, since this analysis is still being used by the AEC as economic justification

---

[6]Except Fermi-I, a 61-Mw LMFBR, which was closed in 1972 for lack of funds. In nine years, the facility operated at full capacity for a total of only 378 hours.

for the program.[7] Particular attention is given to the sensitivity of the results of this 1970 Analysis to changes in some of the most important or critical input variables.

Probably the most critical variables are the capital costs of nuclear plants, namely, the LMFBR, the light water reactors (LWRs), and the high temperature gas-cooled reactor (HTGR). These costs are examined, along with the fuel cycle costs and reactor performance assumptions, in Chapter 2. The sensitivity of the 1970 Analysis results to changes in electrical energy demand assumptions is examined in Chapter 4.

Any discussion of whether to implement or postpone commercial availability of the LMFBR more than one or two decades beyond the currently proposed date (1986) should include a more accurate assessment of available uranium resources and consideration of alternate electrical energy generation programs, including other breeder reactor programs, coal gasification, fuel cells, geothermal and solar energy, and fusion. The availability of uranium resources is discussed in Chapter 3. A thorough analysis of alternative energy programs is not made,[8] nor is an attempt made to justify alternative priorities for federal and nonfederal energy research and development expenditures. However, in Chapter 5 a brief discussion is devoted to the high temperature gas-cooled reactor. The HTGR is currently entering the commercial market and, assuming its commercial success, it could be the principal competitor to the LMFBR despite the fact that it is not a breeder. The gas-cooled fast breeder reactor (GCFBR) is also discussed briefly in the same chapter. Even though it is less well developed, the GCFBR appears to have economic, performance, and safety advantages over the LMFBR, and, with commercial development, it could give the LMFBR strong competition in the 1990s and beyond.

The second part of this volume is devoted to a discussion of environmental aspects of an energy economy that includes reliance on the LMFBR as a principal source of energy. Chapter 6 examines

[7]See for example, "Liquid Metal Fast Breeder Reactor, Proposed Determination Pending Preparation of Environmental Impact Statement," *Federal Register,* 38 (June 29, 1973), pp. 17263-17264.

[8]The thermal breeders, that is, the light-water breeder and the molten-salt breeder, are not discussed further in this report. The light-water breeder is currently being developed by the AEC's Division of Naval Reactors. The molten-salt breeder was under development at Oak Ridge National Laboratory until the AEC dropped this program in fiscal 1973 because of budget priorities. Congress has authorized additional funding for this program in fiscal 1974.

the routine releases of residuals from LMFBRs and other nuclear plants, and for the most part dismisses these as being relatively unimportant to LMFBR development strategy. Chapter 7 examines what I believe are the most critical environmental problems, or risks, associated with an LMFBR economy, namely, those that arise from unscheduled events. Particular attention here is given to: (1) reactor accidents, (2) the release into the environment of one of the most carcinogenic materials known to man—the plutonium fuel— which is also the material bred by LMFBRs, and (3) the possible unauthorized use of this material to construct nuclear weapons or plutonium dispersal devices.

Readers not wishing to labor through the details of the discussion may find it useful to read the summary and conclusions in Part III.

I

Economic Considerations

Introduction to Part I

LMFBR PROGRAM EXPENDITURES: ACTUAL AND ESTIMATED

According to official sources, federal expenditures on the LMFBR from 1969 through 1972 totaled $682 million (see Table 1). This includes expenditures for research and development, as well as operating, equipment, and construction costs; it does not include costs of research on environmental and health hazards from low-dose radiation exposure. During these four years, the proportion of federal R&D energy expenditures attributable to the LMFBR increased from 37 percent to 45 percent. However, according to one estimate, the actual resources committed may have been much higher because many of the AEC's general reactor technology and safety programs have been diverted to solving problems specific to the breeder.[1]

In Table 1, federal expenditures for the LMFBR program are compared with other federal energy R&D funding during the 1969-73 fiscal-year period. As the table shows, federal energy R&D expenditures for fiscal 1973 will be about $622 million. About $260 million of this (42 percent) is allocated to the LMFBR program; $95 million (15 percent) to all other civilian nuclear power programs; $94 million (about 15 percent) to coal, one-third of which is for health and safety research; $65 million (10 percent) to fusion

---

[1] Allen L. Hammond, "Management of U.S. Breeder Program Draws Criticism," *Science,* 174 (Nov. 19, 1971), p. 809.

9

TABLE 1.   Federal Energy Research and Development Funding,
Fiscal Year 1969 Through 1973

(millions of dollars)

Energy type	1969	1970	1971	1972	1973
Coal resources development (total)	23.3	30.4	49.0	76.8	94.4
Production and utilization R&D	21.0	26.7	34.2	45.8	64.3
Mining health and safety research	2.3	3.7	14.8	31.0	30.1
Petroleum and natural gas (total)	13.5	14.8	17.5	23.8	26.1
Petroleum extraction technology	2.6	2.7	2.7	3.2	3.1
Nuclear gas stimulation[a]	2.4	3.7	6.1	7.0	7.5
Oil shale	2.5	2.4	2.7	2.6	2.5
Continental shelf mapping	6.0	6.0	6.0	11.0	13.0
Nuclear fission (total)	277.1	253.4	265.6	328.1	356.3
LMFBR[a]	132.5	144.3	167.9	237.4	261.5
Other civilian nuclear power[b]	144.6	109.1	97.7	90.7	94.8
Nuclear fusion (total)	31.8	37.5	41.6	47.2	65.4
Magnetic confinement[b]	29.7	34.3	32.3	33.2	40.3
Laser-pellet[a,b]	2.1	3.2	9.3	14.0	25.1
Energy conversion with less environmental impact (total)	12.3	22.9	22.8	33.4	55.3
Cleaner fuels R&D—stationary sources	10.7	19.8	17.4	24.5	29.5
SO$_x$ removal				2.6	15.2
Improved energy systems	0.3	0.8	3.0	2.4	2.8
Thermal effects R&D	1.3	2.3	2.4	3.9	2.8[c]
General energy R&D (total)	3.0	4.2	8.7	15.4	24.1
Energy resources research[d]		1.1	5.0	9.8	13.4
Geothermal resources	0.1	0.2	0.2	0.7	2.5
Engineering energetics research	2.9	2.9	2.7	4.0	4.7
Underground transmission			0.8	0.9	1.0
Cryogenic generation					1.0
Nonnuclear energy R&D					1.5
Total	361.0	363.2	405.2	524.7	621.6

SOURCE: Edward E. David (then director of the Office of Science and Technology), in *Liquid Metal Fast Breeder Reactor (LMFBR) Demonstration Plant,* Hearings before the U.S. Congress, Joint Committee on Atomic Energy, 92 Cong. 2 sess. (Sept. 7, 8, 12, 1972), pp. 164–65.

NOTE: The funding listed in these tables covers the federal R&D programs in development exploration and production, conversion, and transmission of our energy resources. This funding includes energy conversion R&D for stationary applications only; R&D funding for improved mobile applications (e.g., automotive, rail, seagoing) are not included. Fundamental research on environmental health effects of combustion products and low-dose radiation exposure is not included.

[a]This funding includes operation, equipment, and construction costs.

[b]The primary applications of the multipurpose laser-pellet effort are for other than energy production.

[c]This entry includes $1,500,000 for dry cooling tower R&D under the AEC's new nonnuclear energy R&D category. Other related work is carried out under other civilian nuclear power.

[d]The NSF RANN program includes research on solar energy as well as fundamental energy policy studies.

energy; and $26 million (4 percent) to petroleum and natural gas. Some $4 to $5 million—less than 1 percent—is being spent for solar energy research with terrestrial applications.[2]

The AEC and the Office of Management and Budget (OMB) break down the total LMFBR program expenditures for fiscal 1972 and 1973 as follows:[3]

	1972	*1973*
	(millions of dollars)	
Operating budget	190	204
Capital equipment	7	10
Construction	42	47
Total	239	261

The operating budget includes the LMFBR base ($122 million for 1972 and $132 million for 1973), the LMFBR portion of the general reactor technology budget (about 75 percent), the fast reactor safety budget ($14.5 million for 1972 and $19.7 million for 1973), and the LMFBR demonstration plant budget ($1.8 million for 1972 and $8 million for 1973).

The Memorandum of Understanding (discussed earlier) estimates the total demonstration plant project cost, including 30 percent escalation, as $700 million.[4] Privately and publicly owned U.S. electric utilities have pledged, through the Breeder Reactor Corporation, approximately $250 million toward the plant's financing. In addition, an estimated $4 million in administrative costs will be incurred by TVA and Commonwealth Edison for which the two utilities will not be reimbursed.

Through the AEC, the government has already authorized about $100 million toward the project. Eight million dollars of this has already been spent for design studies. The remaining $92 million is available for actual construction costs. Under the Memorandum of Understanding, the AEC is obligated to put up the additional

[2]George P. Miller, Representative from California, in "A Focus for Solar Energy," *Congressional Record* (May 31, 1972), p. H 5130.

[3]U.S. Office of Management and Budget staff, oral response to inquiry.

[4]This is $150 to $200 million higher than an AEC estimate only six months earlier. See Milton Shaw, Director of AEC's Division of Reactor Development and Technology, at Hearings before the U.S. Congress, Joint Committee on Atomic Energy, on *AEC Authorizing Legislation—Fiscal Year 1973*, Part 2 (February 22, 1972), p. 1157.

FIGURE 1. Anticipated LMFBR Program Expenditures

(a)   LMFBR Program
Government vs. Private Industrial Estimated Annual Expenditures, 1972-1978

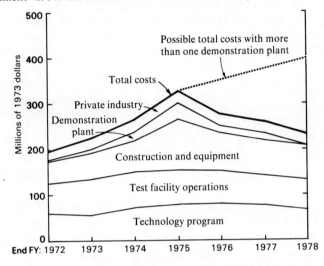

(b)
Anticipated Cumulative Governmental Expenditures vs. Utility Commitments
for LMFBR

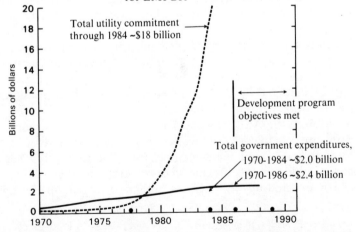

SOURCE: Part (a): *AEC Authorizing Legislation—Fiscal Year 1974,*
Hearings before the Joint Committee on Atomic Energy, 93 Cong., 1 sess.
(1973), p. 1760. Part (b): *AEC Authorizing Legislation—Fiscal Year 1972,*
Hearings before the Joint Committee on Atomic Energy, 92 Cong., 1 sess.
(1971), p. 96.

$350 million in estimated costs plus any cost overruns. The AEC will assume all costs of decommissioning the plant unless TVA decides to buy the plant, a decision TVA does not have to make until five years after completion of operational testing, which TVA will conduct.

The Administration's fiscal 1974 budget includes $772 million for energy-related R&D, of which $323 million (42 percent) is for the LMFBR program. Robert Gillette, whose breakdown of budget categories and budget figures differs slightly from those of E. E. David in Table 1, estimates that the LMFBR 1974 budget is up $50 million from 1973.[5]

At the request of the Administration, the AEC has prepared a study detailing where an additional $100 million on energy R&D will be spent in fiscal 1974.[6] Half of this will go to coal, $7.3 million to geothermal, and $3.5 million to solar energy. Only $6.5 million of these additional funds will be spent on nuclear R&D, and all of this is to go to the gas-cooled reactor programs.

Projected budget requests for the LMFBR program were presented by Milton Shaw in hearings before the Joint Committee on Atomic Energy. Figure 1(a) shows the estimated annual costs for the LMFBR program through 1977. Figure 1(b) shows the anticipated cumulative governmental and utility expenditures through 1986 and 1984, respectively.

An AEC summary of estimated civilian nuclear power R&D costs, which appears to have been prepared about the same time, is presented in the *Updated (1970) Cost-Benefit Analysis of the U.S. Breeder Reactor Program*[7] (referred to in this report as the

---

[5]Robert Gillette, "Energy," *Science,* 179 (Feb. 9, 1973), pp. 549-50. According to Gillette, the fiscal 74 budget also includes: $120 million for the production and utilization of coal—up $25 million; $9 million for production of other fossil fuels (petroleum and natural gas); $88 million for fusion, of which $44 million (up $7 million) is for nonmilitary R&D (this would imply that much of the laser-pellet R&D in Table 1 is for military application); $62 million for nuclear fuel process development; $90 million for other nuclear power; $16 million for solar and geothermal energy—double the fiscal 73 figure; and $63 million for other energy-related programs. The fuel process development and other (than LMFBR) nuclear power funds include $7 million for the HTGR; $2 million for thorium utilization; and $1 million for the GCFBR.

[6]The breakdown of this spending proposal is presented in *Weekly Energy Report* (Sept. 17, 1973), pp. 6-8.

[7]U.S. Atomic Energy Commission, Division of Reactor Development and Technology, *Updated (1970) Cost-Benefit Analysis of the U.S. Breeder Reactor Program*, WASH 1184 (Jan. 1972).

1970 Analysis). These data are reproduced in Table 2.

Comparing the estimates from the 1974 hearings and those in the 1970 Analysis with the budget estimates by David (shown in Table 1), several observations can be made. First, the estimated costs for fiscal 1970–73 in Figure 1(a) are lower than the LMFBR program expenditures in Table 1. This is because the term

TABLE 2. Summary of Estimated AEC Cumulative Research and Development Costs, Mid-1971 to 2020

(billions of dollars)

Reactor type	Date of LMFBR introduction				
	1984 (B-1)	1986 (B-2)	1990 (B-3)	1994 (B-4)	1986 with parallel breeder in 1994 (B-5)
Breeders					
LMFBR	2.3	2.5	3.1	3.7	2.5
Other breeders	0.1	0.1	0.1	0.1	1.9
Supporting technology	1.0	1.2	1.4	1.6	1.6
Total breeders	3.4	3.8	4.6	5.4	6.0
Nonbreeders					
Converters	0.1	0.1	0.1	0.1	0.1
Supporting technology	0.4	0.4	0.4	0.4	0.4
Total nonbreeders	0.5	0.5	0.5	0.5	0.5
General support	2.7	2.5	2.3	2.1	2.6
Grand total	6.6	6.8	7.4	8.0	9.1
	Cost of total breeders discounted to mid-1971				
Discount rate (percent)					
5	2.5	2.7	3.1	3.4	4.0
7	2.3	2.4	2.7	2.9	3.6
10	2.0	2.1	2.3	2.4	3.0
12.5	1.8	1.9	2.0	2.1	2.6

SOURCE: U.S. Atomic Energy Commission, Division of Reactor Development and Technology, *Updated (1970) Cost-Benefit Analysis of the U.S. Breeder Reactor Program,* WASH 1184 (Jan. 1972), pp. 10–11.

NOTE:

LMFBR commercially introduced in:*

B-1   Accelerated breeder program   1984
B-2   Currently planned breeder program   1986
B-3   Four-year delay in breeder development program   1990
B-4   Eight-year delay in breeder development program   1994
B-5   PBR program with parallel breeder introduced in 1994   1986

*Commercial introduction is defined as the date when a significant number of commercial-size LMFBR power plants become operational.

"LMFBR Program" in Figure 1(a) describes a budget category and does not include LMFBR-related costs in other budget categories, e.g., "Nuclear Safety" and "General Reactor Technology." To this extent, then, the estimates embodied in Figure 1(a) are understated.

According to the 1970 AEC estimate reproduced in Table 2, the U.S. breeder program was to eventually cost (from mid-1971) an additional $3.4 billion to $6.0 billion in federal funds alone, and, as seen from Figure 1(b), may influence the way in which the utility companies will spend billions more per year on energy systems by the end of the century. However, the projected LMFBR program expenditures in Table 2 (up to $6.0 billion) are understated to the extent that a major share of the funding in the "General Support" category is also directed toward support of the LMFBR program. In October 1973, it was reported the AEC's unofficial estimate of LMFBR costs was $5.1.[8] This estimate (in 1973 dollars) covers the fourteen-year period 1974 to 1988, and, as reported, includes $1 billion for "general" R&D that would indirectly benefit the LMFBR and $90 million that would be spent in direct assistance to utilities to help them buy their first four commercial-size breeder power plants.[9]

It is not clear whether the $2.4 billion, labeled in Figure 1(b) as the cumulative governmental expenditures between 1970 and 1986, is consistent with the data presented in Table 2. If, for example, it is the same as the estimated total breeder expenditures discounted at 7 percent in Table 2, then the values for the discounted cost of the breeder program, which were used to calculate net benefits and benefit-to-cost ratios in the 1970 Analysis represent expenditures through 1986 (or the appropriate LMFBR market entry date) and exclude further expenditures, such as the light-water reactor (LWR) program is incurring today (e.g., Power Burst Facility, Loss of Fluid Test Facility, etc.). In any case, it is clear that the net benefits and benefit-to-cost ratios in the 1970 Analysis exclude the nonfederal breeder R&D costs provided by the nuclear industry.

The total utility commitment through 1984 is estimated in Figure 1(b). While it is unclear how much of this represents capital

[8]Robert Gillette, "One Breeder for the Price of Two?" *Science* 182 (October 5, 1973), p. 38.
[9]Ibid.

equipment and other expenditures that should not be included as
R&D costs, it does suggest that if nonfederal R&D costs were
included in the 1970 Analysis, the net benefits and benefit-to-cost
ratios would be considerably lower.

Based on past experience with nuclear reactor programs, the
LMFBR program is likely to continue to experience considerable
cost overruns. Paul MacAvoy, reporting on the ratio of realized-
to-forecast construction expenditures for AEC reactor programs
prior to 1967 (see Table 3) noted, "all projects failed to stay within

TABLE 3.   Ratio of Realized to Forecast Reactor Construction Costs

Reactor type	Ratio of realized to forecast expenditures on construction, for all reactors of that type completed before 1967	Number of reactors
Pressurized water reactor	1.2	3
Boiling water reactor	1.4	5
Heavy water reactor	1.7	1
Gas-cooled reactor	1.9	1
Sodium graphite reactor	2.4	1
	>2.0	Canceled
Homogeneous reactor	1.6	1
Organic-cooled reactor	2.1	1

SOURCE: Paul W. MacAvoy, *Economic Strategy for Developing Nuclear Breeder Reactors* (Cambridge: M.I.T. Press, 1969), p. 114.

predesignated levels of capital costs; ... the average ratio of
actual-to-design costs was greater than 1.5 for all projects."[10] This
of course does not of necessity imply that the LMFBR program will
suffer similar results. However, the total cost estimate for the Fast
Flux Test Facility (FFTF), an integral part of the LMFBR program, has increased by at least $167 million in the past four years,
1.9 times the fiscal 1970 estimate.[11] This does not include another

[10]Paul M. MacAvoy, *Economic Strategy for Developing Nuclear Breeder Reactors*
(Cambridge: M.I.T. Press, 1969), p. 115.
[11]The total cost estimate—Plant and Capital Equipment (PACE) and R&D costs
related to construction—increased $83 million, from $192.5 million in fiscal 70 to
$275.9 million in fiscal 73. See "FFTF Total Cost Estimates Face $83 Million Over-
run," *Nuclear Industry*, 19 (Aug. 1972), pp. 15-16 [no author indicated]. The
Administration's fiscal 74 budget estimate for total FFTF PACE funds is $187.85
million, up $85 million from the fiscal 73 estimate.

$300 million or so for related hardware and R&D that is hidden in the base program budget category. Likewise, in March 1971, the AEC estimated the total cost of the LMFBR demonstration plant to be $400 to $500 million;[12] in February 1972, $450 to $550 million;[13] and seven months later, in September 1972, $538 to $756 million.[14] If cost overruns continue to plague the LMFBR program, they could significantly alter the benefit-to-cost estimates in the 1970 Analysis.

THE DEVELOPMENT OF AEC COST-BENEFIT STUDIES

In 1966, as part of its continuing program assessment and at the request of the Joint Committee on Atomic Energy (JCAE), the AEC initiated an overall review of the U.S. civilian nuclear program. The Division of Reactor Development and Technology established a number of task forces to consider the technical prospects for reactor concepts under consideration and to provide the initial development of an analytical program for a model of the U.S. electrical power economy. The application of this model would be used to evaluate the benefits of alternate courses of electric power system development.

The Model

The power economy model that was developed simulates the U.S. electrical energy economy, using a cash-flow basis to establish the relationship between the various participants in the construction and operation of power plants. The analysis centers around a linear programming model used to calculate the (discounted) minimum cost of supplying U.S. electrical energy needs for the next fifty years (mid-1970 to 2020).

It should, perhaps, be noted here that the model was primarily designed to study trade-offs among nuclear power plants. For this reason, the AEC devoted less attention to analysis of fossil-fuel-related inputs. (For a brief discussion of the economic structure of the model, see Appendix A.)[15]

[12]*AEC Authorizing Legislation–FY 1972*, p. 702.
[13]*AEC Authorizing Legislation–FY 1973*, pp. 1156-1159.
[14]*Liquid Metal Fast Breeder Reactor Demonstration Plant*, Hearings, p. 44.
[15]Appendix A is reproduced from U.S. Atomic Energy Commission, *Reactor Fuel Cycle Costs for Nuclear Power Evaluation*, WASH 1099 (December 1971), prepared

TABLE 4. Summary of AEC's Cost-Benefit Analyses of LMFBR

(a) 1970 results			*(billions of dollars)*
	No breeder	LMFBR intro. '86	Savings
Power cost			
Undiscounted	$2,704	$2,346	$358
Discounted at 7%	437.4	415.9	21.5
Cost of breeder R&D program discounted at 7%		2.4	
Net savings, discounted at 7%			19.1
Benefit-to-cost ratio at 7% discount rate = 9			

(b) 1968 results			
	No breeder	LMFBR intro. '84	Savings
Power cost			
Undiscounted	$1,539	$1,332	$207
Discounted at 7%	214.7	205.6	9.1
Cost of breeder R&D program discounted at 7%		2.5	
Net savings, discounted at 7%			6.6
Benefit-to-cost ratio at 7% discount rate = 3.6			

SOURCE: *AEC Authorizing Legislation—Fiscal Year 1972,* Hearings before the Joint Committee on Atomic Energy of the U.S. Congress, 92 Cong. 1 sess. (1971), p. 690.

NOTE: In addition to other tangible benefits not listed above, the AEC indicates in the 1970 Analysis that 2,360,000 metric tons of U_3O_8 and 139,000 metric tons per year of separative work demand would be saved.

An indication of the sensitivity of the model is illustrated by the following AEC figures (discounted at 7% to mid-1971):

Delaying breeder beyond 1986	loss of $2.00 bill. per year
50% increase in uranium availability	loss of $1.4 bill.
20% decrease in energy demand	loss of $6.7 bill.
20% increase in energy demand	gain of $4.5 bill.
10% increase in total plant cost (equivalent to a 30% increase in steam supply system capital costs)	loss of $10.4 bill.

---

by the staff of Oak Ridge National Laboratory (ORNL). There are minor differences among the models used in the AEC's cost-benefit studies, newer versions of these models, and similar models used at ORNL. The differences are not important to this discussion.

More detailed descriptions of the model and the methods used in the cost-benefit analyses are contained in: M.J. Whitman, A.N. Tardiff, and P.L. Hofmann, "U.S. Civilian Nuclear Power Cost-Benefit Analysis" (presented at the Fourth United Nations International Conference on the Peaceful Uses of Atomic Energy, Geneva, Switzerland, Sept. 6-16, 1971); D.E. Deonigi, "A Simulation of the U.S. Power Economy, *"Proceedings American Power Conference,* 32 (1970), pp. 105-115; U.S. AEC, *Potential Nuclear Power Growth Patterns;* R.W. Hardie, W.E. Black, and W.W. Little, *ALPS, A Linear Programming System for Forecasting Optimum Power Growth Patterns,* HEDL-TME 72-31, Hanford Engineering Development Laboratory (April 1972).

TABLE 5. Estimated Increase (Decrease) in 1970 Analysis Benefits Compared
with 1968 Analysis, Discounted at 7 Percent to Mid-1971[a]

| | *(billions of dollars)* |
| | Increase (+) or decrease (−) |
Variable	in benefits
Energy demand	+12.4
Separative work cost[b]	+ 6.7
Fossil-fuel costs and capital costs	+ 7.1
Delay in date of introducing LMFBR	− 2.6

SOURCE: *AEC Authorizing Legislation—Fiscal Year 1972,* Hearings before the
Joint Committee on Atomic Energy of the U.S. Congress, 92 Cong. 1 sess. (1971),
p. 689.
[a]The benefits to the year 2020 were estimated at $9.1 billion in the 1969 Analysis
and $21.5 billion in the 1970 Analysis.
[b]A separative work unit is not a quantity of material, but a measure of the effort
expended in gaseous diffusion plants to separate a quantity of uranium of a given
assay into two components, one having a higher percentage of U-235 and one
having a lower percentage.

Initial results of the overall review were available in 1968, and,
in 1969, the AEC published its *Cost-Benefit Analysis of the U.S.
Breeder Reactor Program*[16] (referred to in this report as the 1968
Analysis). In December 1970, the AEC published the initial find-
ings of the Systems Analysis Task Force,[17] and, in May 1972, the
AEC released its 1970 Analysis.

According to the AEC, the analysis was updated two years after
the initial report to take into account a number of changes in the
variables.[18] Table 4 shows the 1970 Analysis results reflecting the
AEC's judgment of the most likely values of the parameters varied,
and the comparable 1968 results; Table 5 compares the two sets
of figures. As can be seen, the 1970 Analysis approximately doubles the benefits estimated two years before, even though the post-
ponement of the entry of the LMFBR by two years would cost an

[16]U.S. Atomic Energy Commission, Division of Reactor Development and
Technology, WASH 1126 (April 1969).
[17]U.S. Atomic Energy Commission, Systems Analysis Task Force under direction
of Division of Reactor Development and Technology, *Potential Nuclear Power
Growth Patterns,* WASH 1098 (December 1970).
[18]Shaw, in *AEC Authorizing Legislation, FY 1972,* p. 689, states: "The principal
reasons for updating it are the cost increases in fossil fuel; the increase in electrical

estimated $2.6 billion more. The re-estimate of energy demand alone increased benefits by $6.7 billion, and $7.1 billion more was saved by the re-estimate of fuel and capital costs (see Table 4). On the other hand, a mere 10 percent increase in estimated LMFBR plant costs (other things being equal) would reduce benefits by $10.4 billion (see note to Table 5).

While the AEC clearly recognizes that fifty-year economic projections should not be construed as absolute forecasts,[19] a real question as to the value of the model arises when a two-year update of a fifty-year analysis produces changes of this magnitude. One might be particularly suspicious when the results are so favorable to the cause espoused.

Methodology

In the 1970 Analysis, the AEC applied the model to sixteen hypothetical cases divided into seven groups (see Table 6).

The calculations estimate the benefits accrued from an economy with an LMFBR as compared to an economy with only fossil-fuel (coal), light water reactor (LWR), and high temperature gas-cooled reactor (HTGR) power plants. . . . The seven groups were designed to determine the effect of varying the date of introduction of the breeder, varying uranium resources, varying energy demand, increasing the capital cost of the breeder, and the ability of the HTGR to penetrate the market.[20]

Six of the seven groups consist of a base case without a breeder and cases with a breeder represented by the LMFBR. In the first group the date of LMFBR introduction was parameterized for 1984, 1986, 1990, and 1994 (cases 2, 3, 4, and 5). Case 3 reflects the AEC's judgment of the most likely values of the parameters varied in the 1970 Analysis.

There are of course many parameters that were not varied in the 1970 Analysis and others that were not included. For example, some of those held constant were fossil-fuel (coal) and nuclear

---

demands; the increased cost of separative work; increase in the availability of low-cost uranium; the addition of environmental-related systems induced some changes, the capital cost of nuclear plants and fossil plants increased, and the fact that our LMFBR program was not proceeding as quickly as we had planned previously."

[19]U.S. AEC, *Updated (1970) Analysis*, WASH 1184, p. iii. See also statements by the late George M. Kavanagh and Milton Shaw (op.cit., p. 693) where the limitations of the cost-benefit analysis are brought to the attention of the JCAE.

[20]U.S. AEC, *Updated (1970) Analysis*, WASH 1184, pp. 7, 9.

TABLE 6. Characteristics of the AEC's Seven Groups and Sixteen Cases

Case no.	Uranium reserves vs. cost (1)	Energy demand (2)	Date of introduction LMFBR (3)
1	1/70 Est.	Probable	None
2	1/70 Est.	Probable	1984
3	1/70 Est.	Probable	1986
4	1/70 Est.	Probable	1990
5	1/70 Est.	Probable	1994
6	Optimistic	Probable	None
7	Optimistic	Probable	1986
8	Unlimited	Probable	None
9	Unlimited	Probable	1986
10	1/70 Est.	Low	None
11	1/70 Est.	Low	1986
12	1/70 Est.	High	None
13	1/70 Est.	High	1986
14[a]	1/70 Est.	Probable	1986
15[b]	1/70 Est.	Probable	None
16[b]	1/70 Est.	Probable	1986

SOURCE: U.S. Atomic Energy Commission, Division of Reactor Development and Technology, *Updated (1970) Cost-Benefit Analysis of the U.S. Breeder Reactor Program,* WASH 1184 (Jan. 1972), p. 29.

NOTE: The identification of the three uranium supply curves in column 1 and the three energy demand curves in column 2 ("probable," "low," and "high") are discussed in Chapters 3 and 4, respectively.

[a]With 10% higher LMFBR plant capital costs.

[b]Without HTGR.

(LWR, HTGR, and LMFBR) plant design characteristics, fossil-fuel costs, nuclear fuel cycle costs as functions of nuclear fuel demand, and generating capacity load factor histories. While the more important of these parameters are discussed briefly in the 1970 Analysis, many of them are not analyzed here for one or more of the following reasons: (1) it is thought that the results of the cost-benefit analysis are not sensitive to changes in these parameters (see discussion of fossil-fuel plants on p. 145); (2) lacking sensitivity data, it would be difficult to judge the effect of changes in these parameters; (3) the author accepts the AEC measures of these parameters as reasonable approximations or projections; (4) a lack of time.

The AEC's basic estimates of nuclear fuel cycle costs as functions of demand are accepted in this analysis. However, for a given nuclear fuel process, the estimation of a curve of unit cost versus time is heavily dependent, due to economies of scale, on the amount of nuclear capacity need as a function of time. For this reason, in the AEC's cost-benefit analyses initial growth projections for each reactor type were assumed, and fuel cycle costs were estimated. In addition, one of the AEC ground rules was that the potential effect of possible future regulations regarding siting, effluent control, waste disposal, and safeguards against the diversion of special nuclear materials, except to the extent that plant sizes may be limited by such regulations, would not be included in the cost estimates.[21] Therefore, nuclear fuel cycle costs are examined in this report only to the extent that LMFBR capital costs and design characteristics affect nuclear fuel cycle economies of scale, and to the extent that fuel cycle costs for all nuclear plants may increase due to future regulations.

SUMMARY

It is clear that expenditures for the LMFBR have been almost as great as for all other energy sources combined—and this heavy weighting in favor of the fast breeder reactor is expected to continue. The enormous sums already spent, as well as those anticipated for the next twenty to thirty years in both the public and private sectors, are justified by the AEC and the Administration on the basis of a series of cost-benefit analyses, culminating in the latest 1970 Analysis. The most recent two analyses clearly indicate the sensitivity of some of the variables to rather slight changes in re-estimating them.

In the following chapters, I explore these analyses to determine whether they do in fact support the vastly superior qualities claimed for the LMFBR.

[21]U.S. AEC, *Reactor Fuel Cycle Costs*, p. 6.

1

The Choice of Discount Rate

Expenditures and revenues occurring in different years cannot, from an economic standpoint, be added or subtracted directly because of the time value of money. This value is variously referred to in economic analysis as rate of return, interest rate, or discount rate.

In the 1970 Analysis, four discount rates were considered: 5, 7, 10, and 12.5 percent. The results for two of these rates, 7 percent and 10 percent, are shown in Table 7. Figure 2 shows the sensitivity of the 1970 Analysis to these discount rates with all other parameters fixed at what the AEC judged were the most probable values, that is, case 3 in Table 6. Notice that the reported net benefits (discounted savings in power costs minus the R&D costs) are reduced by 77 percent when the discount rate is increased from 7 percent to 10 percent. The reported benefits are negative for discount rates above about 13 percent.

Of the rates considered, the AEC prefers the 7 percent rate because:

The LMFBR program can be identified with the utility sector of the U.S. economy, and the rate of return applicable to that sector has been considered as the criterion rate for evaluation of public investments in this area. The discount rates applicable to the electric utility industry would most nearly comply with this criterion.[1]

---

[1]U.S. AEC, *Cost-Benefit Analysis,* WASH 1126 (April 1969), p. 38.

TABLE 7. Costs, Benefits, and Benefit-Cost Ratio to Year 2020 for Breeder Program, Undiscounted, and Discounted at 7% and 10% per Year

(dollar figures in billions)

Case no.	Undiscounted		Discounted to mid-1971 at 7%/yr					Discounted to mid-1971 at 10%/yr				
	Energy cost	Gross benefit	Energy cost (1)	Gross benefit (2)	R&D cost (3)	Net benefit (2)−(3) (4)	Benefit-to-cost ratio (2)÷(3) (5)	Energy cost (6)	Gross benefit (7)	R&D cost (8)	Net benefit (7)−(8) (9)	Benefit-to-cost ratio (7)÷(8) (10)
1	2704	—	437.4	—	—	—	—	247.8	—	—	—	—
2	2316	388	413.3	24.1	2.3	21.8	10.5	240.4	7.4	2.0	5.4	3.7
3	2346	358	415.9	21.5	2.4	19.1	9.0	241.4	6.4	2.1	4.3	3.0
4	2398	306	424.1	13.3	2.7	10.6	4.9	244.4	3.4	2.3	1.1	1.5
5	2485	219	430.3	7.1	2.9	4.2	2.4	246.4	1.4	2.4	(1.0)	0.6
6	2667	—	433.5	—	—	—	—	246.2	—	—	—	—
7	2328	339	413.4	20.1	2.4	17.7	8.4	240.3	5.9	2.1	3.8	2.8
8	2244	—	409.6	—	—	—	—	238.5	—	—	—	—
9	2234	10	408.4	1.2	2.4	(1.2)	0.5	238.2	0.3	2.1	(1.8)	0.1
10	2096	—	349.2	—	—	—	—	200.4	—	—	—	—
11	1842	254	334.4	14.8	2.4	12.4	6.2	196.2	4.2	2.1	2.1	2.0
12	3332	—	523.3	—	—	—	—	293.1	—	—	—	—
13	2857	475	497.3	26.0	2.4	23.6	10.8	285.7	7.4	2.1	5.3	3.5
14[a]	2449	255	426.5	10.9	2.4	8.5	4.5	245.4	2.4	2.1	0.3	1.1
15[b]	3466	—	461.7	—	—	—	—	254.8	—	—	—	—
16[b]	2387	1079	419.4	42.3	2.4	39.9	17.6	242.8	12.0	2.4	9.6	5.0

SOURCE: Same as Table 6, p. 21.
[a] With 10% higher LMFBR plant capital costs.
[b] Without HTGR.

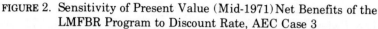

FIGURE 2. Sensitivity of Present Value (Mid-1971) Net Benefits of the
LMFBR Program to Discount Rate, AEC Case 3

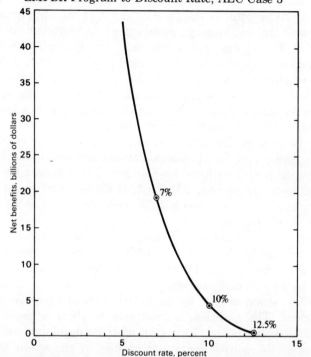

SOURCE: AEC, Division of Reactor Development and Technology, *Up-dated (1970) Cost-Benefit Analysis of the U.S. Breeder Reactor Program,* WASH 1184 (Jan. 1972), pp. 28-31.

*The circles represent case 3 of the 1970 Analysis (see Table 6). Case 3 reflects the AEC's judgment of the most likely values of the other parameters varied in the analysis.

However, the mere fact that the LMFBR will be used to generate electricity, and that the utilities produce and sell electricity, does not lead logically to a conclusion that the appropriate discount rate for a federally funded LMFBR R&D program is equivalent to the federally regulated rate of return of the utility industry.

According to the guidelines established in March 1972 by George P. Shultz, while he was director of the Office of Management and Budget (OMB), all agencies of the executive branch of the federal government, except the U.S. Postal Service, ought to use a 10 percent discount rate for program analyses submitted to OMB in support of legislative and budget programs.[2]

The Federal Water Resources Council in December 1971 also arrived at 10 percent as the best estimate of the appropriate discount rate for evaluating government investment decisions. Because of its cogency and conciseness, the Council's analysis is reproduced in Appendix B. The Council points out that a discount rate lower than 10 percent might be used for political or social purposes—to subsidize incomes in specific regions, for example. But even for such purposes, the Council indicates that a lower discount rate is often an inefficient instrument.

If the 10 percent discount rate represents the best estimate of the opportunity cost for all federal investment activities, then one could assume that it includes an average of risk factors for federal and nonfederal investments. If the LMFBR program has a higher than average risk associated with it, then perhaps the 10 percent discount rate is too low.

While some might argue that the government should take a risk-neutral position with respect to LMFBR expenditures, it would appear that the financial risks of the program are not borne equally by everyone in society. The utilities, and in some cases the vendors, stand to gain by the federal expenditures for LMFBR development. The utilities are unlikely to show a profit loss if the LMFBR is not competitive soon after its development. On the other hand, the consumers stand to lose in the event that the LMFBR energy costs are higher than anticipated. They lose not only the LMFBR R&D expenditure, but there is also evidence to suggest that the utilities may buy the LMFBRs anyway,[3] in which case the consumers may be victims of additional rate increases. Competitors for program funds as well as consumers stand to lose when funds are directed away from alternate R&D (or other) programs. In this regard, it is interesting to examine the views of the utility industry.

In a panel discussion at the Atomic Industrial Forum's annual meeting in October 1971, Herman M. Dieckamp, president of Atomics International Division of North American Rockwell, stated:

[2]Circular No. A-94, Revised, March 27, 1972, to the heads of executive departments and establishments from George P. Shultz, Director, Office of Management and Budget. Exceptions to this rule are allowed where some other rate is prescribed by or pursuant to law, Executive Order, or other relevant circulars.

[3]See discussion of Averch-Johnson effect in Chapter 5.

There is ... considerable variation in judgment about the imminence of the need to introduce fast breeders on a large scale. This variation in judgment is evidenced by the leisurely pace of the program and the uncertainty in planning beyond the first demonstration plant.

This range of judgment about the immediacy of the need is, in my mind, a result of the fact that the introduction time, that is, the time from now to the point of significant impact on power generation, is at least 15 or probably more like 20 years, which is longer than the industry planning cycle, and I think Dr. Netschert [vice president, National Economic Research Associates, Inc.] has also indicated to us the many uncertainties associated with the kind of long-range projections that are necessary to clearly identify the need for a new source of power generation.

The breeder does not have the optimism about a nuclear panacea that aided the introduction of the light water reactor. On the contrary, its requests for support come at a time when the industry is painfully aware of the cost of introducing nuclear power and also gruelingly aware of the public acceptance problem.[4]

Similar views have been expressed with respect to financing the LMFBR demonstration plant. Thomas G. Ayers, president of Commonwealth Edison Co., recently declared:

The biggest obstacles to going ahead with the demonstration plants are raising the money, allocating the financial risks, and satisfying environmental requirements. ... The huge initial cost estimates for the demonstration plants, together with the risks of cost overruns and capacity unavailable, impose special problems for the breeder demonstration plants.[5]

Westinghouse's John Simpson, president of Power Systems, suggested in 1971 that if Westinghouse invested $72 million in the LMFBR demonstration plant, it would not make its first dollars on the breeder until 1987, and would not be accumulatively in the black until 1995. At that time a manufacturer would have to have at least 40 percent of the market to make it pay off.[6] Wallace R. Behnke, Commonwealth Edison vice-president, has estimated that "the most a utility can pay for a demonstration plant is the cost of equivalent conventional capacity, discounted for risk and lower plant availability in the earlier years of operation."[7]

---

[4]Herman M. Dieckamp at the annual conference of the Atomic Industrial Forum in Miami Beach, Florida, October 17-21, 1971, *Nuclear Industry,* 18 Part I (Oct.-Nov. 1971), p. 19.

[5]Thomas G. Ayers at the Annual Convention of the Edison Electric Institute, Cleveland, Ohio, June 1971, *Nuclear Industry,* 18 (June 1971), p.4.

[6]John Simpson at a press conference of the American Power Conference Symposium in Chicago, Illinois, April 1971, *Nuclear Industry,* 18 (April 1971), p.6.

[7]Wallace R. Behnke at the annual conference of the Atomic Industrial Forum in Washington, D.C., November 1970, *Nuclear Industry,* 17 (Nov.-Dec. 1970), p.25.

While these statements are not intended to imply that these gentlemen are opposed to breeder development on a timely basis, they do provide evidence that the financial risk of the breeder program and the breeder demonstration plant is high. When this risk is reflected in their discount rate, it is easy to understand their

FIGURE 3. Cumulative Present Value Gross Benefits, and R&D Expenditures as a Function of Time

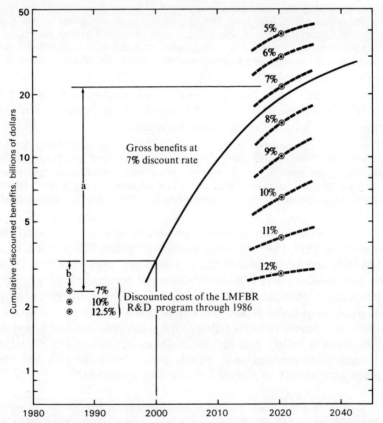

SOURCE: Solid curve: P.L. Hofman, Hanford Engineering Development Laboratory, Richland, Washington, private communication. Dashed curves: estimated from Figure 2.

NOTE: Results are for the 1970 Analysis, case 3 assumptions (see note to Figure 2). The solid curve is approximately equivalent to the 1970 Analysis results, except discounted to 1970 instead of mid-1971.

reluctance to commit funds for the necessary LMFBR R&D that is needed if the AEC's schedule is to be met.

One of the reasons that the risk is high—and this goes back to Simpson's statement above—is that the discounted cumulative benefits, even under the AEC's assumptions, are not larger than the discounted costs until around 1995. Less than 8 percent of the discounted benefits through the year 2020 will have been accumulated by 2000. This is shown in Figure 3, lines a and b.

There is extensive economic literature that argues that the government can take on more risky projects than private industry because of the greater breadth and depth of its R&D portfolio. The implications here are that a project of the scale of the LMFBR program could not be undertaken by private industry because of the implied risk of default for a large number of corporations in the private sector; moreover, even the private capital markets might not be able to diversify that much risk away through private holdings of balanced portfolios of stock in these companies. The thought is that the government can diversify more easily. In this regard, it is interesting to recall that the LMFBR program represents over 40 percent of the government's energy R&D portfolio.

If the program is to be justified on the basis of dollar savings to society, i.e., on a social accounting basis, then some economists would argue, as the AEC acknowledges in its 1968 Analysis,

... one would calculate benefits and costs on a pre-tax basis and use a discount rate representing the pre-tax rate of return of the relevant portion of the private sector.[8]

One calculation, in 1968, when the rate of inflation was less than it is today and when the accounting rate of return for those electric utilities deriving less than 10 percent of their revenues from gas operations was around 7.5 percent, was that the average social rate of return for these utilities was about 14 percent.[9]

---

[8]U.S. AEC, *Cost-Benefit Analysis,* WASH 1126, p. 38.
[9]Paul S. Brandon, "The Electric Side of Combination Gas-Electric Utilities," *The Bell Journal of Economics and Management Science,* 2 (Autumn 1971), pp. 688-703. Brandon chooses as a measure of the social rate of return the net income before taxes and before interest payments, divided by the average of beginning and end-of-year values of net plants in service.

2

LMFBR Generating Costs

LMFBR power plants will be economical provided the total cost of electricity generated by these plants, averaged over the thirty- to forty-year plant lifetime, is comparable to, or less than, the generating cost from existing power plant alternatives.

One of the alternatives will be fossil-fueled plants. On the basis of AEC cases 1, 3, and 4, the 1970 Analysis predicts that fossil-fueled (coal) plants will represent, respectively, only 9 percent, 0.4 percent, and 2 percent of the *base-load* generating capacity placed in operation between 1990 and 2020.[1] The same source infers that the LMFBR's principal competition between 1990 and 2020 will come from other nuclear plants, namely, LWRs and the HTGR.

While the AEC may not have devoted sufficient attention to the cost assumptions related to the fossil-fueled plants, it would be difficult to argue that there will be many more, or substantially fewer, fossil-fueled plant additions than predicted by the 1970 Analysis, at least not enough to alter appreciably the benefits of the LMFBR program.[2] For this reason, I do not examine the AEC's

---

[1]U.S. AEC, *Updated (1970) Analysis*, WASH 1184, Table 9, p. 34. Cases 1, 3, and 4 are the only cases for which the AEC has tabulated the generation capacity placed in operation as a function of time.

[2]It is interesting to note, however, if the additional fossil-fueled plant base-load capacity added between 1990 and 2020 is *less* than predicted by the 1970 Analysis, the percentages noted above suggest that the resulting error as far as LMFBR benefits are concerned would not be more than a few percent. If the fossil-fueled plant capacity is *more*, the benefits of the LMFBR could be anywhere from slightly to considerably less than projected.

cost assumptions pertaining to these plants.

When comparing the LMFBR energy costs with costs using alternative nuclear plants, it is convenient to consider the contributions to the total generating cost due to: (1) capital costs, (2) fuel cycle costs, and (3) operation and maintenance costs. A thorough examination of operation and maintenance costs of nuclear plants is not included in this study, since this contribution will probably represent no more than about 5 percent of the total generating cost for each of the nuclear plant types (LWR, HTGR, and LMFBR) considered. It is assumed that the operation and maintenance costs of the three nuclear plant alternatives are comparable, although the use of sodium as a coolant may make these costs slightly higher for the LMFBR.

The comparison of LMFBR capital costs and fuel cycle costs with those of the LWR and HTGR would not be complete without taking future uranium prices into consideration. While this will be discussed in some detail in Chapter 3, it is explainable briefly (and simplistically) as follows: Under current technological conditions, the capital costs of the LMFBR are estimated to be higher than those of the other two reactor types, but its fuel cycle costs are estimated to be lower, and, according to the AEC, may well be offsetting. As improvements in technology and design for all three types develop, however, the differential may become less (or greater). Indeed, as indicated in the following section, it may well be that the capital cost estimates are significantly understated. But, even if the higher capital costs of the LMFBR cannot be offset by lower fuel cycle costs, the future depletion of uranium resources (and, therefore, the expectation of higher uranium prices) could be the decisive factor, since the LMFBR is much less dependent on uranium supply than the other two reactor types. (It would be well to note here, though, that the gas-cooled fast breeder would also have this advantage, with perhaps less disadvantage in capital costs.)

Capital Cost Estimates

The projected capital costs of the power plants included in the AEC's 1968 and 1970 cost-benefit studies are shown in Figure 4.

In the 1970 Analysis only the LMFBR capital cost curve was varied (see case 14 in Table 6); the capital cost curves of other plant types were fixed for all cases. According to this analysis, a

FIGURE 4. Projected Power Plant Capital Costs Used
in AEC's Cost-Benefit Analysis

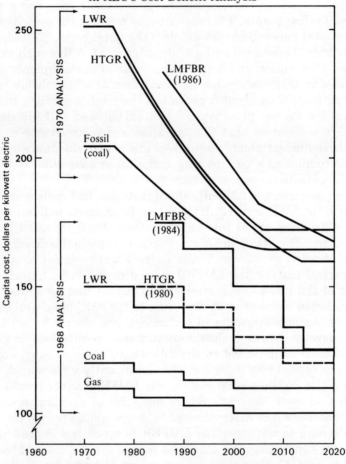

SOURCE: AEC, *Updated (1970) Analysis*, WASH 1184, p. 37.

10 percent increase in the capital costs of the LMFBR power plant[3]
decreases the $21.5 billion benefits to $10.6 billion.

By simple extrapolation, one might conclude from this statement
that a 20 percent increase in LMFBR plant cost (equivalent to a
50-60 percent cost increase in the nuclear steam-generating system) decreases the net benefits of the LMFBR program to zero.

[3]According to the AEC estimates, this is equivalent to a one-third increase in
the cost of the nuclear island (see note to Table 4).

However, a better approach is to examine these sensitivity results in terms of the LMFBR–LWR and LMFBR–HTGR capital cost *differentials*. It was noted earlier that this is one of the critical factors that will determine the success or failure of the LMFBR.

Estimates of LMFBR–LWR capital cost differences are plotted in Figure 5(A); LMFBR-HTGR cost differences in Figure 5(B). The curves are the differences in plant capital costs (as indicated in Figure 4) as a function of the year the plants become available, that is, the end of the construction period. The curves labeled (a) in both parts of Figure 5 are differences in the appropriate 1968 Analysis curves; the curves labeled (b) are differences in the 1970 Analysis curves. The dotted curve (c) represents the arbitrary addition of a 10 percent increase in LMFBR capital costs.

As seen from curve (b) in both parts of Figure 5, the 1970 Analysis assumes that the initial follow-on LMFBR will cost no more than about $18/kw more than LWRs and HTGRs, and this cost differential will be reduced gradually in subsequent years. Curve (c) represents an initial $42/kw capital cost differential, decreasing to about $15/kw by 2020 in the LMFBR–LWR case and to about $25/kw in the LMFBR–HTGR case.

The capital cost curves used in the 1970 Analysis represent late-1970 estimates generated by the Capital Cost Evaluating Group at Oak Ridge National Laboratory (ORNL). The method used to generate these curves is described in a March 5, 1971, ORNL technical memorandum by Bowers and Myers.[4] Capital costs for the 1000-Mw PWR (one of the two LWR types), HTGR, and LMFBR nuclear plants, provided with run-of-river cooling and with cooling towers, were calculated in term of mid-1970 dollars. Costs were based on ideal siting conditions of the AEC standard, hypothetical, Middletown site. Start of construction was mid-1970, and five-year construction time for nuclear plants was assumed. The costs did not include escalation during construction since the power economy model is based on constant dollars.[5] Bowers and Myers reported the total plant capital costs as: PWR—$252/kw; HTGR—$238/kw; and LMFBR—$272/kw.

In order to project these costs over the fifty-year period, 1970 through 2020, ORNL took into account estimated increases in unit

---

[4]Howard I. Bowers and M.L. Myers, *Estimated Capital Costs of Nuclear and Fossil Power Plants,* Oak Ridge National Laboratory, ORNL-TM-3243 (March 5, 1971).
    [5]Additional ground rules appear in ibid., p.8.

FIGURE 5. Estimates of Nuclear Plant Capital Cost Differential as a
Function of Year of Introduction

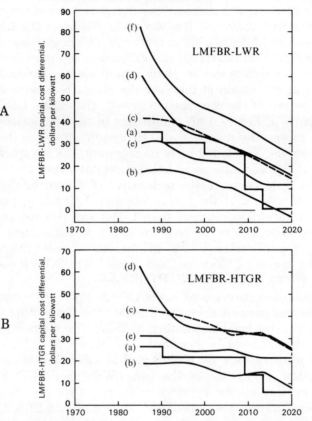

SOURCES AND NOTES: Curve (a): 1968 Analysis, with 1984 LMFBR
introduction, mid-1970 dollars. Curve (b): 1970 Analysis, with 1986
LMFBR introduction, AEC middletown site, natural draft hyperbolic
cooling towers, mid-1970 dollars. Curve (c): Same as (b) but with LMFBR
capital costs increased by 10 percent, cost of other plants held constant.
Curve (d): Howard I. Bowers and M.L. Myers, "Estimated Capital Costs
of Nuclear and Fossil Power Plants," Oak Ridge National Laboratory,
ORNL-TM-3243 (March 5, 1971); with AEC middletown site, natural
draft hyperbolic cooling towers, and mid-1970 dollars. Curve (e): Same as
(d) but with modified LMFBR learning curve and modified curve of
LMFBR unit size versus year; these modifications reflected suggestions
of AEC Division of Reactor Development and Technology, Office of Program
Analysis. Curve (f): Same as (d) but with preliminary CONCEPT-II estimates of LMFBR and PWR reference plant costs.

FIGURE 6. Estimated Unit Sizes

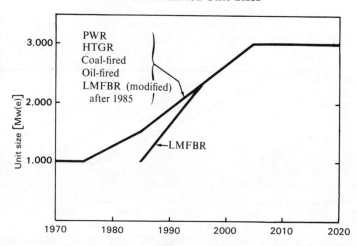

SOURCE: Howard I. Bowers and M.L. Myers, "Estimated Capital Costs of Nuclear and Fossil Power Plants," Oak Ridge National Laboratory, ORNL-TM-3243 (March 5, 1971), p. 18.

size and assumed learning curves for the different types of plants. To account for unit size, unit capital costs (in $/kw) were first scaled from 1000 Mw to 3000 Mw, using

$$\text{cost}_2 = \text{cost}_1 \left(\frac{\text{size}_2}{\text{size}_1} \right)^n,$$

where cost_1 and size_1 refer to the 1000-Mw reference plant, and n is a scaling exponent.[6] The scaling exponent for each plant type was derived from rough cost estimates by examining trends in the historical data and projected costs through about 1980. The exponents for all nuclear plants were approximately -0.3.[7] Next, projections were made of plant unit size as a function of year over the fifty-year period. These projections are reproduced in Figure 6. At the suggestion of the AEC's Office of Program Analysis, Division of Reactor Development and Technology (AEC-DRDT), an alternate LMFBR curve was also considered. AEC-DRDT sug-

[6]Ibid., p. 9.
[7]Ibid., p. 16.

FIGURE 7. Assumed Learning Curves

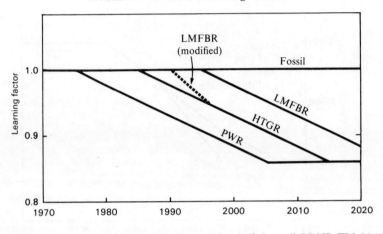

SOURCE: Bowers and Myers, "Estimated Capital Costs," ORNL-TM-3243, p. 20.

gested that the LMFBR be introduced at a unit size of 1500 Mw in 1985, and thereafter follow the same curve as all other types of plants. From the scaling equation above and the projections in Figure 7, plant cost reductions per year due to increases in plant size are calculated in the obvious manner.

The learning curves used by ORNL (see Figure 7) were estimated by Bowers and Myers as follows:

A 95% learning curve (5% improvement per decade) based on a 10-year period starting in 1975 and extending for 30 years ending in 2005 was assumed for PWR plants. The learning curves for HTGR plants and LMFBR plants were assumed to start in 1985 and in 1995, respectively, lagging the PWR learning by 10 and 20 years, respectively, each extending for 30 years. The 10-year period was selected on the basis of approximately doubling of generating capacity every 10 years. No assumptions were made in regard to relative numbers of different types of reactors. To allow for initial problems the learning process was assumed to start approximately 10 years following the assumed introduction dates. An alternate modified learning curve ... was also assumed for LMFBR plants.[8]

The modified learning curve (dashed line in Figure 7) was again the suggestion of AEC-DRDT, Office of Program Analysis.

[8]Ibid., p. 19.

With the learning curves and unit size cost assumptions above, ORNL took the base-year plant costs, applied the unit size correction, and then multiplied by the appropriate learning factor to obtain the plant capital cost curves.

The curves in the 1970 Analysis, reproduced in Figure 4, represent preliminary (late 1970) cost estimates using this technique. The cost curves reported by Bowers and Myers (early-1971 estimates) for the PWR and HTGR, together with the LMFBR curve incorporating the modifications suggested by AEC-DRDT, differ from the respective curves of the 1970 Analysis due to revisions that were made in the scaling exponents. While the capital cost curves presented by Bowers and Myers are not reproduced in this paper, the LMFBR–PWR and LMFBR–HTGR capital cost differentials have been calculated from their curves and are shown in Figure 5. The cost differentials labeled (d) in Figure 5 are calculated from the Bowers and Myers data with the ORNL estimates of plant unit size and learning rates. The cost differentials labeled (e) are from the Bowers and Myers data that include the AEC-DRDT modifications.

Three observations from Figure 5 are made at this point. First, the capital cost differentials, and therefore the benefits of the LMFBR program, are very sensitive to changes in the scaling exponent. This accounts for the difference between curves (b) and (e) in each part of the figure. (Note that the curve labeled (e) is about midway between (b) and (c), and recall that gross benefits of the LMFBR program corresponding to (c) are only half the benefits corresponding to (b).) Second, the capital cost differentials, and therefore the LMFBR benefits, are very sensitive to the assumptions of unit size growth and learning rate, accounting for the difference between curves (d) and (e) in the figure. Third, after about 1990—comparatively few LMFBRs will be built before this date—curves (c) and (d) closely follow one another. Hence, if one were to accept the more recent ORNL scaling exponent and the ORNL assumptions of unit size and learning rate, rather than the AEC-DRDT assumptions, then the gross benefits of the LMFBR program would be about one-half of the benefits reported in the 1970 Analysis, all other assumptions remaining the same.

Since the Bowers and Myers paper was published, the Capital Cost Evaluation Group at ORNL has sought to improve its methods of estimating capital costs of steam electric power plants. A brief discussion of this ongoing effort is contained in the AEC's environmental impact statement for the LMFBR demonstration plant.[9] As part of this effort, the CONCEPT computer program,[10] used to calculate the PWR costs reported by Bowers and Myers, has been revised. The new version, called CONCEPT-II, relies on detailed cost estimates for PWR, BWR, HTGR, and LMFBR nuclear plants and coal-, oil-, and gas-fired plants, which are stored internally for a specified location and construction time period. The program then uses other stored cost data to adjust the reference cost model to a specific plant size (electrical rating), site location, and a construction time period. The stored economic data reflect locational factors (such as material price indices and labor rates) for some twenty U.S. and two Canadian localities, plus an additional hypothetical location—the AEC reference site, Middletown, U.S.A.[11]

It is reasonable to ask what the latest CONCEPT-II capital cost predictions are for the nuclear plants, and what effect these newer estimates would have on estimated benefits of the LMFBR program. The structure of the CONCEPT code and some of the underlying assumptions, together with example calculations (including sensitivity calculations) for the PWR and the fossil-fueled plants

[9]U.S. Atomic Energy Commission, *Liquid Metal Fast Breeder Reactor Demonstration Plant Environmental Statement,* WASH 1509 (April 1972), pp. 245-46.

[10]A preliminary users manual is available, entitled "CONCEPT—Computerized Conceptual Cost Estimates for Steam-Electric Power Plants," U.S. AEC Report ORNL-TM-3276 (Oct. 1971).

[11]United Engineers & Constructors, Inc., "Liquid Metal Fast Breeder Reactor Plant," No. UEC-AEC-720630, a 1000-Mw Central Station Power Plants Investment Cost Study performed for the U.S. Atomic Energy Commission (June 1972), p. 1-1. The BWR, PWR, LMFBR, and coal- and oil-fueled power plant data incorporated in CONCEPT-II are based on cost analyses conducted by United Engineers and Constructors, Inc., under contract to AEC-DRDT. See U.S. Atomic Energy Commission, *1000-Mwe Central Station Power Plants Investment Cost Study, Vol. I—Pressurized Water Reactor Plant; Vol. II—Boiling Water Reactor Plant; Vol. III—Coal-Fired Fossil Plant; Vol. IV—Oil-Fired Fossil Plant,* WASH 1230 (June 1972).

United Engineers' cost estimates for the LMFBR are based on the 1000-Mw LMFBR follow-on conceptual study reference design by Babcock and Wilcox Co. See United Engineers and Constructors, Inc., "LMFBR Plant." Because the current U.S. LMFBR demonstration plant is a loop- rather than a pot-design, one might question the validity of using a pot-design for assessing future LMFBR costs. Since the pot-design appears less complicated (requiring less plumbing) than the loop-design, it appears reasonable to assume that it would also be less costly. Cost estimates for cooling towers (mechanical and natural draft) and near-zero release radioactive waste systems for the LWRs have been made by the AEC. Since United Engineers has not completed its HTGR cost estimates, the present HTGR data used in Concept-II represent ORNL estimates. The gas-fueled power plant costs appear also to represent ORNL estimates.

have been summarized from AEC source material by F. C. Olds, editor of *Power Engineering*.[12]

The following are the ground rules.

1. Costs are based on 1000-Mw plants and ideal siting conditions of the AEC standard hypothetical Middletown site.

2. A mid-1972 start of construction and a 7½-year construction period are assumed (commercial operation in 1980).

3. Costs exclude escalation during construction.

4. Costs are in mid-1972 dollars.

5. First-of-a-kind, or prototype, cost effects are excluded.

6. Costs include allowance for mechanical draft cooling towers (e.g., $20 million for PWR).[13]

7. PWR cost includes $4 million allowance for near-zero rad-waste system.[14]

Based on these assumptions, CONCEPT-II plant cost estimates are $336/kw for the PWR[15] and $373/kw for the pool-type LMFBR.[16]

While existing nuclear plants and those under construction provided a basis for estimating PWR direct costs in CONCEPT-II, no similar LMFBR data existed. Consequently, the LMFBR direct costs in the CONCEPT-II program are probably not accurate to more than ±25 percent. Coupling this with the fact that the figures quoted above represent preliminary unpublished estimates, appropriate care should be taken when drawing conclusions from them. With this in mind, it is useful nevertheless to reexamine the LMFBR cost-benefit results using these newer capital cost estimates, because these newer figures in effect represent an updating of the estimates of the ORNL group that furnished the curves used in the 1970 Analysis.

If one assumes a 7 percent average annual increase in nuclear power plant costs due to escalation,[17] the mid-1970 dollar equivalent of the preliminary CONCEPT-II plant cost estimates quoted above would be $293/kw for the PWR and $326/kw for the LMFBR. When the reference PWR and LMFBR plant costs used in the Bowers and Myers paper (i.e., PWR, $252/kw and LMFBR,

---

[12]F. C. Olds, "Capital Cost Calculations for Future Power Plants," *Power Engineering* (Jan. 1973), pp. 61-65.

[13]Ibid., p. 62.

[14]Ibid.

[15]Ibid.

[16]Based on unpublished information.

[17]The analysis presented here is not particularly sensitive to this assumption.

$272/kw) are replaced by these higher figures, the capital cost differentials increase. In Figure 5(A), curve (d), corresponding to the unmodified Bowers and Myers LMFBR and PWR capital cost curves, increases to curve (f). Likewise, were it shown, curve (e), which includes the AEC-DRDT modifications, would increase to approximately the position of curve (c). Similar results would be realized in an analysis of the LMFBR–HTGR capital cost differential. Other estimates of future nuclear power plant capital costs can be found in the literature.[18]

Probably all of the U.S. manufacturers vying for the future LMFBR market have made their own economic analyses of the incentives for developing the LMFBR on a timely basis. For the most part, their data are either unpublished or difficult to normalize to the ground rules used in the 1970 Analysis. In a recent GE cost-benefit study reported by P. M. Murphy, the capital cost differential between the LWR and LMFBR was taken as $30/kw when the breeder was introduced, dropping to $15/kw by 1990, "as the Breeder technology matures and the unit size increases into the 2000-Mw range and beyond."[19]

There is clearly too much uncertainty in all of these cost estimates to make energy strategy decisions based on these results alone, but there are reasons to believe the actual LMFBR–LWR and LMFBR–HTGR capital cost differentials are more likely to be even higher than the predictions discussed above. Below, I examine several factors to support this hypothesis. If nothing else, these factors should increase one's awareness of the uncertainties surrounding these cost estimates.

First, estimates of breeder capital costs depend heavily on cost estimates for commercially available nonbreeders. The cost data for numerous components and systems in existing nuclear plants are used as references, and the marginal differences in the costs

[18]See, for example, Edison Electric Institute, *Report of the EEI Reactor Assessment Panel*, EEI Publication No. 70-30 (New York, 1970). Because the methodology of their cost estimates is not well documented, and because this 1969 utility view is no longer current, the results are not presented here, but are summarized in Appendix F.

[19]P. M. Murphy, "Incentives for the Development of the Fast Breeder Reactor," Breeder Reactor Department, General Electric Company. The date of this study was not given and it is unknown whether GE still uses a comparable cost differential in its base-case estimates.

of the similar systems in the breeders are estimated.[20] As the costs of the conventional nuclear plants increase, the cost estimates of the LMFBR have also increased. Since the LMFBR is expected to cost more than the conventional plants, one might also expect the capital cost differential between the LMFBR and the conventional plants to increase, although not necessarily by the same percentage.

From Figure 4 (see page 32), it is noted that, for all plant types, the 1970 capital cost predictions (in constant dollars) are higher than the 1968 predictions. The CONCEPT-II data suggest that the costs as predicted in 1972 are even higher. If this trend in rising plant capital costs (in constant dollars) continues over the next few years, one might expect the cost differentials to increase, and it is the absolute differentials and not the percentage differentials that are crucial.

A counter-argument here would be to note that, while capital cost estimates for all plant types increased between the 1968 Analysis and 1970 Analysis, the cost differentials decreased slightly (see Figures 4 and 5). While such an effect could occur again, due to either the discovery of new information or more accurate cost estimates, the opposite effect could also occur, as it in fact already has since the 1970 Analysis (cf. CONCEPT-II data).

A second reason the cost differentials may be higher is illustrated by the record of cost estimates during the development of other AEC reactor programs. The commercial light water reactors are considerably more costly than originally estimated. Analysts for Gilbert Associates have noted:

> About eight years ago it was believed light water reactor plants could be built for about $125 per kilowatt, or less. Today, plants to be completed about eight years hence are generally being estimated at close to $400 per kw. That's more than a 300 percent increase in expected cost over an eight-year period.[21]

Their analysis indicated that the 1968 estimates for nonturnkey LWR plants to be completed in the early 1970s were about $150/kw lower than will actually be experienced for those plants.[22] A table

---

[20]For example, the cost of LMFBR reactor vessels has been estimated by multiplying the weight of the unit by a specific cost per unit weight determined from previous experience with LWRs. See ibid.

[21]Peter J. McTague, G. J. Davidson, R. M. Bredin, and A. A. Herman, "The Evolution of Nuclear Plant Costs," *Nuclear News*, 15 (Feb. 1972), p. 31.

[22]Ibid.

they presented that breaks down this cost increase shows only a small fraction of the cost overruns due to added inflation. While McTague et al. suggest that $110 of the $150/kw increase is due to two unanticipated factors—stretchout of construction schedule and added scope of the work required—they believe that "neither of these factors should have much additional cost impact on future [light water] plants."[23]

It seems likely that the LMFBR program will experience similar cost increases during its initial development period. Unlike other plant types (e.g., fossil, LWR, and HTGR[24]) which are already on the market, commercial LMFBR power plants have not been built. The LMFBR program faces unanticipated development problems, and we know from experience with light water reactors that large-scale development projects of this type can easily encounter subtle and unforeseen interacting circumstances that result in costly solutions in terms of commercial design.[25]

Additional reasons to support the suspicion that the capital cost differentials from the 1970 Analysis are low concern projections of plant unit size, learning rates, and environmental costs as related to capital expenditures. These are discussed in turn below.

[23]Ibid.

[24]While the HTGR has not actually penetrated the market, the 330-Mw Fort St. Vrain unit, should be operational in early 1974. In addition, Gulf General Atomics has sold commercial-size HTGRs at the time of this writing, although none of these is scheduled to produce power before 1980.

[25]For example, a significant aspect of LMFBR safety analysis is the potential release of plutonium to the environment under hypothetical "design basis accident" (DBA) conditions. DBA describes a hypothetical accident that is used as a basis for designing the reactor containment and engineering safeguards that must function under emergency conditions. The issue here is not the probability of such accidents but the consequences should they occur. Plutonium release is of principal interest as opposed to the release of uranium or the volatile and solid fission products, since bone and lung doses from plutonium ingestion at the site boundary can be shown to be controlling factors under DBA conditions. In models of plutonium transport from core disassembly to aerosol release from the primary and secondary containment to the site environs, there are several variables about which there is substantial uncertainty. These uncertainties in some cases translate into order-of-magnitude (or more) uncertainties in the calculated plutonium leakage fractions following fast reactor DBAs (discussed in more detail in Chapter 7). While future studies assessing the reality of a plutonium release hazard may show it to be insignificant, it is conceivable that it could be a problem with large LMFBRs. In the latter case it is possible that this could lead to additional unanticipated capital expenditures to provide safety margins such that the calculated plutonium leakage following DBAs is reduced to acceptable levels. Other examples of uncertainties in the LMFBR design that could lead to higher costs are presented in the United Engineers cost study for the LMFBR (United Engineers, "LMFBR Plant," pp. 5-8 through 5-12).

Plant Unit Size

Light-water reactor plants of 1100 Mw to 1200 Mw are already under construction, and there are studies that indicate that 3000-Mw to 4000-Mw reactors of this type are feasible.[26] In a panel discussion at the 1972 American Nuclear Society Conference at Atlantic City, Ruble Thomas of Southern Services observed that the forced outage rate for commercial nuclear plants appears to increase with plant size. Furthermore, given the same outage rate, from the standpoint of reliability it is more economical for a utility to purchase two smaller plants than one large plant. Thomas concluded that because plant reliability is one of the most important variables when computing energy costs, we may see a saturation in plant size, or at least a slower increase in plant size than previously predicted.[27]

The staff of the FPC in a case before the Securities and Exchange Commission argued in 1972 that large electric power plant units (including nuclear) are not as reliable as smaller units, and that the existence of economies of scale with larger plants has not been demonstrated.[28]

Other factors that could limit the trend toward larger nuclear plants would be restrictions to standardize design or to provide additional assurance of public safety.[29] In March 1973 the AEC announced procedural options for standardizing nuclear power plant designs and licensing reviews.[30] One of the ground rules limits LWR power levels to approximately 1300 Mw. With respect to plant costs, this cuts both ways, since one of the goals of standardization is to reduce unit costs. It is noted, however, that cost reductions through standardization should be achieved in LWRs and the HTGR long before a standard LMFBR design is chosen. With respect to the need to limit plant size for reasons of safety, arguments supporting such a policy can be found in the AEC's

---

[26]Bowers and Myers, "Estimated Capital Cost," p. 16.

[27]Ruble Thomas at the American Nuclear Society Conference, Aug. 22-25, 1972, Atlantic City.

[28]Brief prepared by the Division of Corporate Regulations, Federal Power Commission, in the matter of American Electric Power Company, Inc., Administration Proceeding File No. 3-1476 (Aug. 25, 1972).

[29]Alternatively, capital costs could be increased to achieve the same level of safety with the larger plants.

[30]"Standardized Design Licensing," *Nuclear Industry* (March 1973), p. 16. [No author indicated.]

emergency core-cooling system hearings.[31] Similar arguments can be raised with respect to LMFBR safety.

Learning Curves

According to Bowers and Myers:

Classical learning curves in manufacturing industries are based on producing many standardized components. The design and construction of a relatively small number of electric power plants is not exactly analogous to the production of many standardized components. Not only are relatively few power plants constructed but also they are not fully standardized. In addition, the power plant design and construction industry has been going through a period of instability and rapid change due to several factors such as increasing unit size, increased escalation rates, increased quality assurance requirements, changing designs due to licensing and regulation requirements, added features for protection against environmental effects, decreased labor productivity, delays in construction schedules, and increased interest rates. All of which make it next to impossible to deduce learning curves from historical cost data. Obviously, extrapolation of power plant costs by the learning curve technique is risky and probably naive. If attempted at all, it should be restricted to a finite number of similar plants because of the rapid changes which take place in design from plant to plant and in many cases increase costs rather than decrease costs. Based on these considerations, a strong argument could be made for assuming no cost reduction to learning.[32]

The AEC is not alone in assuming that future LWRs as well as other plant types will cost less in terms of constant dollars. MacAvoy notes, "improvement by repetition" in the production of components should produce a 3 to 5 percent reduction in cost each year, which should be reflected in at least a 1 percent discount of present values.[33] As seen from Appendix F, the EEI Reactor Assessment Panel also predicted a learning trend for all plant types. Contrary to expectations, the downtrend in LWR plant investment costs has not been maintained. In fact, we have witnessed just the opposite effect. Over the last seven years, nuclear plant capital costs (in constant dollars) have roughly tripled. Fossil-fueled plant costs have increased rapidly also. Vann, Whit-

---

[31]The AEC's rule-making hearings on acceptance criteria for emergency core-cooling systems for light-water reactors.

[32]Bowers and Myers, "Estimated Capital Cost," p. 21.

[33]Paul MacAvoy, *Economic Strategy,* p. 111.

FIGURE 8. Capital Cost Effect of "Learning" on Commercial LWR Power
Plants in the United States

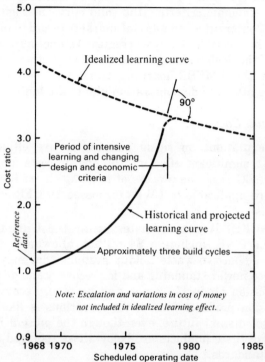

SOURCE: H.E. Vann, M.J. Whitman, and H.I. Bowers, "Factors Affecting
Historical and Projected Capital Costs of Nuclear Power Plants in the
United States," paper presented at the Fourth UN Conference on Peaceful
Uses of Atomic Energy (Geneva, Sept. 6-16, 1971).

man, and Bowers[34] suggest that although history has not been kind
to nuclear plant investment costs (as demonstrated by the rapidly
rising curve in Figure 8), nuclear plants (LWRs) beginning operation in 1978, should include all of the significant design and
economic escalatory costs, thus leading to cost stabilization shortly
after that date. This of course remains to be seen.

[34]H. E. Vann, M. J. Whitman, H. I. Bowers, "Factors Affecting Historical and
Projected Capital Costs of Nuclear Power Plants in the United States" (Paper presented at the Fourth United Nations International Conference on Peaceful Uses
of Atomic Energy, Geneva, Sept. 6-16, 1971).

It is noteworthy that the capital cost curves in the 1970 Analysis do not include a similar "period of intensive learning and changing design and economic criteria" (the solid curve in Figure 8) when the LMFBR enters the commercial market. In order to accept the cost curves in the 1970 Analysis (Figure 4), one must hypothesize that most of the design changes and the host of other factors which could offset the LMFBR learning trend will be under control immediately after the demonstration plants are built.

Environmental Costs

Future regulations on siting and radioactive effluent control could have a significant effect on the energy costs for all reactor types. The AEC is in the process of revising the radiation protection standard applicable to LWRs (proposed 10 CFR 50 Appendix I regulations).

The CONCEPT-II cost estimates (using the United Engineers data) for the PWR, include a $4 million allowance ($4/kw)[35] for additional radioactive waste holdup systems that may be needed to meet these newer standards and for recovery and disposal of the noble gas fission products—xenon and krypton. Recovery of these gaseous fission products from LWR operations is likely to begin in the not-too-distant future, even though the present release concentrations of these products are below those required to meet the new AEC standards..

The cost of radioactive gas recovery systems, including tritium removal, should be significantly less for HTGRs. The fission product release from proposed HTGRs is already well below the proposed 10 CFR 50 Appendix I numerical limits.

The United Engineers cost estimates for the LMFBR in CONCEPT-II include the cost of radioactive gas recovery systems. The industry for several years has assumed that LMFBRs will have near-zero radioactive release.

In summary, since the 1970 Analysis the AEC has continued to update its cost data and improve its methods of estimating capital costs of steam electric power plants. The effect of these newer data has not been favorable to the LMFBR. For example, *without changing any other assumptions,* if one were to replace the capital cost curves used in the 1970 Analysis by curves based on CONCEPT-II

---

[35]Actual cost may be as high as $6/kw.

reference plant capital cost estimates and the ORNL assumptions of unit sizes and learning rates presented by Bowers and Myers, then the predicted net benefits of the LMFBR program would be close to, if not less than, zero, and the model would probably predict that the LMFBR would not be competitive in 1986 even if it were commercially available. Furthermore, the competitive position of the LMFBR is likely to be even worse than this would indicate, since this estimate does not reflect development problems (some unforeseen), which the LMFBR program faces and which we know from experience can result in costly solutions in terms of commercial designs.

REACTOR PERFORMANCE DATA

As shown in Table 8, two LMFBR designs having appreciably different performance characteristics were included in the 1970 Analysis: the 1000-Mw follow-on designs by Atomics International (AI) and General Electric (GE).

With the AEC's assumption that 1900-Mw LMFBRs based on the GE design will be on-line in 1990, the 1970 Analysis projects that only 24 million kw of capacity (equivalent to 24 nominal size—1000-Mw—plants) will be supplied by the AI follow-on plants that are built between 1986 and 1990. In 1990, large advanced reactors of the GE design are projected to capture the market, and the 2,924 million kw of capacity added between 1990 and 2020 are expected to be supplied by these reactors.[36] Thus, in this model, over 99 percent of the LMFBR capacity is supplied by advanced oxide reactors. Therefore, for all practical purposes, the 1970 Analysis is based on 2000-Mw to 3000-Mw LMFBRs of the GE design.

The questions that arise are (1) What are the characteristics of the two designs and how do they differ in cost-benefit terms? (2) In what way is the GE design superior? and, most important, (3) Is it likely that production of this design will indeed be feasible as early as anticipated, if at all?

The significance of the differences in these two designs lies in the large economic incentive to design fast breeder reactor cores

---

[36]Saul Strauch of staff of Division of Reactor Development and Technology, private communication.

TABLE 8. Typical Reactor Characteristics Used in 1970 Analysis

Reactor design	Plant net thermal efficiency (%)	Fuel	Equilibrium fuel exposures Mwd/tonne heavy metal	Specific power Mwt/tonne	Net yield kg/Mwe-yr Fissile Pu	Net yield kg/Mwe-yr U^{233}	Net consumption U^{235}	Initial specific inventory kg fissile per Mwe	Plutonium doubling time (simple interest) (years)	Net U_3O_8 tonnes/ Mwe-yr	Net separative work (kg/Mwe-yr)
LWR Non-recycle	32.5	Enriched uranium for 30 yrs	30,000—1970 20,000—1990	34.9	.272	—	.867	2.17	—	.24	148
Pu-recycle	32.5	Pu in natural uranium — 4 yrs then enriched uranium	30,000—1970 20,000—1990	34.9	.107	—	.690	2.20	—	.19	115
Pu-recycle	32.5	Pu in natural uranium — 10 yrs then enriched uranium	30,000—1970 20,000—1990	44.8	-.009	—	.550	1.48	—	.13	105
HTGR Reference	43	Highly enriched uranium carbide (U^{235} in U^{238}) in ThC with recycling of bred U^{233}	63,000	57.0	.001	.064	.293	1.77	—	.09	98
LMFBR Early[a]	42	PuO_2-UO_2	Core—68,000 Blanket—6000	50.2	.217	—	—	2.67	12	—	—
Advanced[b] reactors	42	PuO_2-UO_2	Core—104,000 Blanket—9000	53.8	.358	—	—	1.96	6	—	—

SOURCE: U.S. Atomic Energy Commission, Division of Reactor Development and Technology, *Updated (1970) Cost-Benefit Analysis of the U.S. Breeder Reactor Program*, WASH 1184 (Jan. 1972), p. 40.
[a]Based on AI follow-on design performance data.
[b]Based on GE follow-on design performance data.

with optimum fuel geometries. That is, the cores of such reactors would be so designed that the efficiency of the reactor could not be increased by changing the core configuration, within reasonable constraints imposed by physical characteristics and safety considerations. Given this optimal design, plant safety must then rely on engineering safeguards to provide the equivalent margins of safety, rather than the inherent physical properties of the fuel and core configuration. This is necessary because of the large energy release estimated for disassembly accidents associated with the advanced core designs having these optimum or near-optimum fuel geometries.

The GE follow-on design capitalizes on the benefits of a near-optimum fuel geometry. It assumes that accidents leading to complete core voiding[37] and major meltdown of the fuel must either be prevented by sophisticated accident detection and protection devices, or must be shown to be "incredible" (of acceptable low probability) by further development effort.[38] Since very large accidents are prevented from occurring solely through the use of core safety instrumentation and protective systems in the GE design, blast shields to absorb large quantities of energy during a hypothetical fuel meltdown or large sodium voiding accident are not provided within the vessel structure.[39] This is in contrast to the AI follow-on design and other more conservative LMFBR designs, which assume that major voiding and meltdown accidents could occur, but the severity of such accidents would be minimized by designing particular characteristics into the reactor core. The AI design is based on containment of a disassembly accident.[40]

The advanced GE design represents the most optimistic technology of the AEC-sponsored 1000-Mw LMFBR design studies.[41]

---

[37]Core voiding refers to loss of liquid coolant, in this case sodium, from the reactor core, generally through vaporization. An excellent layman's discussion of sodium voiding, the sodium void coefficient, and other reactor power coefficients, reproduced from "The Fast Breeder Reactor," by A. S. Gibson, is contained in Appendix C. This paper as well as others presenting economic and ecological arguments for developing the LMFBR can be obtained by writing Manager-Marketing, Breeder Reactor Department, General Electric Co., 310 DeGuigne Drive, Sunnyvale, California 94086.

[38]GE, "Conceptual Plant Design, p. 1.

[39]Ibid, p. 13.

[40]Atomics International, *AI Follow-on Study*, Vol. I, p. 68.

[41]See reports cited in Paul R. Huebotter, "Effects of Metal Swelling and Creep on Fast Reactor Design and Performance," *Reactor Technology*, Vol. 15, No. 2 (Summer 1972), p. 180.

It is designed to operate at a peak fuel temperature of 5100°F.[42]
At 1.10 times rated power, the maximum temperature is 5200°F,
which is right at the melting point of the fuel, i.e., 5206°F. By
comparison, the peak fuel temperature of the AI design during normal operations is 4420°F,[43] safely under the fuel melting
point. Unlike the AI design, the GE fuel pins are the vented type
to prevent internal pressure buildup due to fission product gases.
As a result, the fission products are released directly to the sodium
coolant rather than remaining trapped in the elements until the
fuel is reprocessed after removal from the core. The reactor core
of the GE design operates at a high average specific power, 155
Mw(t)/mt of U+Pu, compared with 116 Mw(t)/mt for the AI
design.[44] As seen from Table 8, the GE design has a higher average
core burnup, 104,000 Mwd/mt of U+Pu, compared with the AI
design's 68,000 Mwd/mt, and a much lower fuel inventory, initially
1.96 metric tons of fissile U+Pu, compared with the AI design's
2.67 metric tons.

Due to its near-optimum fuel geometry and higher specific
power, the GE design has a much larger positive sodium void coefficient. Reactors designed to operate with high sodium void coefficient will have to be highly instrumented—much more so than
present-day reactors with negative void coefficients—in order to
counter the loss of what is otherwise an attractive safety factor.
This, in turn, leads to the requirement for the GE design's accident
control strategy discussed above.

By operating at higher peak fuel and cladding temperatures,
higher specific power and core burnup, and with a lower fuel inventory, the advanced oxide design proposed by GE has lower fuel
cycle cost and a shorter fuel doubling time, i.e., seven and three-
quarter years[45] compared with thirteen years[46] for the AI design
(Table 8 reports six and twelve years respectively).

Even with advances in instrumentation in the next two decades,
advanced LMFBR designs, such as the GE follow-on, would still not
be consistent with the Commission's "defense in depth" approach

---

[42]U.S. AEC, "An Assessment of the LMFBR," WASH 1100, unpublished (1970),
p. 96.
[43]Ibid.
[44]See Glossary for definition of technical terms and abbreviations.
[45]GE, "Conceptual Plant Design," p.13.
[46]Atomics International, *AI Follow-on Study,* Vol. II, p. 258.

to reactor safety.[47] It does not appear that an ultra-high performance LMFBR design like the GE design will be built at an early
date, if at all, thereby compromising reactor safety and the success
of the LMFBR program. It seems more likely that the GE design's
peak fuel and cladding temperatures and other design characteristics eventually must be traded against a wider safety margin, in
the latter's favor.

One difficulty that the GE design, as well as other fast breeder
designs, has encountered is dimensional instability of the fast
breeder reactor fuel and structural materials, due to radiation-
induced swelling and radiation-induced creep. The British in 1967
discovered that high neutron doses over long periods of time, a
combination of conditions planned for commercial LMFBRs, can
result in dangerous amounts of swelling over the projected lifetime
of the fuel, typically two or more years.[48] Since the swelling was
discovered, the major challenge in the field of fast reactor core
design has been to predict the nature of the dimensional changes
in reactor components and to accomodate these properties of reactor materials, the general characteristics of fast reactors, and the
objectives and constraints of specific reactors.[49]

Paul Huebotter of Argonne National Laboratory recently
reviewed the effects of metal swelling and creep on fast reactor
design and performance. In reference to $(U,Pu)O_2$-fueled LMFBR
with stainless steel core structures, Huebotter says, " . . . it appears
that the swelling phenomenon has thwarted the development of
core features that could have produced a step increase in core-fuel
fraction with resultant increases in breeding ratio and specific
power." He goes on to note that the core design features of the
GE follow-on designs now seem impractical in view of the need
to accommodate swelling, while the AI and Babcock & Wilcox
1000-Mw concepts now seem to be more practical designs.[50]

---

[47]As discussed by William O. Doub, in "The Future of the Breeder, Its Impact
on the Environment, and Its Regulatory Aspects" (remarks before the 35th Annual
Meeting of the Washington Public Utility Districts Association, Seattle, Washington, Dec. 9, 1971), *AEC News Release,* Vol. 2, No. 50 (Dec. 15, 1971), p. 4.

[48]For a typical mixed-oxide fuel element in a commercial LMFBR, the maximum
radiation-induced swelling has been estimated at about 12 percent ($\Delta V/V$) at a
peak fuel burnup of 100,000 Mwd/metric ton. The assumptions on which this
estimate is based are given in Huebotter, "Effect of Metal Swelling," p. 159.

[49]Ibid., p. 157.

[50]Ibid., pp. 178,179.

The GE design also faces numerous technological uncertainties associated with the design and development of specific instruments required for safety systems, as well as with the reactor structure, the sodium pumps and valves, sodium to sodium heat exchanger, and steam generator.[51]

Although the 1970 Analysis does not report the sensitivity of the LMFBR net benefits to changes in reactor performance data, one can estimate applicable results from the 1968 Analysis and the LMFBR capital cost sensitivity data presented in the 1970 Analysis. As shown in Figure 9, any change in the LMFBR design characteristics that would result in a change in the plant power cost on the order of 1 mill/kwh (10 to 15 percent of the generating cost from LWRs on order today) would have a devastating effect on the net discounted benefits.

It was noted previously that industry estimates place the AI follow-on design fuel cycle costs at 0.5 mills/kwh greater than the fuel cycle costs of the GE design. An independent estimate can be found by comparing the "levelized cost of power"[52] for the two LMFBR designs having comparable start-up dates. Levelized cost of power for the plants is printed out by the power economy model used in the 1970 Analysis. While these data have not been published, I have learned that the difference in levelized cost of power for the two designs is closer to 1 mill/kwh.

Thus, if the AEC's Division of Reactor Licensing chooses not to license reactor designs with large positive void coefficients that rely solely on instrumentation for plant and public safety, the LMFBR energy cost could easily increase by 0.5 mills/kwh or more.

Discussing the economic implications of accommodating radiation-induced swelling and radiation-induced creep, Huebotter notes:[53]

The general view of fast reactor designers is that the need to accommodate swelling and creep will increase the cost of energy production, but not by so much as to undermine the role of the breeder reactor as a major future energy source for the world.

[51]GE, "Conceptual Plant Design," p.5.

[52]The levelized cost of power is defined as that constant number of mills/kwh which will yield a flow of cash to the generating companies sufficient to recover their investments, pay all operating and fuel cycle expenses, including taxes, and earn the required rate of return on investment. See Appendix A for further details.

[53]Paul Huebotter, "Effects of Metal Swelling" p. 178.

Capital costs are subject to increase from (1) larger reactor size resulting from space needed to accommodate swelling in the core and (2) complex reactor internals not heretofore utilized, e.g., core clamps.

The only component of the energy-cost increase calculable on first principles is the cost of the enlarged interassembly gap reflected through decreased breeding ratio and specific power. This cost has been calculated as~0.08 mill/kwh for 15% swelling accommodation and proportionately less for lesser amounts of swelling. The upper boundary on fuel-cycle cost increase has been suggested as 0.35 mill/kwh, based on the worst-case assumption that fuel burnup would need to be reduced by half.

Several design approaches have been suggested that represent more radical departures from preswelling LMFBR design practice. All involve penalties in fuel-cycle costs which generally fall between the limits given above [footnotes omitted].

FIGURE 9. Sensitivity of Discounted Benefits to LMFBR Energy Costs

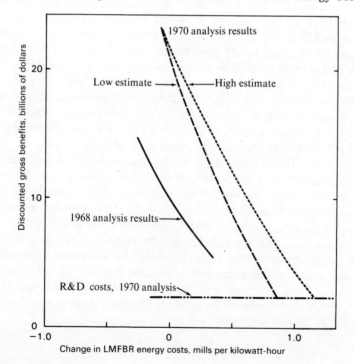

NOTE: 1970 Analysis results based on case 3 assumptions (see Table 6).

Elsewhere, Huebotter notes:[54]

Taking the "physics" value of increased interassembly sodium gaps as the minimum cost of accommodating swelling and a 50% burnup reduction as the maximum cost, a cost-benefit analysis for development of low-swelling alloys has been made. The analysis indicated that the cost savings of having to accommodate only 5% $\Delta V/V$ in U.S. breeder reactors to be built over the period 1970-2020.., rather than 15% $\Delta V/V$, have a 1970 present worth of from $860,000,000 to $5,600,000,000.

These present-worth estimates are based on the 1968 Analysis. If based on the 1970 Analysis, as seen from Figure 9, the lower and upper limits would be about $2 billion and $8 billion, respectively. Since the GE follow-on was not designed to accommodate significant swelling, in the context of the 1970 Analysis, these represent limits on the cost penalty of having to make such an accommodation.

In the 1970 Analysis the GE design is brought on-line in 1990, four years after the first follow-on plant enters the market. Construction on the first LMFBR demonstration plant will not start before 1974 at the earliest. It is not expected to start generating power before 1980. After that date, there may be one or two more demonstration plants. At present, the period between initial planning and operation of light water reactors is approaching ten years, with a seven-and-one-half year construction period. Even if an AI follow-on design is on-line by 1986, and twenty-four follow-on plants are completed by 1990, within the present scope of the LMFBR program plan it is inconceivable that an advanced oxide LMFBR meeting the GE specifications will be on-line by 1990. Even if the GE design were built, discounting the adequacy of safety provisions, it would not be available before the mid- or late-1990s at the very earliest. Such a delay would be costly in terms of projected net benefits. Using 1970 Analysis results, a ten-year delay in the entry dates of both LMFBR designs would reduce present value benefits by $20 billion, more than the estimated net benefits of the program. Delaying only the advanced oxide design by ten years would represent a sizable fraction of that amount.

While I have not made a comparable analysis of LWR and HTGR performance characteristics used in the 1970 Analysis, a few brief observations are worth noting.

[54]Ibid., p. 179.

Three of several types of LWRs were used in the 1970 Analysis (see Table 8). The data for the first LWR, using only enriched uranium feed, approach closely the performance of today's commercial plants.

The HTGR data in the same table are optimistic relative to present commercial designs which have been purchased by utilities. Specifically, the HTGR in the 1970 Analysis includes an on-line refueling machine and has a higher conversion ratio[55] than in present commercial designs. In addition, it has a net thermal efficiency of 43 percent, while today's designs are closer to 39 percent.

While development of an on-line refueling machine and high conversion ratios and higher efficiencies probably can be achieved in subsequent HTGRs, development of these factors will probably be dictated by economic optimization of the entire reactor plant to produce power at minimum cost.

The initial core of the 40-Mw HTGR prototype at Peach Bottom experienced an excessive—in fact, intolerable—fuel failure rate. While this problem appears to have been corrected, to date there is simply not enough operating experience to confirm that the fuel particles and fuel elements of large HTGRs will operate within required technical specification, under commercial HTGR operating conditions, over the projected lifetime of the fuel. If commercial HTGRs were to experience unanticipated excessive fuel failures in the future, this could result in a reduction in the actual performance. A similar effect has already occurred with LWRs. The Advisory Committee on Reactor Safeguards recommended in 1972 that the power levels of several large LWRs be limited to less than full power.[56] This resulted from the discovery of an unanticipated fuel degradation problem in unpressurized fuel elements removed from the 420-Mw PWR at Ginna. Similarly, several PWRs have been derated because of the effect of fuel densification on meeting licensing requirements related to the emergency core cooling system.

Since one cannot predict the severity of fuel failure problems, regardless of the reactor type, it is difficult to measure the economic

[55]The conversion ratio for a reactor can be defined as: mass of nonfissile material converted to fissile material/mass of fissile material burned, or simply the ratio of fuel bred to fuel burned. A breeder reactor has a conversion ratio greater than one, and the ratio is called the breeding ratio.

[56]The two-unit Zion (twin 1050-Mw PWRs) was restricted to 85 percent full power for the lifetime of the fuel core in unit 1.

impact should such fuel failures occur. In any case, should the fuel failure rate be greater than anticipated, the principal impact would probably result not from any reduction in plant performance but from a decrease in plant reliability, which in turn affects marketability.

FUEL CYCLE COSTS

The achievement of an economically competitive LMFBR is predicated on its ability to attain low fuel cycle costs, since, as indicated earlier, it does not appear possible at present to reduce the capital cost of the LMFBR to values approaching those of the

TABLE 9.   Reactor Fuel Cycle Costs

(a) 1000-Mw LMFBR equilibrium cycle fuel cost

Cost component		Cost, mill/kwh
Fabrication		0.334
Reprocessing and reconversion		0.166
Shipping		0.038
Plutonium carrying charge of which		0.546
Inpile	0.432	
Outpile	0.114	
Fabrication carrying charge		0.061
Reprocessing carrying charge		−0.042
Plutonium credit		−0.348
Total		0.755

(b) Estimated fuel cycle costs for a model
1000-Mw light-water reactor today

Cost component	Cost, mill/kwh
Mining and milling	0.38
Conversion to UF_6	0.07
Enrichment	0.58
Reconversion and fabrication	0.33
Spent-fuel shipping	0.02
Reprocessing	0.12
Waste management	0.04
Plutonium credit	−0.25
Uranium credit (includes a 0.03 mill/kwh cost of reconverting to UF_6)	−0.12
Fuel inventory carrying charge	0.57
Total	1.74

SOURCE: Part (a), U.S. Atomic Energy Commission, *An Assessment of the Liquid Metal Fast Breeder Reactor,* WASH 1100 (unpublished), p. 124. Part (b), U.S. Atomic Energy Commission, *The Nuclear Industry,* WASH 1174-71 (1971), p. 92.

LWR. The AEC assumes that there is a high probability of achieving the fuel cycle costs indicated in Table 9.

According to 1968 AI estimates, the AI follow-on design, with average core fuel burnups of 68,000 Mwd/mt of U+Pu, would have fuel cycle costs on the order of 0.9 mills per kilowatt-hour (kwh).[57] The more efficient GE design, operating at a 104,000 Mwd/ton average core burnup, would require less fuel inventory in the fuel cycle. According to GE estimates in 1968, it could achieve a fuel cycle cost of approximately 0.4 mills/kwh.[58] There are grounds, however, for believing these to be very optimistic, and probably unrealistic estimates because: (1) they are based on a large LMFBR economy with advanced fuel fabrication and reprocessing facilities; (2) they do not include future environmental and materials safeguard costs; and (3) they are based on a thirty-day time period between reactor refueling and shipment of the spent fuel to the reprocessing plant. These factors will be discussed in more detail below.

One of the principal factors influencing fuel cycle costs is reactor design (see previous section). However, I am not challenging most fuel cycle cost data, which are treated in detail in the literature.[59] The discussion here is limited to those fuel cycle costs that are external to the reactor, e.g., fuel fabrication and reprocessing costs, and among those, only the costs that were not included in the 1970 Analysis or that could significantly alter the difference between LMFBR and LWR (or HTGR) fuel cycle costs.

Technological Uncertainty

Technological uncertainties can exist in establishing a large-scale commercial plutonium recycle capability for LWRs and fast reactors. Here, the head-end, solvent extraction and to some extent the fabrication steps, will benefit from commercially available experience with LWR fuel. Significant differences will be due primarily to: (1) the higher enrichment of the LMFBR fuel requir-

[57]Atomics International, *AI Follow-on Study,* Vol. I, p. 66.
[58]GE, "Conceptual Plant Design," p. 27.
[59]Oak Ridge National Laboratory, *Siting of Fuel Reprocessing Plants and Waste Management Facilities* (compiled and edited by the ORNL staff), ORNL-4451 (July 1971), p. 362; U.S. AEC, *An Assessment of the LMFBR;* U.S. AEC, *Reactor Fuel Cycle Costs for Nuclear Power Evaluation,* WASH 1099 (Dec. 1971); U.S. AEC, *LMFBR Program Plan,* Vol. 8, *Fuel Recycle,* WASH 1108 (Aug. 1968), pp. 8-28, 8-29.

ing greater criticality control; (2) higher concentrations of volatile fission products (principally iodine) if the LMFBR fuel is reprocessed after a short cooling period; and (3) the remote fabrication requirement due to the relatively high concentrations of various plutonium isotopes other than Pu-239 (i.e., Pu-236, -238, -240, -241, and -242) and their daughter products in the core fuel. The intrinsic neutron- and gamma-radiation levels are likely to be fairly high, and some degree of remote fabrication will be required, even if the fuel is fully decontaminated from fission products.

These technological uncertainties could affect the size of the fuel business, which is one of the most significant factors in establishing fuel fabrication and reprocessing costs. General Electric reported that a more conservative estimate that arbitrarily doubles the fabrication and reprocessing unit costs and increases the cost of capital from 10 to 13 percent would increase the LMFBR fuel cycle costs of the GE design by almost 0.5 mills/kwh.[60]

Doubling fabrication and reprocessing unit costs is not unrealistic. For example, the cost of reprocessing LWR fuels drops from about $31/kg in a 1-metric ton/day plant to less than one-half of this figure in a 5-metric ton/day plant, and to a little more than one-third of the 1-metric ton/day cost at 17 to 18 metric tons per day.[61] Similar economies of scale can be found in HTGR and LMFBR fuel fabrication and reprocessing plants.

As can be seen in Table 10, the AEC's economic model includes such economies of scale. In fact, the 1970 Analysis predicts that fabrication and reprocessing costs for all reactor types will drop significantly over the next fifty years. Since the 1970 Analysis does not predict high "first-of-a-kind" LMFBR costs during the initial period of commercialization, and since it anticipates that the very optimistic GE design will be introduced in 1990, the 1970 Analysis predicts that LMFBRs will be built as rapidly as possible for the first ten years.[62] As a result the LMFBRs are expected to be able to profit rapidly from the economies of scale in the fuel cycle.

By other AEC estimates, near-term (late 1980s and early 1990s) fuel cycle costs for LMFBRs are expected to be about 2 mills/kwh

[60]GE, "Conceptual Plant Design," p. 5.

[61]Ibid., pp. 2-9.

[62]In the 1970 Analysis, it is arbitrarily assumed that 8000 Mw of LMFBR capacity will be built in the 1986-87 biennium, with the limitation that the capacity could no more than double in any succeeding two-year period. AEC, *Updated (1970) Analysis*, p. 41.

TABLE 10. AEC Estimate of Representative Fuel Fabrication and Reprocessing Costs Used in 1970 Cost-Benefit Analysis of the LMFBR Program

Reactor	Fabrication cost including fuel preparation, $/kg[a]		Reprocessing cost including conversion, $/kg[a]	
	Initial	Year 2020	Initial	Year 2020
LWR (without Pu recycle)	$ 83	$ 42	$ 34	$ 22
LWR (with Pu recycle)	147	48	50	22
HTGR (with LMFBR)	243	89	62	34
LMFBR (intro. 1986)	316	115	38	30

SOURCE: U.S. Atomic Energy Commission, *Updated (1970) Cost-Benefit Analysis of the U.S. Breeder Reactor Program,* WASH 1184 (Jan. 1972), p. 41.

[a]The contribution to the energy cost, C_e (mills/kwh), for a nuclear plant or plant type, due to a fuel cycle cost component, C_f ($/kg), can be calculated using

$$C_e = \frac{KC_f}{\epsilon B},$$

where B is the fuel burnup in Mw(t)−d/metric ton, ϵ is the plant's thermal efficiency, and $K = 1000/24$. Typical values of B for the LWR, HTGR, and LMFBR are 33,000 Mwd/mt, 65,000 Mwd/mt, and 80,000 Mwd/mt, respectively; typical values of ϵ are 0.33, 0.4, and 0.4, respectively.

(about 0.3 mills/kwh higher than LWR fuel cycle costs today).[63] Here, the assumption is that the LMFBR will not be competitive initially. In November 1972 Bertram Wolfe, director of General Electric's Breeder Reactor Division, suggested that it may take subsidization to get commercial breeders going. He said, "Perhaps it will require a commitment to provide a large number of plants where it will be known that the first few will be unprofitable—the kind of commitment that GE and Westinghouse undertook to launch commercial light water reactors."[64] As mentioned earlier, the AEC has earmarked $90 million of its R&D budget to be spent in direct assistance to utilities to help them buy their first four commercial-size breeder power plants. I believe that under more realistic capital cost and design assumptions, the high LMFBR fuel cycle costs may persist for a longer period and further subsidies would be required.

[63]U.S. AEC, *LMFBR Program Plan,* WASH 1108, pp. 8-28.
[64]Bertram Wolfe, "The Influence of Component Development, Prototype Designs, and Construction Experience on the 1000-Mw LMFBR," *Transactions* of the American Nuclear Society's International Conference on Nuclear Solutions to World Energy Problems (Washington, D.C., Nov. 12-17, 1972).

Technological uncertainty could also have a large effect on HTGR fuel cycle costs. For example, we have no large-scale experience with the uranium-233–thorium fuel cycle insofar as uranium 233 recycling is concerned. The processes required for the recycling of uranium-233 from graphite fuels are: (1) a head-end step in which the fuel and fission products are separated from the carbon; (2) a solvent extraction step in which the thorium and uranium are separated from the fission products and from each other; and (3) a refabrication step in which both recycled uranium-233 and fresh fuel are prepared for insertion in the reactor. At present, additional development work is required to demonstrate the head-end step. General solvent extraction technology exists for processing the irradiated fuel, and separation and subsequent decontamination of uranium-233 has been demonstrated in the laboratory. In addition, limited pilot-plant experience has been gained in the recovery of thorium. Recovered thorium and uranium-233, even after removal of fission products, rapidly become radioactive due to the radioactive decay of uranium-232 and subsequent buildup of its daughter products. While several approaches to the problem of decontamination and fabrication of HTGR fuel are under consideration, it appears probable that the HTGR, like the LMFBR, will require some form of remote fabrication of its recycled fuel. There is considerable uncertainty in cost estimates of remote fabrication when on a commercial scale.

In summary, two important unknowns are to what extent the LWR and HTGR fuel cycles will benefit from economies of scale before the LMFBR is introduced in significant numbers and whether the LMFBR can rapidly close the gap if it exists. The 1970 Analysis predicts the LMFBR will be economically attractive initially, will be introduced rapidly, and will quickly benefit by economies of scale in the fuel cycle.

Plutonium Carrying Charge

Another factor that could increase fuel cycle costs of LMFBRs relative to LWRs is related to the out-of-pile plutonium carrying charge. There is a strong economic incentive for making the cooling time as short as possible in order to minimize inventory charges.[65] HTGR and FBR spent fuel (mixed core and blanket) can

---

[65]U.S. AEC, *Reactor Fuel Cycle Costs*, p. 110.

have values of $500 to $1000 per kilogram, depending on fissile uranium and plutonium values.[66] Preprocessing delays can thus cost $5 to $20 per kilogram per month,[67] or a total of $20 to $80 per kilogram for the difference between a "conventional" (LWR) 150-day postirradiation cooling time and a projected economic cooling time of thirty days.[68] The 1970 Analysis assumed a thirty-day cooling time for LMFBR spent fuel. A 150-day cooling period would increase LMFBR fuel cycle costs (assuming an AI design) by about 0.06 mills/kwh to 0.25 mills/kwh.[69] Increasing the LMFBR cooling time to 270 days would of course double these estimates. Alvin Weinberg, director of Oak Ridge National Laboratory, has assumed 0.2 mills/kwh as the penalty for increasing the cooling period to 360 days.[70]

A second incentive for making the cooling time as short as possible is related to the breeder doubling time, that is, the time required for the breeder to produce twice as much fuel as it consumes. For a single reactor the doubling time is proportional to $(t_r + t_o)/t_r$, where t_r is the time interval the fuel is in the reactor, and t_o is the time interval the fuel spends outside the reactor for reprocessing, fabrication, and associated operations.[71] Assuming typical values, t_r = two years and t_o = one year, increasing the cooling time by half a year would increase the doubling time by

[66]Ibid., p. 120.

[67]A. R. Irvine in "An Engineering Evaluation of LMFBR Fuel Shipment" (ORNL-TM-2723, Sept. 1971), p. 3, uses $18/kg per month.

[68]U.S. AEC, *Reactor Fuel Cycle Costs.*

[69]To convert $/kg to mills/kwh, see note in Table 10.

[70]Alvin M. Weinberg, "Social Institutions and Nuclear Energy," *Science,* 177 (July 7, 1972), p. 31. This is not a large cost penalty compared with the total cost of generating electricity, estimated as 8.6 mills/kwh.

[71]Simple doubling time (*SDT*), which is applicable to a single breeder operating alone, is approximated by

$$SDT = \frac{KI_s}{BR-1} ,$$

where K is a constant whose value depends on the load factor, α (the neutron capture-to-fission ratio for plutonium in LMFBRs), and the frequency of refueling; BR is the breeding ratio defined as the ratio of fuel atoms (plutonium) produced (from conversion of U-238) to the fuel atoms burned in the reactor; and I_s is the specific inventory of a reactor *system* (kg fissile material/Mw(t)). Assuming a load factor = 0.8, the constant K is about 3.2 for LMFBRs, although it varies among designs. Breeding ratios can be in excess of 1.6 (a so-called high gain breeder), but for oxide-fueled LMFBRs the current estimates range from 1.1 to 1.3. I_s can be about 17 percent. The breeder doubling time is more sensitive to other factors, primarily the specific inventory of the reactor (kg fissile material/Mw in the reactor) and the fuel burnup (megawatt-days/ton of fuel).[72] The doubling time can affect the rate of market penetration of the breeder if there is a shortage of plutonium for fueling the initial cores of these reactors, and it also affects the ultimate LMFBR fraction of generating capacity and the ultimate demand on uranium resources. With respect to the last, the difference between doubling times of seven and fourteen years can mean the difference of a few million tons in peak cumulative ore requirements for a combination of breeders and nonbreeders.

In the United States a shortage of plutonium is unlikely to be a problem initially and, in any event, achieving minimum power cost is generally considered more important than the total fissile inventory growth criterion. Hence, in selecting the cooling time, the breeder performance as measured by the doubling time is of secondary importance compared with the inventory costs.

Spent-Fuel Costs

There are environmental considerations that could either force the industry toward spent LMFBR fuel cooling times considerably

---

expressed as

$$I_s = \frac{t_r + t_o}{t_r} I_r = \left(1 + \frac{t_o}{t_r}\right) I_r,$$

where t_r and t_o are defined in the text and I_r is the specific inventory of the reactor itself (kg fissile material/Mw(t) in the reactor). The reciprocal of I_r is the specific fuel rating, i.e., specific power (Mw(t)/kg of fissile material) not to be confused with specific power in units of Mw(t)/kg fuel (fissile and nonfissile). For reasons of general economics (inventory charges and doubling time), the fast reactor core requires a specific power on the order of 1 Mw(t)/kg of fissile plutonium.

[72]Referring to the previous notation, the time the fuel spends in the reactor, t_r, can be expressed as $t_r = I_r \cdot BU$, where BU is the burnup. This, together with the expressions in footnote 71, yields:

$$SDT = \frac{K}{BR-1} \left(I_r + \frac{t_o}{BU}\right),$$

which demonstrates the requirement for high burnup, low fuel cycle time, and low specific inventory (i.e., high fuel rating). This also demonstrates some of the trade-off that must be considered in designing a breeder. For example, a high breeding ratio does not necessarily increase the doubling time, if it is at the expense of a high specific inventory.

TABLE 11. Comparison of Decay-Heat Generation Rates and Fission-Product Activity Levels for LWR and LMFBR Fuels

Type of reactor	Specific power[a] (kw/kg of fuel)	Fuel burnup[a] (1000 Mwd/tonne)	Cooling time (days)	Heat-generation rate (kw/kg of fuel)	Total (B+γ) activity (1000 curies/kg of fuel)[b]
LWR	15	20	30	23	5
LWR	15	20	90	12	2
LMFBR	100	50	30	132	33
LMFBR	100	50	90	68	19
LMFBR	200	50	30	230	54
LMFBR	200	50	90	110	28
LMFBR	200	100	30	264	66
LMFBR	200	100	90	136	38

SOURCE: U.S. Atomic Energy Commission, *Liquid Metal Fast Breeder Reactor Program Plan, Vol. 8: Fuel Recycle* (prepared by the LMFBR Program Office of Argonne National Laboratory for the AEC Division of Reactor Development and Technology), WASH 1108 (Aug. 1968), p. 8–54.

[a]Current estimates of fuel characteristics (i.e., specific power and burnup) are given in the text.

[b]As a rough approximation, beta and gamma curies can each be expected to be one-half the total curies.

longer than the thirty-day cooling time assumed in the 1970 Analysis, or significantly increase LMFBR shipping costs, at present estimated to be about 0.04 mills/kwh plus the fuel inventory charge for the LMFBR fuels (see Table 9).

Because LMFBR fuels are burned at high specific power (kw/kg of fuel) and discharged after high burnups, the discharged fuels will contain high concentrations of short-lived fission products —e.g., I-131 and Xe-133. This results in higher rates of decay heat generation and radiation levels than with LWR fuels. The important difference in the severity of the problems in shipping LMFBR fuels and current LWR fuels is illustrated in the last two columns of Table 11. While this table illustrates fairly well the differences between LWR and LMFBR fuels, the numbers themselves are not very accurate, nor is the relative proportion of beta and gamma energies.[73]

[73]U.S. AEC, *LMFBR Program Plan,* WASH 1108, pp. 8-53 and 8-54.

Typical estimates of fuel characteristics today in thermal units are:

Reactor	Specific power (kw/kg of fuel)	Fuel burnup (1000 Mwd/ton)
PWR	37.5	33
LMFBR (AI design)		
Core	116	67.6
Blanket	4.7-8.1	4.7-8.0
LMFBR (GE design)		
Core	156	104.5
Blanket	8.5-13	8.7-9.1

A typical LMFBR spent-fuel shipment might contain roughly equal quantities of core and blanket material. For the AI design this fuel mixture would have an average specific power of 60 kw/kg and an average burnup of 37,000 Mwd/ton.

The AEC's concept for shipping spent LMFBR fuel after a thirty-day cooling time is based in part on a GE proposal and current ORNL designs. Each shipping cask would contain approximately six to eighteen fuel assemblies. The fuel assemblies would be shipped by rail, sealed in individual steel canisters filled with liquid sodium as a heat transfer agent. Each shipment might contain 1.5 tons of spent fuel and would generate up to 300 kilowatts of thermal power.[74]

Each shipment would contain up to 75 megacuries of radioactivity including about 200,000 curies of radioactive iodine, 120,000 curies of xenon, and 15,000 curies of krypton.[75] An accidental release during shipping of all the noble gases and 30 percent of the volatile iodine would be equivalent to the release of 200,000 curies of radioactive material. By comparison, the United Kingdom Atomic Energy Authority (UKAEA) Windscale accident, October 10, 1957, was smaller by a factor of 10; the estimated release dur-

---

[74]Alvin M. Weinberg, "Social Institutions and Nuclear Energy," p. 31.

[75]Ibid. Assuming 1.5 metric tons of spent LMFBR (AI reference oxide design) fuel at thirty-day cooling time. Power = 58.23 Mw/mt; average burnup = 32,977 Mwd/mt; flux = 2.65×10^{15} N/cm^2-sec. See U.S. AEC, *Siting of Fuel Reprocessing Plants*, p. 3-39. The AI reference oxide design is an earlier LMFBR design than the AI follow-on design discussed previously in the text. This does not significantly affect the results.

ing this accident was 21,000 curies, principally from the iodine and the noble gases.[76] The maximum integrated exposure to a person in the open in the vicinity of the Windscale accident was 30-50 mrem. Therefore, it would not be unreasonable to expect individuals not occupationally exposed to receive from an LMFBR spent-fuel shipping accident absorbed doses on the order of 0.5 rem or greater.[77] Larger doses are estimated if one considers iodine reconcentration in the grass–cow–milk food chain. The cost of such an accident could easily run into the tens of millions of dollars. Increasing the postirradiation cooling time to 150 days would effectively eliminate the iodine and xenon hazards. About 97 percent of the radiokrypton would still be present.

A 1968 ORNL staff study projected 9,500 shipments of spent fuel in the year 2000, more than half of these being LMFBR fuel shipments. The same study projected roughly twice the number of LMFBR shipments in 2015 compared with the year 2000, and assumed an average distance from reactor to reprocessing plant of about 500 miles.[78] Weinberg assumed 7,000 to 12,000 spent-fuel shipments per year by 2000, an average shipping distance of 1,000 miles and 60 to 100 loaded casks in transit at all times.[79] The overall accident rate of motor carriers, typically of those that might transport radioactive materials, has declined from 3.2 per million vehicle miles in 1964 to 1.7 per million vehicle miles in 1969.[80] The accident frequency for freight trains (likely to be required for shipping LMFBR spent fuel) increased from 8.2 per million train miles in 1967 to 9.9 per million train miles in 1969.[81] Here the accident rate per car for other than grade-crossing accidents is

---

[76]Theos Thompson, "AEC Technical Review of Selected Portions of *The Careless Atom*," in *Selected Materials on Environmental Effects of Producing Electric Power*, Hearings before the Joint Committee on Atomic Energy, 91 Cong. 1 sess. (1969), p. 356.

[77]The National Council on Radiation Protection and Measurements recommends, "The dose limit for the critical organs (e.g., whole body) of an individual not occupationally exposed shall be 0.5 rem in any one year, in addition to natural radiation and dental exposures" (NCRP Report No. 39, p. 95). By way of comparison, the average per capita dose to the U.S. population due to natural background radiation is 0.13 rem/yr; due to medical and dental exposures the per capita dose is about 0.1 rem/yr.

[78]AEC, *Siting of Fuel Reprocessing Plants*, pp. 2-9, 3-5, 3-54.

[79]Alvin Weinberg, "Social Institutions and Nuclear Energy," p. 31.

[80]AEC, *Environmental Survey of Transportation of Radioactive Materials to and from Nuclear Power Plants* (Dec. 1972), p. 65.

[81]Ibid., p. 66.

TABLE 12.   Accident Probabilities Per Vehicle Mile for Truck, Rail, and
Barge, by Accident Severity Categories

Accident severity category	Vehicle speed at impact (mph)	Fire duration (hr)	Accident probabilities
Minor	0—30	0—1/2	2×10^{-6}
	30—50	0	
Moderate	0—30	1/2—1	3×10^{-7}
	30—70	<1/2	
Severe	0—50	>1	8×10^{-9}
	30—70	1/2—1	
	>70	0—1/2	
Extra severe	50—70	>1	2×10^{-11}
	>70	1/2—1	
Extreme	>70	>1	1×10^{-13}

SOURCE: U.S. Atomic Energy Commission, *Environmental Survey of Transportation of Radioactive Materials to and from Nuclear Power Plants* (Dec. 1972), pp. 70–71.

about 0.8 car accidents per million car miles.[82] Similar data are available for barge accidents.

The AEC has calculated the probability of truck, rail, and barge accidents of various degrees of severity, in terms of velocity of vehicle impact and incident and duration of fire. These data are summarized in Table 12.

Assuming 5,000 LMFBR spent-fuel shipments per year (corresponding roughly to the AEC estimates for the year 2000), an average shipping distance of 1,000 miles, and using the severe accident probability in Table 12, LMFBR spent-fuel casks would be involved in a serious accident at the rate of 0.04 per year. By AEC estimates the probability would double to 8 percent by 2015. This estimate is somewhat lower than a preliminary EPA estimate indicating that by 1990 about fifty accidents per year could occur involving the shipment of spent fuels from nuclear power plants to fuel reprocessing plants, perhaps three to five involving serious damage to the shipping cask.[83]

[82]Ibid., pp. 66-67. This calculation is based on the following information: (1) roughly 58 percent of the rail accidents are other than grade-crossing accidents; (2) the average train length is seventy cars; and (3) each accident involves an average of ten cars.

[83]Contract No. 68-01-0555 issued by Environmental Protection Agency on June 29, 1972, to Holmes and Narver, Inc., Anaheim, California (unpublished), p. 1.

Since the liquid sodium burns spontaneously on contact with air, it would not be unreasonable to assume that those serious accidents where the cask seal is broken would be associated with fires of several hours duration. This in turn could cause the release of most of the noble gases and other volatile fission products, perhaps 1 percent of the semivolatile products (Ru, Cs, Te, Tc, and Se),[84] and very small percentages of the plutonium and nonvolatile fission products.

At present, LWR spent-fuel shipping casks are designed to meet Department of Transportation (DOT) and AEC shipping regulations (10 CFR 71). They must withstand a sequence of hypothetical conditions: a 30-foot free-fall drop (30 mph terminal speed) onto a flat, essentially unyielding surface; followed by a 40-inch free drop onto a 6-inch diameter steel pin; followed by a 30-minute exposure to a 1475°F fire; followed by an 8-hour immersion in 3 feet of water.[85]

It is always possible to hypothesize accident conditions more, or less, severe than these. The critical questions concern the frequencies of these more severe classes of accidents and the probabilities that the cask seals will break or the cooling system will be lost under these more extreme conditions. To date, there is simply not enough information, particularly about the latter factor, to conclude that currently contemplated LMFBR cask designs are adequate, considering the projected frequency of spent-fuel ship-

---

[84]AEC, *Siting of Fuel Reprocessing Plants,* p. 8-46.

[85]The amount of damage to a package in an accident is not directly related to the accident severity. Package damage depends on the form and amount of energy sustained by the package and the ability of the package to withstand those forces. The ability of a package to withstand accident forces depends on the design of the package and the quality assurance exercised in its manufacture, use, and maintenance. Various factors limit the effect accident conditions will have on a package. For instance, the 30-foot free-fall drop test is representative of the damage sustained in most real accidents in which the vehicle speed at the time of impact is greater than 50 mph. Although the velocity at the time of impact in the drop test is about 30 mph, the test requires dropping the package, including the protective shield if it is part of the package, on an unyielding surface. In a real accident, the forces the package sustains are mitigated by the angle of impact of the vehicle, the crushing of the vehicle, which absorbs much of the impact, and the fact that, for impacts of heavy objects such as transporting trucks, the object with which the truck collides in most cases yields and thus absorbs some of the impact. See "Testimony and Exhibits of Robert F. Barker in the Environmental Phase of the Hearings before the Atomic Safety and Licensing Board," AEC Docket Nos. 50-348 & 50-364 (October 15, 1969).

ments. Most assuredly, if LMFBR spent fuel is shipped in thirty days or less, the casks will have to be designed so that the probability of a cask seal break and an associated fire of several hours duration is considered "incredible," in which case the 8 percent per year probability of severe accident estimated above would appear to be unacceptable.

A study of the hazard associated with spent-fuel transportation was performed at ORNL in 1971 under AEC-DRDT direction.[86] This latter study received limited in-house distribution but has not been published. However, the *Environmental Survey of Transportation of Radioactive Materials to and from Nuclear Power Plants,* which applies only to light water reactors, and the following analysis by Weinberg[87] appear to be based in part on this study.

... The derailment rate in rail transport (in the United States) is 10^{-6} per car mile. Thus, if there were 12,000 shipments per year, each of a distance of 1000 miles, we would expect 12 derailments annually. However, the number of serious accidents would be perhaps 10^{-4}- to 10^{-6}-fold less frequent; and shipping casks are designed to withstand all but the most serious accident (the train wreck near an oil refinery that goes into flames as a result of the crash). Thus the statistics—between 1.2×10^{-3} and 1.2×10^{-5} serious accidents per year—at least until the year 2000, look quite good. Nevertheless the shipping problem is a difficult one and may force a change in basic strategy. For example, we may decide to cool fuel from LMFBRs in place for 360 days before shipping: this reduces the heat load sixfold, and increases the cost of power by only around 0.2 mills per electric kilowatt hour. Or a solution that I personally prefer is to cluster fast breeders in nuclear power parks which have their own on-site reprocessing facilities.

In conclusion, if more stringent cask designs or cooling time longer than thirty days are required for LMFBR spent-fuel shipments, or both, the transportation costs in the 1970 Analysis would understate the true costs by 0.06 mills/kwh to 0.25 mills/kwh.

---

[86]In June 1972, EPA contracted with Holmes & Narver, Inc., to perform a similar study.

[87]Alvin Weinberg, "Social Institutions and Nuclear Energy," p. 31. Weinberg notes further that clustering reactors in nuclear parks would make both cooling and transmission of power difficult; also such parks would be more vulnerable to common mode failure, such as acts of war or earthquakes. These difficulties must be balanced against the advantage of not shipping spent fuel off-site, and of simplifying control of fissile material against diversion. While Weinberg's view that the advantages of clustering outweigh its disadvantages is shared by many in the nuclear community, there have been no detailed studies of this trade-off and none are under way.

Effluent Control Costs at Fuel Reprocessing Plants

In a previous section I discussed the AEC's revised radiation protection standards applicable to LWRs (10 CFR 50 Appendix I) and capital costs associated with future regulations on radioactive effluent control at the power plant. If, or when, similar radioactive effluent standards are applied to fuel reprocessing plants, reprocessing costs will increase. In any event, more stringent measures would be required to control the routine release of radionuclides from processing fast breeder reactor fuel than LWR or HTGR fuels, if, for economic reasons, the shorter cooling times proposed for these fuels are used. For example, today, plants that reprocess LWR fuels after 150-day cooling periods routinely release 0.1 percent of the radioactive iodine to the atmosphere. However, plants for reprocessing LMFBR or GCFBR fuels after 30-day cooling periods would require techniques for maintaining the fractional iodine-131 release in the range of 10^{-7}.[88] Likewise, reducing the LMFBR spent-fuel cooling period from 150 days to the proposed 30 days increases the noble gas activity by an order of magnitude. This will be shown in Part II, Chapter 6, where the routine radioactive releases from fuel reprocessing plants are discussed in more detail.

The technology for krypton retention now exists. Identification of an effective and practical disposal method is a major, if not the controlling, consideration regarding whether to remove the Kr-85 at existing LWR fuel reprocessing plants, particularly in view of the low reduction of radiation exposure that would be realized by Kr-85 removal.[89] The cost of a krypton retention system is estimated to be $0.75/kg (about 0.003 mills/kwh).[90] The technology for tritium removal does not exist at present; however, General Electric has estimated for the Midwest Fuel Recovery Plant (1,500 metric tons per year) a cost of $10 million for recovery and less than $1 million for deep-well disposal.[91] Together these costs cor-

---

[88]U.S. AEC, *Siting of Fuel Reprocessing Plants*, p. 8-15.

[89]*Applicants Environmental Report, Supplement No. 1*, Midwest Fuel Recovery Plant, NEDO 14504-2, Class 1 (November 1971).

[90]This assumes $3 million in capital costs, a 24 percent fixed charge rate; $320,000/yr operating expenses (eight people); $40,000/yr for shipping (eighty-one cylinders at $500/cylinder); $48,000/yr for disposal ($600/cylinder) for a plant reprocessing 1,500 metric tons of fuel per year.

[91]*Applicants Environmental Report*, p. II-11.

respond to about \$2.2/kg (0.01 mills/kwh). Other effluent control technologies, such as air filtration and iodine retention at fractional releases in the range of 10^{-4} to 10^{-5}, have been developed and are less costly.

As noted earlier the additional effluent control costs, in \$/kg of fuel processed, are likely to be more at fast breeder reactor fuel reprocessing plants than at equivalent-size LWR fuel reprocessing plants, if spent fuel is shipped after a short cooling time. However, when the fuel cycle costs in \$/kg are converted to mills/kwh (see note to Table 10), due to higher fuel burnups and thermal efficiencies, the LMFBR and HTGR have an advantage over the LWR. For equivalent fuel cycle costs in \$/kg, the energy costs for the LMFBR and HTGR are about one-third the LWR value.

In summary, additional effluent controls at the fuel reprocessing plants are not likely to result in more than a 0.01 to 0.02 mills/kwh increase in energy costs regardless of the plant type, and, therefore, will probably have a negligible effect on the competitive positions of the plant alternatives.

Safeguarding Costs

Safeguarding against diversion of fissile material to unauthorized use could affect how fuel recycle operations will be performed and undoubtedly will increase the fuel cycle cost of all reactor types. The LWRs in operation today and those planned for the next thirty years will be fueled with natural or slightly enriched uranium and will produce plutonium as a by-product. The slightly enriched uranium (about 2 to 4 percent U-235) is not usable for nuclear weapons, but the plutonium (approximately 70 percent fissile) is so usable.[92] Plutonium produced in LWRs is discharged at a typical rate of 250 kg of plutonium, of which 180 kg is fissile, each year from each 1000-Mw reactor. The plutonium is being stockpiled at present, since it is not yet economical to introduce a large-scale plutonium recycle capability. The major safeguard problems are expected to occur in the transportation sector (after spent-fuel processing) and at the fuel preparation and fabrication plants. Hence, safeguarding the plutonium should be more difficult

[92]The critical mass of a plutonium sphere surrounded by a good reflector is about 6 kg. Such a sphere would have a radius no greater than about 4.5 cm (i.e., less than 2 inches). See E. D. Clayton, "Plutonium Criticality Experiments," *Physics Today*, Vol. 18, No. 9 (Sept. 1965), p. 47.

with the introduction of a complete plutonium fuel cycle (for the LMFBR and/or LWR-HTGR with Pu recycle) than if the plutonium were simply stockpiled after reprocessing the LWR spent fuel. It has been predicted that commercial reactors will cause civilian plutonium stores in the United States to rise from the 1971 figure of 600 kilograms to 720,000 kilograms or more by the year 2000.[93] This stockpile will be used to fuel the first LMFBRs.

In the HTGR fuel cycle, for each 1000-Mw plant there will be about 340 kg/yr of fissile U-235 (as 93 percent enriched uranium) shipped from the gaseous diffusion plant. Discharged from the reactor and leaving the spent-fuel reprocessing plant will be roughly 200 kg/yr of fissile uranium, about 90 percent of which is U-233. As noted earlier, U-233 is highly radioactive and therefore difficult to handle. This and the make-up uranium from the diffusion plant will be sent to the fuel preparation and fabrication plants and ultimately reach the reactor as new fuel rods.

At equilibrium, that is, after the third or fourth refueling, approximately 790 kg/yr (GE design) to 1200 kg/yr (AI design) of fissile plutonium for each 1000-Mw LMFBR will be shipped to the fuel preparation and fabrication plants and ultimately to the reactor. Discharged from the reactor and fuel reprocessing plants will be 1100 kg/yr (GE design) to 1400 kg/yr (AI design) of fissile plutonium.

Thus, on a per plant basis, there will be roughly six to seven times as much fissile plutonium in the LMFBR fuel cycle as in the LWR fuel cycle (without Pu-recycle), and several times as much as in an equivalent HTGR cycle. The fast breeders will generate more fissile plutonium than they consume, and with a large enough breeding ratio they could eventually produce more highly enriched plutonium than is required to fuel the nuclear economy, although this is not inevitable. In theory, since the breeding ratio is not fixed, one can have a mix of breeders and non-breeders such that there is no excess plutonium.

At present, the AEC assumes that the LMFBR core and blanket spent-fuel discharge rates will be comparable and that the core and blanket spent fuels will be mixed during reprocessing. Because of the widely differing characteristics of core and blanket fuels, it may be economically advantageous to process the two fuels

[93]Deborah Shapley, "Plutonium: Reactor Proliferation Threatens a Nuclear Black Market," *Science*, 172 (April 9, 1971), pp. 143-46.

separately, regardless of the location of the reprocessing plant.[94] If processed separately, whether for economic or some other reasons, this would introduce an additional factor into the safeguards problem. The plutonium bred in the LMFBR blanket will have a rather low content of the troublesome isotope, plutonium-240. The more fissile plutonium from the blanket can be used for weapon production with particular ease. On the other hand, the plutonium produced from LWRs, like that recovered from mixed LMFBR fuel reprocessing, contains a higher fraction of non-fissile plutonium and is therefore less useful for weapons.

Because of the larger inventory of fissile material, safeguarding should be more difficult in the LMFBR fuel cycle than in the LWR, and to a lesser extent HTGR, fuel cycles. This is difficult to quantify because of: (1) the differences in the fuel cycles; (2) enriched fuel inventories in those sectors of the fuel cycles where theft is likely, and (3) inherent safeguards of the materials, e.g., radioactivity in the fuel.

It is likely that the entire LMFBR fuel cycle will be subject to international safeguards.[95] There is considerable uncertainty as to the exact costs of safeguarding, due in part to the lack of definitive studies. There are two approaches to safeguarding under consideration. The first approach, the principal basis for international safeguards, requires an exact accounting of all fissile material throughout the fuel cycle. This might require, for example, extensive bookkeeping and highly accurate nondestructive analysis techniques to inventory fissile material in fuel rods. This approach does not prevent theft; it discovers it after the fact. The second method is based on a security system that makes it extremely difficult to remove material from the system, e.g., it provides armed guards and personnel monitoring. The actual safeguards cost depends on which approach, or mix of these, is utilized. If, for example, one assumes that the inventory procedure for safeguarding might require shutting down frequently enough so that the throughput of the plant would be reduced by 20 percent, then the additional fabrication, reprocessing, and reconversion costs increase the LMFBR fuel cycle cost by about 0.1 mill/kwh. Having armed guards accompany all shipments of fissile material (except possibly spent-fuel shipments from the reactor, which are unlikely

[94]U.S. AEC, *LMFBR Program Plan,* WASH 1108, p. 8-39.
[95]Ibid., p. 8-218.

to be stolen) could significantly increase the transportation cost. Whether safeguard costs are borne by the federal government or the industry, they are legitimate costs associated with the fuel cycles and should be included in cost-benefit analyses of the LMFBR and other nuclear power programs.

3

Uranium Supply and Demand

Since the economic arguments discussed thus far indicate that the breeder will probably not be competitive with other nuclear plants initially, uranium prices may be a dominant factor in determining the appropriate timing for commercial introduction.

Aside from the breeder's relative insensitivity to uranium prices, another attractive feature (often cited) is that it increases the total amount of fissile material available from a given quantity of uranium.

While both these issues will be considered in this chapter, the resource conservation argument is less important, since, as will be shown, its effectiveness does not depend on the date of commercial introduction.

Whether deflated uranium prices will rise appreciably in ensuing years depends largely on the availability of uranium, whether the uranium mining industry remains competitive, and whether low-cost uranium reserves can be proven rapidly enough to meet the anticipated demand. One also needs to consider externalities, such as environmental costs, which could increase uranium mining costs.

Deflated uranium costs versus supply were estimated by the 1970 Analysis and are shown in the three curves of Figure 10.

The cases A, B, and C in Figure 10 are labeled in Table 13, column 1, "1/70 Estimate," "Optimistic," and "Unlimited," respectively. Case B, however, is no longer considered optimistic by the AEC's Division of Raw Materials. Rather, it is considered that the true uranium supply curve lies somewhere between case B and case C. The reasons for this will become apparent in the subsequent discussion.

With all other assumptions (e.g., capital costs, plant performance characteristics, energy demand) unchanged from the case 3

FIGURE 10. Uranium Ore Available at Given Prices

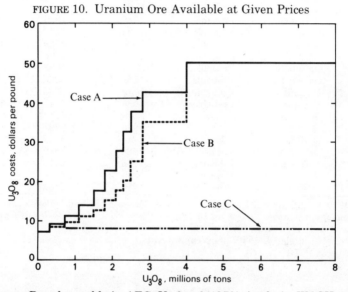

SOURCE: Based on table in AEC, *Updated (1970) Analysis,* WASH 1184, p. 42.

NOTE: According to the 1970 Analysis, case A is based on current domestic uranium reserves and estimates of additional available resources in recognized favorable geological environments. To achieve this uranium availability would require continued expeditious exploration and exploitation of known and estimated resources.

Case B is an alternative analysis based on the premise that resources may be larger than presently estimated. Historic patterns of resource development for other metals suggest that this can be expected if adequate time is allowed for discovery and exploitation. This case might be considered as "optimistic" because it goes beyond current knowledge. On the other hand, time is a critical factor because of the likelihood that the uranium demand will peak during the next thirty years.

Case C assumes unlimited uranium availability at \$8/lb of U_3O_8. While an unlimited amount of uranium is not expected to be available at this price, this case was included to examine the competitive position of the breeder if the cost of uranium does not increase.

TABLE 13. Uranium Requirements

Case no. (1)	Uranium reserves vs. cost (1)	Energy demand (2)	Date of introduction LMFBR (3)	U_3O_8 required to year 2020 (kilotons) Required (4)	Savings (5)
1	1/70 Est.	Probable	None	4531	—
2	1/70 Est.	Probable	1984	1929	2602
3	1/70 Est.	Probable	1986	2171	2360
4	1/70 Est.	Probable	1990	2589	1942
5	1/70 Est.	Probable	1994	3129	1402
6	Optimistic	Probable	None	4639	—
7	Optimistic	Probable	1986	2320	2319
8	Unlimited	Probable	None	6636	—
9	Unlimited	Probable	1986	3043	3593
10	1/70 Est.	Low	None	3740	—
11	1/70 Est.	Low	1986	1798	1942
12	1/70 Est.	High	None	5327	—
13	1/70 Est.	High	1986	2419	2908
14[a]	1/70 Est.	Probable	1986	2216	2315
15[b]	1/70 Est.	Probable	None	4540	—
16[b]	1/70 Est.	Probable	1986	2152	2388

SOURCE: U.S. Atomic Energy Commission, Division of Reactor Development and Technology, *Updated (1970) Cost-Benefit Analysis of the U.S. Breeder Reactor Program*, WASH 1184 (Jan. 1972), p. 15.
[a]With 10% higher LMFBR plant capital costs.
[b]Without HTGR.

assumptions, as shown in Table 6, and using a 7 percent discount rate, the 1970 Analysis shows present value of net benefits decreasing from $19.1 billion to $17.7 billion to negative $1.2 billion, as one varies the uranium supply curve from A to B to C. At a 10 percent discount rate, the present value of net benefits decreases from $4.3 billion to $3.8 billion to a negative $1.8 billion (see Table 7).

Whitman et al., noting that the use of case B rather than case A decreases the present value of benefits by only $1.4 billion, suggested that "this small decrease and lack of sensitivity to uranium supply reflects the breeder's efficient utilization of uranium resources."[1]

[1]M. J. Whitman, A.N. Tardiff, and P.L. Hofmann, "U.S. Civilian Nuclear Power Cost-Benefit Analysis" (presented at the Fourth United Nations International Conference on the Peaceful Uses of Atomic Energy, Geneva, Sept. 6-16, 1971).

It is true that the breeder, when compared with LWRs and HTGRs, is much less sensitive to the price of uranium. This can also be seen from Figure 11. Based on the 1970 Analysis assumption that the LMFBR capital cost will never be more than about $20/kw above the HTGR cost, the LMFBR will be competitive even at existing uranium prices. If one assumes that the small reduction in uranium prices in going from case A to case B will not affect

FIGURE 11. Sensitivity of Nuclear Energy Generating Cost to Price of Natural Uranium

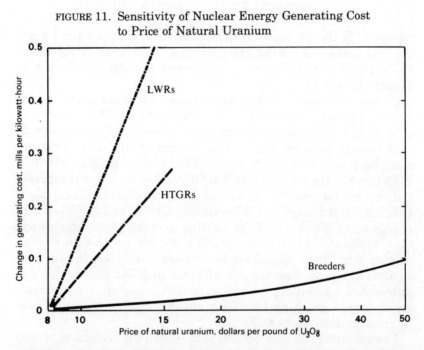

SOURCE: Robert D. Nininger, "Nuclear Resources," paper presented at Energy Resources Conference, College of Engineering, University of Kentucky (Lexington, May 11, 1971).

NOTE: The HTGR curve (linear slope = 0.035 $\frac{\text{mills/Kwh}}{\text{\$/lb}}$) was recalculated for 7% rather than 10%, using data from "HTGR Fuel and Fuel Cycle, Summary Description" by L.J. Colby, R.C. Dahlberg, and S. Jaye, Gulf General Atomic Company, Doc. No. GA-10233 (May 25, 1971), p. 20. The LWR curve is based on a plant capacity of 80% and a 7% discount rate.

appreciably the mix in plant types (i.e., the number of LMFBRs and HTGRs in a given year) that provide the required generating capacity,[2] then the only factor remaining to which to attribute the decrease in discounted benefits is the decrease in the value of uranium. In fact, the $1.4 billion decrease in discounted benefits can be explained largely in terms of differences in discounted uranium costs, i.e.,

$$\Delta = \left[C(\text{without LMFBR}) - C(\text{with LMFBR})\right]_{\text{Case A}}$$
$$- \left[C(\text{without LMFBR}) - C(\text{with LMFBR})\right]_{\text{Case B}}$$

where Δ is the decrease in discounted benefits, and the Cs are the discounted costs of the uranium used. The Cs can be estimated using the 7 percent discount factor and the data presented in Figures 10 and 12.

On the other hand, if the United States continues to rely on fission as a primary source of energy and if the LMFBR is not competitive initially, then future uranium prices could have a significant bearing on when it does become competitive. The important point here is that it will require an increase of roughly $14/lb of U_3O_8 to offset the 0.5 mill/kwh LMFBR-HTGR energy cost differential, or an increase of $8.3/lb of U_3O_8 to offset an equivalent LMFBR–LWR energy cost differential.[3] Given the LMFBR–HTGR energy cost differential, if the deflated uranium price remains less than $20/lb of U_3O_8 (roughly $12/lb above the present price) after mining 4 million to 5 million tons of uranium, then the increase in uranium price would be insufficient to offset the energy cost differential. According to the projected uranium requirements under case A (with no LMFBRs), this uranium tonnage will not be reached until about 2020.

The remainder of this section is devoted to a discussion of why uranium prices may not rise nearly as rapidly as suggested by the supply curves A and B in Figure 10.

---

[2]Note from Figure 10 that the uranium price differential between case A and case B is never more than $12.50/lb.

[3]Likewise, since $1/kw in capital costs is equivalent to 0.02 mills/kwh, it will require an increase of roughly $6/lb of U_3O_8 to offset a $10/kw LMFBR–HTGR capital cost differential; or an increase of $3.3/lb of U_3O_8 to offset an equivalent LMFBR–LWR differential.

FIGURE 12. Effect of LMFBR Introduction on Uranium Commitments

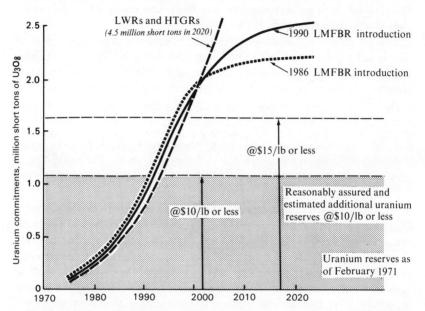

SOURCE: Robert D. Nininger, "Nuclear Resources" (May 11, 1971). The data are based on the 1970 Analysis.

URANIUM AVAILABILITY

The primary factor influencing uranium prices is the availability of low-cost uranium; that is, how much low-cost uranium is in the ground.[4]

James R. Schlesinger, in October 1971 when he was chairman of the Atomic Energy Commission, stated that the availability of low-grade uranium reserves was "not too substantial," and that at the present rate of nonbreeder reactor use, "it will be exhausted in several decades."[5] Six months later, however, Robert Nininger, assistant director for raw materials at the Commission, stated: "We

[4]Those unfamiliar with the definitions of uranium price and ore categories, e.g., "reasonably assured reserves" and "estimated additional resources," may find the definitions in the Glossary helpful.

[5]James R. Schlesinger, "Expectations and Responsibilities of the Nuclear Industry," as quoted in the New York Times (Jan. 15, 1972), p. 25.

have not attempted to assess the total resources of the country and the lack of such an assessment has been the cause of some confusion about uranium supply."[6]

The executive vice-president of Kerr-McGee Corporation, one of the leading uranium companies in the United States, explains some of the confusion, pointing out that the AEC's estimates of reserves have been based on "known uranium districts." He adds:

There are large areas prospective for uranium in the U.S. that have had little or no exploration. The [AEC] estimates total 1.07 million tons (U_3O_8 in ore) compared to a cumulative estimated requirement of 450,000 tons of U_3O_8 through the year 1985. While the history of the uranium raw material industry is short, the industry has shown the capability to supply the market when given sufficient lead time and adequate economic incentives.[7]

V. E. McKelvey, director of the U.S. Geological Survey, notes that thus far there have been two principal approaches to estimating undiscovered mineral resources. One is to extrapolate observations related to rate of industrial activity, such as annual production of the commodity; the other is to extrapolate observations that relate to the abundance of the mineral in the geologic environment in which it is found. The essential features of the first approach are to analyze the growth in production, proved reserves, and discovery per foot of drilling over time and to project these rate phenomena to terminal values in order to predict ultimate production. The second approach involves the extrapolation of data on the abundance of mineral deposits from explored to unexplored ground on the basis either of area or of the volume of broadly favorable rocks.[8]

The inherent weakness of the first approach, as noted by McKelvey, is that the phenomena being analyzed reflect human activities that are strongly influenced by economic, political, and other factors bearing no relation to the amount of material lying in the ground. Moreover, it makes no allowances for major breakthroughs that might transform extensive low-grade resources into recover-

[6]Robert D. Nininger, "Uranium Reserves and Requirements," paper presented at the Atomic Industrial Forum, Oak Brook, Illinois, March 27, 1973.

[7]Remarks by George H. Cobb, Kerr-McGee Corporation, at the Atomic Industrial Forum Annual Conference, Miami Beach, Florida, October 17-21, 1971, *Nuclear Industry*, 18, Part I (Oct.-Nov. 1971), p. 22.

[8]V. E. McKelvey, "Mineral Resource Estimates and Public Policy," *American Scientist*, 60 (Jan.-Feb. 1972), p. 37.

able reserves or environmental and other factors that might have the opposite effect, nor does it provide a means of estimating the potential resources of unexplored regions.

Domestic Uranium Reserves

The curves plotted in Figure 13 show both the historical trends in domestic uranium production and the projected requirements based on the AEC's case 1 assumption (no LMFBR).[9]

The actual demand may be lower if the AEC and FPC electrical energy forecasts are high or if the nuclear fraction of the required generating capacity is less than the AEC anticipates.[10] It may be higher (as shown in Table 13) if the uranium supply curve is lower, i.e., if it lies between curves B and C in Figure 10 (see, for example, case 8 in Table 13, which corresponds to curve C). For the sake of argument, I assume that the 1970 Analysis base case 1— projected uranium demand without the LMFBR—must be met.

It goes without saying that $10/lb reserves will be exhausted when curve 4 in Figure 13 intersects curve 2 (the projected demand curve). The 1970 Analysis estimates that, with no LMFBRs, this would occur shortly after 1990 with case A uranium prices, and shortly after 1995 with case B prices; in other words, roughly when we exhaust the known $10/lb reserves and $10/lb estimated additional resources.

If uranium mining develops in a manner similar to other ores, we can reasonably expect that the sum of the cumulative production, $10/lb reserves, and $10/lb estimated additional resources will continue to grow as our exploratory efforts continue. Historically, as can be seen from Figure 13, the sum of the uranium cumulative production, reserves, and additional resources generally follows the exploratory effort measured by the cumulative feet of surface drilling. In other words, the amount of uranium found generally reflects the amount of effort put into exploration. This behavior is characteristic of the mining of all minerals early in the history of their development.

Most minerals mined in the United States have experienced exponential demand growth rates during the initial fifty, or so,

[9] The projected commitment data are from the curve labeled "LWRs and HTGRs" in Figure 12 and the case 1 U_3O_8 requirement in Table 13.

[10] See Chapter 4 for the discussion of why electrical energy demand may be lower than the AEC anticipates.

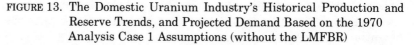

FIGURE 13. The Domestic Uranium Industry's Historical Production and
Reserve Trends, and Projected Demand Based on the 1970
Analysis Case 1 Assumptions (without the LMFBR)

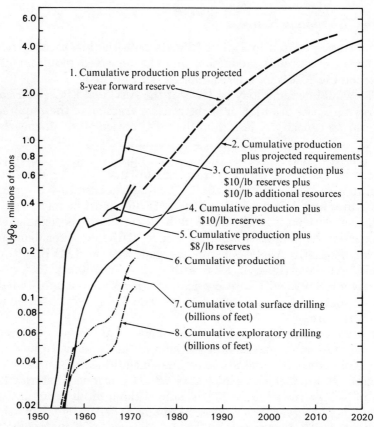

SOURCE: The historical data are based on the AEC's *Statistical Data of
the Uranium Industry* (January 1, 1972).

"Based on 1970, case 1 assumptions.

*b*Reserve estimates prior to 1961 are based on the price of U_3O_8 in ore as
set forth in AEC "Domestic Program Circular 5" (revised).

years of their mining history. Almost without exception, these
minerals have shown either declining or relatively constant
deflated price trends during this period of initial development.[11]

[11]Neal Potter and Francis T. Christy, Jr., *Trends in Natural Resource Commodities* (The Johns Hopkins Press for Resources for the Future, 1962), pp. 32-52.

Petroleum, natural gas, coal, iron, copper, lead, zinc, bauxite (aluminum), molybdenum, silver, and sulfur are included in this list. New districts are still being discovered for nearly every mineral, and large areas favorable for the occurrence of minerals of all kinds are covered by alluvium, volcanics, glacial drift, seawater, and other materials that conceal possible mineral-bearing rocks or structures.[12]

On the other hand, there are two crucial characteristics that distinguish uranium from most minerals. First, the uranium deposits are radioactive. This makes deposits near the surface of the ground comparatively easy to locate and it makes uranium ore easy to assay. During the 1950s there was a big uranium "rush" in the United States. The western states were explored extensively for surface deposits. Because of this, one might conclude that the whereabouts of most of the low-cost uranium ore at or very near the surface may be known by private individuals, mining companies, etc., and that much of this ore either has already been mined or is in the proven reserve and estimated additional resource categories. Second, in contrast to many other minerals, for example iron ore, the concentration of uranium in the ore is small, averaging about 0.2 percent. If we have indeed found most of the strippable low-cost ore at or near the surface, then the cost of mining new finds at greater depths could become increasingly expensive. Thus, it is possible to understand the concern over whether there is enough low-cost uranium in the United States at any depth that can be found and mined rapidly enough to meet our demands beyond the next few decades, unless, of course, breeders are introduced.

One can obtain an entirely different view when the data on the abundance of uranium are extrapolated from explored to unexplored ground on the basis of favorable geologic settings.

As of January 1, 1972, the AEC's estimate of proven reserves, available at a cost of $15/lb of U_3O_8, was 600 thousand tons. When past production of 229 thousand tons and potential (estimated additional resources) of 1 million tons is added, the total "resource" is 1.829 million tons. The AEC's estimates of additional resources, or potential, are much smaller than one might expect because they reflect only possibilities supported by tangible geologic evidence in areas where exploration, including exploratory drilling, has been

[12]McKelvey, "Mineral Resource Estimates."

relatively extensive. In fact, by AEC estimates, about 85 percent of the potential is in currently producing districts. The AEC-estimated additional resources, or potential, have, from the viewpoint of regional exploration, already been discovered. The magnitude of these reserves has not been proven, but there is little question as to their existence.

Ninety-five percent of the uranium discovered in the United States is in sedimentary rocks, principally sandstones, and sandstone formations will probably provide the basis for the U.S. uranium producing industry in the foreseeable future. Most of the uranium occurrences in sedimentary rocks in the United States are found in a 450-thousand square-mile region in the West (see Figure 14, double cross-hatched regions). The reserves reported by the AEC have been discovered as a result of still incomplete exploration of less than 10 percent of that region.[13] These smaller areas in which exploration has been concentrated are in the locale of the major districts, and are shown as solid areas in Figure 14. The majority of the exploration effort today is still concentrated in the vicinity of the producing districts, with less than 15 percent of that effort directed toward new prospects in nonproducing areas. There is little compulsion on the part of mining companies exploring for uranium to leave the proximity of the known producing districts as long as ample exploration opportunities to fill current demand are available.

With the expected increase in demand, there should be an increase in wildcat exploration. There is no reason to assume that the results of this exploration will be any more or less successful than that conducted in the vicinity of the known districts. Although it would be incorrect to conclude that all of the unexplored areas would contain as much uranium as those which have been explored, it would seem most unlikely that the bulk of the known deposits would be confined to the already developed areas within the favorable geologic environment. The Nuclear Task Group of the National Petroleum Council's (NPC's) Committee on U.S. Energy Outlook reported that the prospects for locating other

---

[13]National Petroleum Council, "U.S. Energy Outlook, An Initial Appraisal, 1971-1985," Vol. Two, Summaries of Task Group Reports (Nov. 1971).

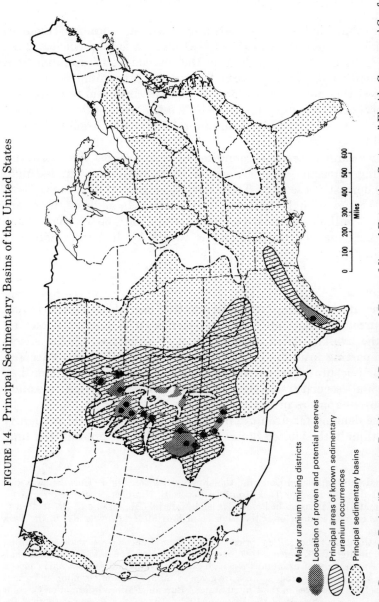

FIGURE 14. Principal Sedimentary Basins of the United States

• Major uranium mining districts

Location of proven and potential reserves

Principal areas of known sedimentary uranium occurrences

Principal sedimentary basins

SOURCE: George B. Parks, "Important Problems and Prospects of Energy Mineral Extraction Systems," Florida Governors' Conference on Energy Supply and Use, Tallahassee, Fla. (March 13-14, 1973).

uranium ore bodies in partially explored and unexplored areas are good.[14]

Uranium industry estimates of low-cost uranium resources (equal to or less than $15/lb of U_3O_8), made for the Nuclear Task Group by extrapolating data on the abundance of uranium from explored to unexplored areas favorable for uranium occurrence, suggest that our ultimate domestic low-cost uranium resources are several times greater than the AEC's estimate. In fact they exceed the AEC's estimated U.S. uranium requirements through the year 2020 by several fold.

If we cannot meet our commitment from low-cost free-world (including domestic) supplies, we can start mining low-grade (high-cost) domestic resources. There may be several million tons of low-grade conventional, e.g., sandstone, sources. In addition, there are several million tons of U_3O_8 available in Chattanooga shale, some of which may be minable in the future for less than $50/lb of uranium.[15]

Foreign Uranium Reserves

The desirability of considering the use of foreign uranium resources for the United States depends on a number of factors: (1) the availability of uranium in other countries; (2) the effects of importing uranium on our economic position; (3) the effects of importing uranium on our political or military position, i.e., national security. (A detailed discussion of foreign uranium resources appears in Appendix D.)

The demand for uranium in the rest of the free world is slightly less than in the United States, although with the present lead time

---

[14]National Petroleum Council, "U.S. Energy Outlook," p. 4. The AEC was represented in the Nuclear Task Group by Robert D. Nininger, assistant director for raw materials, Division of Production and Materials Management. Dr. Rafford L. Faulkner, retired director of the Division of Raw Materials, was also in the Task Group.

[15]Estimates of the selling price of U_3O_8 from Chattanooga shale, containing approximately 0.007 percent U_3O_8 uranium, range from $50/lb to $70/lb. Cost analyses for recovery of uranium from high-grade conventional sources, Chattanooga shale, and other low-grade sources are given in "Availability of Uranium at Various Prices from Resources in the United States," Bureau of Mines Information Circular 8501, U.S. Department of the Interior (1971). The reader is cautioned that the Bureau of Mines estimates of domestic uranium resources from conventional deposits are based on AEC estimates and are correct only to the extent that the AEC estimates are correct.

necessary for constructing and licensing new reactor facilities in the United States, it may equal or slightly exceed the U.S. demand in a few years. The free world at present has about a fourteen-year forward reserve. As in the United States, the free-world uranium market is currently soft, with uranium prices slightly lower than U.S. prices. Over 90 percent of the free world's known uranium resources is in six countries; the rest of the free world's resources are largely unexplored. Seventy percent of the foreign free-world reserves are in Canada and South Africa, countries with limited power requirements.

It is often argued that foreign uranium reserves will be needed to meet foreign demand, and that the United States should therefore not rely on them. This does not appear to be the case in the foreseeable future, even if all countries relying on nuclear power delay breeder introduction. If U.S. demand is limited only to back-up quantities, our position is even more favorable. And, if other countries introduce breeders in substantial numbers before the United States does, our position with respect to the utilization of foreign uranium as a back-up will be improved.

The economic effects of importing uranium are usually discussed in terms of balance-of-payments problems. However, even assuming that our adverse import-export balance remains a problem, projections to the year 2000 of both demand for uranium and import growth in general indicate that uranium imports would not have a statistically significant effect on the balance of payments. It is, of course, highly speculative to make any assumptions about our balance-of-payments position twenty or thirty years hence, and it is certainly beyond the scope of this paper to pursue this aspect of the problem.

It is equally beyond the scope of this report to analyze the political problems inherent in relying on foreign sources of uranium. Suffice it to say that 20 to 25 percent of known uranium resources are in Canada, large deposits are being discovered in Australia, and uranium is not nearly as sensitive as oil to the threat of embargo, since it takes far longer to exhaust the supply already in the fuel cycle at any one time.

Uranium Tails

Still another small source of uranium is the depleted uranium set aside at the enrichment plants. Natural uranium contains

0.711 percent U-235. The percentage of U-235 in the uranium tails at the gaseous diffusion plants is determined by optimizing the cost of the enriched fuel (i.e., the cost of the feed plus the enrichment). In fiscal 1972, to provide enriched uranium for LWRs, the AEC operated these plants at an actual tails assay of 0.30 percent (U-235). Beginning in fiscal 1973, the AEC will operate at 0.275 to 0.30 percent until it has disposed of its surplus stock, which could take about a decade.[16] Subsequently, the AEC may revert to the previously planned level of 0.25 percent. If the enrichment facilities were operated at a tails assay of 0.20 percent instead of 0.25 percent, or higher, and the entire stockpile of enrichment tails were recycled, the United States could reduce its cumulative uranium demand by about 10 percent. For instance, in the year 2000, if we are at the commitment level of 2 million tons of U_3O_8 and we discover we are unable to meet the annual U_3O_8 production requirement (assume it to be 100 thousand tons per year), then we could make up the difference by recycling the enrichment tails (about 2 million tons of depleted uranium in this case). Under these assumptions, the entire tails stock would be equivalent to an additional 200 thousand tons of U_3O_8, a two-year supply at this annual demand level. Thus, we see that the tails provide an additional uranium-235 resource that can be used to supplement pro-

---

[16]On October 13, 1971, the AEC announced for comment a proposal for disposition of the surplus by annual offerings of quantities of uranium for competitive bid between 1974 and 1984. Comments from the uranium-producing industry have persuaded the AEC to revise its plan. In March 1972, the AEC announced that beginning in FY 1973 it would dispose of the surplus by operating the gaseous diffusion plants with a somewhat higher tails assay (0.275 to 0.30 percent) than the previously planned level of 0.25 percent, while charging its customers as if it were operating the plants with tails assay of 0.20 percent. (Statement by J. R. Schlesinger before JCAE on Nuclear Fuel Supply, FY 1973 Authorizing Hearings, March 7-8, 1972.) Operating in this manner, the surplus can be gradually reduced in a way which will avoid direct competition by the government in the private uranium market. According to Daniel Shaw, if the AEC continued to operate the gaseous diffusion plants with the same amount of electrical power as would have been required for operation at 0.25 percent, the 50,000 tons of surplus could be converted to approximately 4 million kg of 2.6 percent enriched material in the next eight years. See "AEC Uranium Policy," *Nuclear Industry*, 19 (February 1972), Part II, p. 18. The resulting enriched stockpile would be available in a form which can more readily be used to hedge against a shortage of uranium or separative capacity, or both. An alternative would be to operate the plants at the power level necessary to meet enriched uranium requirements. In this case, the stockpile would be consumed over a longer period (fourteen years) and the government would benefit by buying less energy and postponing capital commitments for additional enrichment capacity.

duction requirements, if low-cost uranium resources are in shorter supply than anticipated. Since a lower tails assay requires more separative work, at existing separative work prices, it would not be efficient to operate at a 0.2 percent tails assay until the price of uranium reached \$35/lb to \$40/lb of U_3O_8. This feed price depends on the separative work cost and would be lower only if future enrichment costs are lower than present costs. This could occur, for example, if the gas centrifuge technology proved to be less costly than the gaseous diffusion method of enrichment.

MAINTAINING ADEQUATE
FORWARD RESERVES

Simply having an adequate supply of low-cost ore in the ground does not ensure that uranium reserves can be discovered and developed fast enough to meet the much higher demand projected for the future. In order to maintain stable (low) uranium prices, the industry must maintain an adequate forward reserve in a market where the demand is expected to increase rapidly. The AEC believes that an eight-year forward reserve is desirable.

At present, the domestic uranium industry has more than its share of problems. A surplus of U_3O_8 has been building up as nuclear power plants have been delayed, both because of construction delays and, more recently, licensing delays. The government has an additional 50,000 tons of surplus U_3O_8. Buyers have been reluctant to negotiate long-term contracts until the AEC makes a final decision on method and schedule for disposing of this surplus stock (see footnote 15 above). Together, these factors have reduced the demand for uranium. As a result, prices are down and some of the marginal mines, unable to compete, are going out of business. The AEC forecasts an annual U.S. uranium requirement increasing from 10,000 short tons of U_3O_8 in 1973,[17] to 38,400 tons in 1980, 71,500 tons in 1985, 117,900 tons in 1990, and 153,600 tons in 2000.[18] In view of the present soft market, the AEC is concerned

[17]The actual capacity of the domestic uranium industry in 1973 is about 2½ times this demand.

[18]U.S. AEC, *Nuclear Power 1973-2000*, WASH 1139 (72), Dec. 1972, p. 14. This estimate assumes enrichment plant tails assay at 0.30 percent U-235, and recycle of plutonium in reactor loading, beginning with 25 percent in 1977, 50 percent in 1978, 75 percent in 1979, and as much as possible thereafter without limiting

over whether the industry during the next fifteen to twenty-five years can rapidly adjust to the higher demands and maintain an eight-year forward reserve after the existing surplus is exhausted. Since the projected annual uranium demand, assuming breeders are not introduced, will continue to grow,[19] it is further argued that if exploration efforts are not successful during the 1985-95 period, the domestic uranium industry may never be able to meet the demand unless the breeder is introduced forthwith. The specifics of this concern—the technical and economic capability of the industry to meet the demand—have never even been spelled out, let alone adequately assessed. Instead, the concern appears to be based on almost a cursory observation of the soft uranium market and projections of a rapidly increasing demand for uranium after 1980.

Former AEC Commissioner Wilfrid E. Johnson, in remarks at the American Mining Conference in the fall of 1971, noted that exploration during the last five years has resulted in the discovery of about 3½ pounds of uranium concentrate for each foot of drilling. He warned that if this discovery experience continues in the future and drilling is maintained only at the rate planned for 1972 (19 million feet per year), forward reserves in 1985 would be only about a three-year supply.[20] However, Johnson has assumed a constant level of exploration. Historically, we have witnessed just the opposite. The level of uranium exploration has varied in almost direct proportion to the short-term demand in the uranium market for uranium concentrates. Figure 15 shows the annual total surface drilling and the annual additions to $8/lb proven reserves. The growth in drilling between 1948 and 1957 parallels the growth in

---

LMFBR construction. It represents the AEC's "most likely" forecast for these assumptions as of December 31, 1972. To account for uncertainty in nuclear capacity additions, the AEC's estimates of U.S. uranium requirements range from 8,400 to 11,300 in 1973; 36,600 to 44,000 in 1980; 59,900 to 85,500 in 1985; 87,000 to 140,000 in 1990; 100,100 to 173,700 in 1995; and 110,000 to 192,000 in 2000. Without the LMFBR, but with HTGRs, the 1970 Analysis predicts U.S. annual uranium requirements on the order of 100,000 tons of U_3O_8 in 2000 and 150,000 tons in 2010.

[19]The rate of growth of domestic uranium demand without breeders is limited ultimately by the growth rate in electrical energy demand. This becomes noticeable when the nuclear fraction starts saturating the base load generating capacity. With the high nuclear generating capacity growth rates projected by the 1970 Analysis, this occurs around the turn of the century. The 1970 Analysis assumes electrical energy demand growth rates of 4.8 percent during the decade 2000 to 2010, and 3.8 percent from 2010 to 2020.

[20]Wilfrid E. Johnson, "Status of the Uranium Producing Industry," *Mining Congress Journal* (Feb. 1972), pp. 59-64.

FIGURE 15. Annual Additions of Uranium to Proven Reserves ($8/lb U_3O_8), and Annual Uranium Surface Drilling, United States, 1949-71

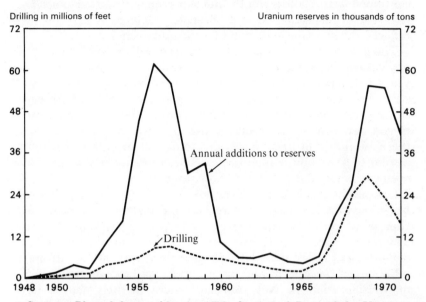

SOURCE: Plotted from tables in AEC, *Statistical Data of the Uranium Industry* (January 1, 1972).

uranium ore purchased by the AEC. Beginning in 1948, the AEC began a program to stimulate domestic production of uranium by guaranteeing to purchase ore at fixed prices, by offering bonuses for initial production from new mines, by undertaking ground and air surveys to locate new deposits, and by undertaking to develop methods for processing ore to concentrates.[21] These encouragements were originally planned to continue to 1962 but, in 1956, the cutoff date was extended to 1966 and, at the same time, the AEC established a flat price of $8/lb U_3O_8 instead of negotiating prices. In November 1958 the AEC announced it would no longer purchase uranium ore but would confine its purchases to yellowcake. As seen from Figure 15, this policy produced a steady decline in surface drilling until the mid-1960s, when the private

[21]Arthur D. Little, Inc., "An Assessment of the Economic Effects of Radiation Exposure Standards for Uranium Miners," Report to the Federal Radiation Council (September 1970), p. 74.

uranium market started developing as a result of the growth in civilian nuclear power plant orders. The growth in surface drilling continued until 1969, when the nuclear economy started experiencing reactor construction and licensing delays, which in turn reduced the short-term demand for uranium concentrate.

The discovery rate in pounds of uranium discovered for footage drilled was the same in the 1966-71 period as for the previous six years, or 3.8 pounds per foot. The success of exploration has demonstrated the capability of the uranium industry to add more reserves through increased exploration effort. The capability of the industry to add new reserves as needed must also necessarily reflect upon the availability of uranium as a resource. If uranium in deposits similar to those now being mined were not available, it would have been extremely difficult to add new reserves.

One might conclude that near-surface, or open pit, deposits will be found with increased exploration, and further exploration will then be concentrated on deeper and deeper underground deposits. This conclusion is only partially true, due to the manner of emplacement of the deposits. The idea that exploration will inevitably be less successful and more expensive, however, is misleading. Exploration in New Mexico, where drilling depths have exceeded 4,000 feet, has resulted in the discovery of 9.7 lb/ft through the 1967-71 period. The discovery rate on the more shallow exploration prospects in Wyoming is considerably less. From these data a case can be made that, with increased depth, exploration is conducted more carefully and with more regard to an early appraisal of the chances of success on any individual prospect. Alternatively, these data may simply reflect a greater abundance of uranium ore in the New Mexico districts than in the Wyoming districts.

The EEI Reactor Assessment Panel has also expressed concern whether the mining industry can meet forward reserve requirements. In Appendix E, I examine the relationship among gross sales, expenditures for exploration and development, and the cost of proving reserves—a relationship used by the Edison Electric Institute (EEI) Panel and others to study this problem. One of the weaknesses of this type of analysis is similar to the weakness of the first approach for estimating unexplored resources outlined by McKelvey.[22] The phenomena being analyzed—the drilling statis-

[22]McKelvey, "Mining Resource Estimates."

tics—are strongly influenced by economic factors. For example, although the major uranium mining companies continue exploration and are making discoveries, due to the lack of demand there is no profit incentive to do the necessary development drilling to convert these finds into proven reserves.[23] The incentive is only to do what is necessary to hold the claims. Similarly, development drilling of only the higher-grade ores influences the dollar yield per foot of drilling. It was noted earlier that the drilling statistics in the uranium industry have been related to short-term uranium demand. Consequently, it is unlikely that the drilling statistics would reflect accurately the capability of the industry to meet future demands.

Probably the most critical drawback to the EEI analysis is the implicit assumption that revenues committed to exploration and development are tied to present gross revenue rather than expected demand and expected revenues. If the industry has some form of solid assurance of the demand ten years ahead, it seems very likely that the necessary funds will be committed. The solid assurance does not need to be in the form of a supported price. It could be found in long-term purchase contracts at mutually acceptable prices. It is reasonable to assume that funds will be committed if the demand is there. A major share of the uranium industry is owned or controlled by major oil companies or other conglomerates having significant fossil fuel interests. According to former Commissioner Johnson,

... the movement of oil companies into exploration, with their large financial and technical capabilities, has been an important positive factor. In 1970, these companies carried out 55 percent of the total drilling effort.[24]

Omitting consideration of the present surplus, i.e., the excess proven reserves over the eight-year forward reserve requirement and the 50,000-ton AEC stockpile, I have estimated the growth in the average rate of proven reserves (assuming an eight-year forward reserve) needed to meet the demand projected by the case 1 assumptions in the 1970 Analysis. Under these assumptions, if the LMFBR is not introduced, the average annual growth rates are less than 11 percent in 1972-82; 6 percent in 1982-92; and 2

---

[23]Larry Werts, Kerr-McGee Corporation, Oklahoma City, Okla., private communication, 1971.

[24]Wilfrid Johnson, "Status of the Uranium Producing Industry," pp. 60-61.

percent in 1992-2002.[25] Consideration of the excess proven reserves and the AEC stockpile reduces the requirement for a high growth rate prior to 1980. Thus, the demand can be met by a lower average growth rate over a longer period. If there is an adequate supply of low-cost uranium in the ground, and if the market is competitive, it seems likely that the industry could maintain these growth rates, particularly the rates required after 1990. If we temporarily fall behind in proven reserves, we can rely on foreign reserves as a back-up. Minor adjustments (10-20 percent) in uranium demand can be made by controlling the uranium enrichment tails assay.

A factor that could reduce the availability of domestic uranium is public pressure to tighten mining regulations and to restrict strip, or even underground, mining in some locations. Pressures of this type are being experienced today, particularly in the coal mining industry. Perhaps up to 25 percent (a rough guess) of the unexplored regions of favorable geology shown in Figure 14 lie on state or federal lands. According to the NPC's Committee on U.S. Energy Outlook, about 50 percent of all proved and currently identified uranium resources are on federal or Indian lands.[26] It would be a mistake to delay the LMFBR program more than a few years without preserving the availability of uranium on both the public and private lands through appropriate state and federal land use policy. Even if the LMFBR program is not delayed, this subject deserves further attention.

MANAGEMENT OF RESIDUALS
IN THE URANIUM INDUSTRY

Management of residuals[27] in the uranium industry will undoubtedly increase uranium prices, but the total increase should be small. At present, about 45 percent of the uranium ore production in the United States is by open pit methods, 53 percent is mined underground, and recovery from mine water and waste heap leaching account for the other 2 percent. The ratio of open pit to

---

[25]These represent upper-limit estimates based on data in Table 13 and Figure 13. Uranium demand data by year were not otherwise available.

[26]National Petroleum Council, "U.S. Energy Outlook," p. 48.

[27]Residuals are the leftovers, the nonmarketable mass and energy, from human production and consumption activities.

underground mining has been relatively constant throughout the history of the industry.

In open pit mining the stripping ratio (ratio of waste, expressed in cubic yards moved, to ore mixed, expressed in tons) is on the order of 35 cu yd/t of ore. Concentrations of U_3O_8 average about 0.2 percent. Assuming an average mine depth of 180 feet and uranium prices of $7/lb of U_3O_8, the open pit mine would contain $200,000 worth of U_3O_8 per acre. If the industry spent 10 percent of this amount, less than $1/lb, on reclamation, the expenditures would average $20,000 per acre. Considerable reclamation, i.e., filling, contouring, and planting, could be accomplished at this level of effort. Average 1964 costs of reclaiming land disturbed by strip and surface mining in the United States have been published by the Department of the Interior.[28] The mean costs were $230 per acre for coal, $870 per acre for clay, $430 per acre for sand and gravel, and $1,700 per acre for stone. The values varied depending upon the geographic area. The maximum value was for stone mined in the West-South-Central region, where the cost for complete reclamation was estimated to be $10,000 per acre. In open pit uranium mining the cost of stripping the overburden to expose the ore varies at present between about 50¢/lb to $1.50/lb of U_3O_8. Assuming that replacing the overburden, contouring, and planting will cost an additional 50¢/lb above this amount, it is estimated that the open pit mines can be completely reclaimed for less than $2/lb of U_3O_8.

As deeper ore bodies are mined by open pit methods, one can expect the stripping ratio and reclamation costs to increase. It would not be unreasonable to expect the relative increase in reclamation costs to be roughly proportional to the relative increase in the stripping ratio. With advances in mining technology it may be reasonable to expect open pit mine depths to double before it becomes more profitable to move underground. Doubling the average open pit depth would double the stripping ratio, and perhaps double the reclamation cost to almost $4/lb of U_3O_8.

In underground mining the problems are different. Most of the material removed from the mine is shipped directly to the mill. The remainder, an amount of mine waste, is piled alongside the mines and subsequently leached to recover U_3O_8. It could be hauled

[28]U.S. Department of the Interior, *Surface Mining and Our Environment* (1967), p. 113.

back into the mines and used as back fill for a few cents per pound of U_3O_8.

The principal environmental cost associated with underground mining is associated with the radioactivity in the mine atmosphere, the radon-daughter hazard. The atmosphere in underground uranium mines contains significant radon-222, resulting from the radioactive decay of radium-226. Radium-226 results from the slow radioactive decay of a series of isotopes, beginning with uranium-238, and is therefore always present in natural uranium deposits. The radon-222 disintegrates radioactively into daughter products, which are isotopes of solid elements. The daughter atoms readily attach themselves to particles of dust or moisture in the air. Subsequently, the radon daughters may be deposited in the miner's lungs during respiration. The radon daughters have been identified as a source of radiation which, in the past, has contributed to excess lung cancers in uranium miners.[29]

The concentration of radon daughters in the mine atmosphere is measured in terms of the "working level" (WL).[30] A miner working in a 1-WL mine atmosphere for 170 hours (one month) will receive a cumulative radiation exposure of one working-level month (WLM).

Protection of mine personnel against overexposure is approached in two ways: (1) the control of radon and radon-daughter concentrations, principally by ventilation, and (2) the control of each miner's cumulative exposure to airborne radon daughters by personnel monitoring and rotation of working locations.

In 1967, agencies responsible for radiation standards and mine safety were issuing conflicting guidelines as to what should be the appropriate radon-daughter exposure standard for underground uranium miners. The principal point of contention was whether an employee should be allowed to receive an exposure of no more than 4 WLM or 12 WLM in any consecutive twelve-month period. The Federal Radiation Council (FRC) contracted with A. D. Little, Inc. to assess the economic effects of compliance with each of these

---

[29]Federal Radiation Council, *Guidance for the Control of Radiation Hazards in Uranium Mining*, Staff Report No. 8, revised (September 1967).

[30]A "working level" is defined as any combination of radon daughters in 1 liter of air that will result in the ultimate emission of 1.3×10^5 MeV (million electron volts) of potential alpha energy released by the radon daughters.

standards. Although the standard is now 4 WLM/yr, at the time of the study the industry was substantially complying with a 12-WLM/yr miner exposure standard. The data provided to Little by the industry showed the following in 1969:[31]

Last-Man Exposure[32] (WLM/yr)	Percent of Mines Sampled
< 4	11.5
4 – 8	27
8 – 12	50
slightly more than 12	11.5

Little found a wide variation in the estimates of the cost of compliance with the WLM/yr standard. Among the mines sampled, the cost ranged from 0 to 76¢/lb of U_3O_8. To meet this standard, Little estimated that the average increase in the cost of production of U_3O_8, weighted in terms of the production quality for each mine in the sample, was 24¢/lb. Similar estimates made by mining companies ranged from agreement to nine times the Little estimates, with "differences . . . explainable in terms of industry's use of larger quantities of air and larger numbers of vent holes than we envisage."[33] Little estimated that the 4-WLM/yr standard would result in a U_3O_8 price increase on the order of 50¢/lb.

Even if 50¢/lb is low by a factor of two, for an additional $2/lb of U_3O_8 one could probably afford another similar reduction in the working level standard. Thus, as long as we continue mining low-cost ore, that is, ore grades comparable to those mined today, $2/lb of U_3O_8 should cover adequately all the anticipated environmental costs associated with underground uranium mining, including handling the mine waste.

The environmental cost associated with underground mining of lower-grade ore should be less, since the radon-daughter hazard would be less in areas with lower uranium concentrations.

One can expect that the uranium mill tailings will also require extensive reclamation. The mill tailings represent the solid residuals after the U_3O_8 has been extracted from the ore. Let us assume:

---

[31]Arthur D. Little, "An Assessment of the Economic Effects," pp. 7-8.

[32]The highest annual exposure value recorded by the companies for anyone in 1969.

[33]Arthur D. Little, "An Assessment of the Economic Effects," p. 8.

(1) concentrations in the ore of 0.2 percent U_3O_8; (2) uranium prices around $8/lb of U_3O_8; (3) a tailing density of 150 pounds per cubic foot; and (4) an average height of the tailings of 30 feet. With these assumptions, an acre of tailings would be produced for every $3 million worth of U_3O_8 processed. If $30,000 per acre were spent on reclamation (an enormous amount), this would represent only 1 percent of the price of the U_3O_8—less than $0.10/lb of U_3O_8 at existing prices.

The tailing could be transported back to the mines for about 4¢ to 6¢ per ton-mile. Assuming an average distance of 10 miles from the mine to the mill, and U_3O_8 concentrations in the ore of 0.2 percent, transportation costs would represent 50¢/ton of ore or 1 to 2 percent of the price of the U_3O_8. Hence, complete reclamation of mill tailings should have a negligible effect on uranium prices.

In the event we are forced to rely temporarily on the Chattanooga shale, the environmental cost probably would still represent a small fraction of the price of U_3O_8. Assume the U_3O_8 concentration in Chattanooga shale is 0.14 lb per ton of ore, the formation is 35 feet thick below 180 feet of overburden, and 1 ton of shale in place occupies 14 cubic feet, and when broken, 25 cubic feet.[34] If uranium prices were $50/lb, under these assumptions 1 acre of land would produce $760 thousand worth of uranium and about 2 acres of tailings, assuming a tailing height of about 30 feet. Average expenditures of $20,000 per acre, both at the mine and the mill, would amount to less than 10 percent of the cost of uranium.

The above calculations of environmental costs associated with the uranium mining and milling industries should be considered as rough first approximations. A more detailed analysis is warranted. However, the results, summarized in Table 14 suggest that by conservative estimates the costs of residuals management in these industries are unlikely to increase the price of uranium significantly in the future. At existing U_3O_8 prices, the increase in the cost of electricity generated by LWRs would be less than about 0.1 mill/kwh, and for HTGRs less than about 0.07 mill/kwh.

One might surmise correctly that these environmental costs give the breeder an economic advantage not considered in the AEC's cost-benefit analysis. However, as noted earlier, the 1970 Analysis

[34]Carl L. Bieniewski, Franklin H. Persse, and Earl F. Brauch, *Availability of Uranium at Various Prices from Resources in the United States*, U.S. Department of the Interior, Bureau of Mines, Information Circular 8501 (1971), p. 71.

TABLE 14. Maximum Residuals Management Cost in Uranium Mining
and Milling Industries

	Mine reclamation	Cost radon-daughter hazard	Mill reclamation	Total
Conventional mine				
Open pit	$2/lb (today) $4/lb (future)	0	$0.20/lb	$2/lb (today) $4/lb (future)
Underground	negligible	$2/lb	$0.20/lb	$2/lb
Chattanooga shale	3% of U_3O_8 cost	negligible	6% of U_3O_8 cost	10% of U_3O_8 cost

also did not consider the effects of future regulations on siting, safeguards, or effluent control on the rest of the nuclear fuel cycles. Since, as I will show in Part II, the environmental hazards in other segments of the LMFBR fuel cycle, e.g., transportation of spent fuel, are greater than the hazards associated with the comparable segments of the LWR or HTGR fuel cycles, future environmental costs associated with these segments could offset any advantage the LMFBR has in the mining and milling segments.

THE EFFECT OF EARLY ENTRY
ON URANIUM RESOURCES

It will be remembered that the argument for the LMFBR included the notion that *early* introduction would be beneficial for the conservation of uranium resources, and one of the questions asked at the beginning of this chapter concerned the necessity of early introduction to achieve the benefits described. It should be noted that, despite lack of quantifiable data on this subject, the fraction of the uranium not converted to energy or plutonium fuel in nonbreeder reactors, that is, the uranium-238, is still readily available for conversion to plutonium fuel and ultimately energy in breeders.

The energy represented by this unconverted fraction of uranium is now stored in the uranium tailings at the enrichment plants and the smaller fraction of uranium recovered from nonbreeder fuel reprocessing.[35] Physically, the same energy will be available regardless of the time breeders are introduced into the economy, assuming they are introduced at all.

If the LMFBR program is postponed for one or more decades, the United States would simply continue stockpiling the uranium tailings at the enrichment plant, as it is now doing.[36] When or if uranium ore prices become sufficiently high to make fast breeders economical, the United States could start breeding fuel (plutonium-239) from the uranium-238 in the enrichment tailings. In effect, postponing the market entry date of the LMFBR until it is economical does not necessarily influence the United States' or the world's ability to meet long-term energy requirements. With respect to uranium conservation, an early LMFBR entry date cannot be viewed as a means of saving an exhaustible resource in the manner that fission, geothermal, and solar energy alternatives reduce the demand for coal or oil.

Plutonium produced in LWRs would be a more efficient fuel in an LMFBR than an LWR, in the sense that more electrical energy would be generated in an LMFBR per kilogram of plutonium depleted. However, the less efficient use of plutonium in an LWR plutonium recycle program during the period the introduction of the LMFBR is delayed appears inconsequential when one considers that the uranium-238 represents an essentially inexhaustible energy resource, which can be tapped if breeders are ultimately introduced. Certainly, the more efficient use of plutonium produced in LWRs should not overshadow economic considerations.

CONCLUSIONS

It will take thirty to forty years to develop and commercialize the breeder and introduce it into the market in sufficient quantity to lower the annual uranium requirement to a small fraction of

---

[35]Most of the enrichment plant tailings and the uranium recovered from spent-fuel reprocessing is uranium-238. The uranium from the spent fuel is supplemented with natural uranium, reenriched and reused as nonbreeder fuel.

[36]The cost of stockpiling depleted uranium at the gaseous diffusion plant in the form of uranium-hexafloride is small—only about $2 per ton per year as compared with U_3O_8 costs on the order of $12,000 to $16,000 per ton; therefore, the cost of storing the stockpile will have no influence on the optimum LMFBR market entry date.

what it would be otherwise (see Figure 12). As long as there are 3 million or possibly 4 million tons of low-cost domestic uranium in the ground, we can afford to delay the introduction of the breeder, as far as low-cost uranium availability is concerned. If the introduction of the breeder is delayed, the annual U_3O_8 requirement (by AEC estimates) will steadily climb, reaching about 100,000 tons per year by 2000; the average annual requirement over the next twenty years is less than half this amount. Therefore, in future years, as one reassesses the need for the breeder from the viewpoint of uranium availability, the required domestic resource (in the ground) will grow from the present estimate of 3 million to 4 million tons. However, our knowledge of domestic resources and costs of recovery will also increase.

Data presented to the Nuclear Task Group of the NPC's Committee on U.S. Energy Outlook, based on extrapolating uranium resources from explored to unexplored regions, indicate that our domestic resources exceed the 3-million to 4-million ton figure several fold.

One can argue that the NPC data may be biased. If there is reasonable doubt, these data could be checked by an independent group. There is ample time to do so. If the LMFBR program is postponed, the risk we are taking is small.

It is important to understand that delaying the breeder entry date and relying on foreign reserves as a back-up for as long as economically possible would have a negligible effect on our ability to meet long-term energy demand. This is because the stockpiled depleted uranium (the U-238 that is set aside at the gaseous diffusion plant) would be used as fuel for the breeders if and when they are finally introduced.

With more realistic estimates of capital cost, plant performance data, and market entry date than were used in the 1970 Analysis, there would be no economic incentive to introduce the LMFBR early, even using case A uranium prices, i.e., $50/lb ore at the 4-million-ton U_3O_8 commitment level. Therefore, even if low-cost uranium ore is exhausted before reaching the 3- to 4-million-ton commitment, and even if our foreign supplies are cut off, we should still not be alarmed at the prospect of having to rely on higher-cost (equal to or less than $50/lb of U_3O_8) ore. In the event that this back-up also fails, that is, if we run out of low-cost ore and we cannot meet the remainder of our needs from either foreign supplies or higher-cost ore, we are still not left without an energy production capability. We still have the options of accelerating the development of the breeder, rapidly converting to a heavier reliance on fossil-fuel plants, or some combination of these. If the United Kingdom, Japan, France, West Germany, or even the USSR continue their LMFBR programs as scheduled, which is very likely, much of the program development work required under the first option already will have been done. In effect, the demonstration plant phase of the U.S. LMFBR program plan could be eliminated, and the thirty- to forty-year required lead time would be reduced by about ten to fifteen years. The uranium requirement would be reduced as well.

Some of these options would be inefficient economically, but the risk seems so small that the economic incentive appears to favor delaying the LMFBR program until the LMFBR looks more favorable economically. This, I believe, probably will not occur until low-cost uranium resources are in much shorter supply.

Finally, I feel that by: (1) judiciously choosing the method and schedule for releasing the AEC's U_3O_8 stockpile and the time when the United States will lift the embargo on foreign U_3O_8, (2) encouraging long-term uranium purchase contracts, and (3) ensuring the availability of domestic uranium resources through state and federal land-use policy, the domestic uranium industry can remain competitive and healthy and can continue to maintain an adequate forward reserve. Under these conditions, I would expect that uranium prices would not fluctuate more than a few dollars per pound of U_3O_8 about the expected price, if future supply and demand were well known. These price fluctuations, due to unanticipated short-term shifts in demand and forward reserves, should have little effect on the average price of uranium over the next fifty years. In addition, lifting the embargo on foreign uranium should increase competition and lower domestic uranium prices slightly.

4

Electrical Energy Demand Forecasts

The AEC's estimates of electrical energy demand in both the 1968 and 1970 Analyses are extensions of a series of forecasts developed by the Federal Power Commission (FPC).

Forecasting energy demand requires that a number of factors be taken into consideration. The following, some of which were considered by the FPC, are among the major ones.[1]

Factors that might decrease demand	*Factors that might increase demand*
1. Reduction in the forecasted population growth rate.	1. Increase in productivity per worker in manufacturing, leading to a growth in real income per capita and a growth in demand for everything, including electrical energy.
2. Shift from single-family homes to multiple dwellings in new residential construction. (A single-family apartment uses about ⅔ of the electrical energy consumption of a single-family home.)	2. Climate control (winter and summer) for houses, patios, and public places.
3. Increase in mobile homes as a percentage of new residences, especially in the price range below $18,000.	3. Urban public transportation (electric) and electric automobiles.

[1]Some of these factors are summarized in P. Borrelli, M. Easterling, B. H. Klain, L. Lees, G. Paulker, and R. Poppe, *People, Power, Pollution*, California Institute of Technology, Environmental Quality Laboratory, Report No. 1 (Sept. 1971); others are from Technical Advisory Committee on Load Forecasting Methodology, "Changed Underlying Factors Influencing Electric Load Growth" (report to the FPC for the *1971 National Power Survey*).

Factors that might
decrease demand

Factors that might
increase demand

4. Slowdown in the rate of growth of the labor force over the next 20 years.
5. Reduction in number of hours in the work week.
6. Shift in labor force from manufacturing to less energy-intensive service and trade occupations.
7. Increase in electrical energy rates (in constant dollars) caused by increasing fuel costs, and by new methods of power plant siting and waste heat and residual management dictated by environmental constraints.
8. Increases in heating, cooling, and lighting efficiencies.
9. Overall change in life style.

4. Increase in pollution control devices which would reduce efficiency, thereby increasing energy requirements.
5. Lack of availability of other fuels for direct use (oil and gas).

Some of these factors could easily be listed in both categories, and it is difficult to estimate just what effect their interaction will have, or indeed, what effect other unlisted factors, which may well be important, will have. What should be clear, however, is the large range of uncertainty associated with any estimate for a period of more than ten to fifteen years.

Attempts to project energy demand have been undertaken by a number of sources using different forecasting techniques and emphasizing different variables. For example, the nine-man Power Requirements Special Technical Committee of the FPC in its 1964 survey felt that electric space heating, population growth, and income growth (as measured by GNP) were the most influential factors. Edwin Vennard[2] found high correlation historically between electric energy demand and GNP alone. Chapman, Tyrrell, and Mount[3] found the most important factors influencing energy demand were a combination of price, population, income, and gas prices.

[2]*The Electric Power Business* (New York: McGraw-Hill Book Co., 2nd ed., 1970). Vennard is the former managing director of the Edison Electric Institute.
[3]Duane Chapman, Timothy Tyrrell, and Timothy Mount, "Energy Demand Growth, the Energy Crisis, and R&D," *Science*, 178 (Nov. 17, 1972), pp. 703-08.

Not only does each source emphasize a somewhat different mix of factors, but their projections of how these factors will behave also vary. Before considering the AEC's results based on FPC data, it would be useful to look at the different estimates mentioned above in order to relate the sensitivity of the variables in the AEC analysis to what these sources consider are plausible future values for them.

FEDERAL POWER COMMISSION FORECASTS

Until the early 1960s the FPC had a poor track record; its electrical energy growth predictions, like nearly everyone else's, were consistently low. With the endorsement of President Kennedy in 1962, the FPC began its first in-depth National Power Survey.

As part of the first survey, the staff of the FPC prepared estimates of load and energy requirements through 1980. The FPC's Power Requirements Special Technical Committee reviewed these forecasts in depth, not only as to the postulates on which they were based but also in comparison with various long-range forecasts which had been made on both regional and national bases by the power suppliers.[4] The 1963 results of this committee represented the forecasts, at five-year intervals, through 1980 which appeared in the 1964 National Power Survey and which comprised the basis for the AEC's projections in their 1968 cost-benefit analysis. The FPC's 1970 National Power Survey was prepared in a similar fashion.

The 1964 National Power Survey projected an electrical energy demand in 1980 equal to 2.7 trillion kwh. However, Hans H. Landsberg, the only member of the 1963 Power Requirements Special Technical Committee not employed by an electric utility, suggested that a number of assumptions basic to the survey were not in agreement with the best estimates at that time. For instance, the 1980 U.S. population forecast of 265 million was higher than the current Bureau of Census estimates—245 million to 260 million. (The 1972 Bureau of Census estimates for 1980 range from 222 million [Series F] to 231 million [Series C].)[5] The 1964 Survey

---

[4]U.S. Federal Power Commission, *National Power Survey, Part II–Advisory Reports* (Oct. 1964), p. 131.

[5]U.S. Dept. of Commerce, "Projections of the Population of the United States, by Age and Sex: 1972 to 2020," *Population Estimates and Projections* (Dec. 1972).

was consonant with a compound rate of growth of GNP of 4 percent, whereas few economists would suggest that the U.S. economy could maintain this rate of growth over a twenty-year period. Landsberg also felt that the Committee's projection of 19 million electrically heated homes in 1980 was high; his projection was 14 million. It was consideration of these factors that led Landsberg to suggest that the 1980 electrical energy demand would be more nearly a figure of 2.3 trillion kwh—lower by 0.4 trillion than the forecast by the Committee. The Committee majority, however, suggested that there were other factors that would offset the points noted by Landsberg. Such factors included but were not limited to: (1) rapid advances in electric power technology which would improve the competitive position of electricity, and (2) the fact that almost invariably utility long-range forecasts have been low.

It is still too early to say which forecast, the Committee majority's or Landsberg's, is more accurate. The 1964 National Power Survey estimate for 1970 was very good, but not necessarily because of the accuracy of the estimates of the trends in *each* of the major factors influencing energy demand. For example, during the short period 1964-70, Landsberg's projections of the trends in population growth and electric space heating were more accurate than those of the Committee majority. Neither Landsberg nor the Committee majority foresaw the high economic growth and high growth in residential and commercial electrical energy sales during this period. In effect, the 1964 National Power Survey forecast for 1970 was correct but for the wrong reason. Thus, we cannot put much faith in this short-term result to measure the reliability of the National Power Survey's long-range forecasts. As the Committee properly noted, "These estimates are not intended to be precise forecasts for any of the five-year points to 1980, but to be broadly indicative of future load growth."[6]

The 1970 National Power Survey benefited from an additional five years of data covering the period 1964 through 1969. As noted above, it was during this short period that the United States experienced high average economic and electrical energy growth rates, 4.5 percent and 7.4 percent per year, respectively. This is not a new phenomenon. Historically, there have been alternate

---

[6]FPC, *National Power Survey, Part II*, p. 131.

periods of relatively high and low rates of growth in electrical energy demand, e.g.,

Period	Rate of Growth in Electrical Energy Demand (percent/year)	Real GNP Growth (percent/year)
1949-56	10.3	4.7
1956-61	5.1	2.2
1961-69	7.3	4.8
1969-71	5.5	1.0

As will be shown later, the high electrical energy growth rate may reflect a short-term, high, real GNP growth rate that cannot be sustained over an extended period. In this regard, it is noted that the average annual rates of growth in real GNP and electrical energy demand during the short period 1969 through 1971 were 1.0 and 5.5, respectively. The rate of growth in electrical energy demand in 1972 was 8 percent. For the period 1970-80, the 1964 Survey predicted an average electrical compound growth rate of 6.1 percent. The 1970 Survey forecast for the same period was 7.3 percent. The later figure is probably more a reflection of the trend during the short period 1964-69, when the average compound growth rate in energy demand was 7.4 percent. Hence, it is difficult to believe that the sustained high annual electrical energy growth rate predicted by the 1970 Survey will be realized, i.e., 7.3 percent for 1970-80, as indicated, and 6.6 percent for 1980-90.

The attractive feature of the forecast method used by the National Power Surveys is that the forecasts represent an aggregate of regional forecasts, which are themselves aggregates of separate utility forecasts; and these, in turn, are aggregates of smaller components or classes, e.g., trends in residential, commercial, and industrial uses. At each level of aggregation the forecasts can be correlated with trends in significant economic, demographic, and climatic factors which have influenced load growth in these classes in the past. Although, a priori, one might expect that this method of forecasting would be the most accurate, there are several major weaknesses in the National Power Survey approach which could offset any advantages in aggregation. Some of these are discussed below.

Electric utilities plan the capacity of their physical system to meet expected peak demand requirements. Total energy requirements are of secondary concern in planning generation capacity. A 1969 survey of practices by electric utilities showed that only about one-half of the reporting utilities prepare an energy forecast as the primary forecast, with a peak demand obtained by use of load factor relationships.[7] The other half prepare peak demand forecasts directly. About one-third of the reporting utilities prepare forecasts on system loads in total. The other two-thirds assemble peak forecasts either by geographic areas, by types of customers, or by some other subdivision of load.[8]

For utilities, the intermediate term (four to six years and often to eight years) covers the most crucial time span in terms of planning physical facilities, since lead times for adding capacity are generally this length.[9] One-fourth of the utilities surveyed report that they do not prepare long-term forecasts. Half of the remaining utilities report that long-term forecasts are extrapolations of intermediate-term forecasts based on judgment, compound rates of growth, fitted curves, or some combination of these.[10] The uncertainty in utility intermediate-term forecasts of total energy requirements, as measured by the average difference between actual results and three- to five-year forecasts, was found to be 4.8 percent.[11] The uncertainty of long-term forecasts by utilities would be even greater. At least one of the difficulties is that long-term population projections, economic growth projections, etc., are very inadequate on a utility area basis and are difficult to make accurately.

Although there is an incentive for utilities to make accurate intermediate-term forecasts, the consequences of error in long-term forecasts are not nearly as great. In fact, from a utility standpoint, it may be desirable to show a high long-term growth rate in order to enable the utilities to obtain capital at a more favorable interest rate and to promote the view in the customers' minds that the

---

[7]Technical Advisory Committee on Load Forecasting Methodology, "The Methodology of Load Forecasting" (report to the Federal Power Commission for the *1969 National Power Survey*), p. V-7.

[8]Ibid., p. V-8.

[9]Ibid., p. II-5.

[10]Ibid., p. V-12.

[11]Ibid., p. V-16.

swing is to electricity. In addition, there may be a spirit of competition between utilities—Who wants to show low growth?

In summary, the long-range subaggregate forecasts, upon which the regional FPC forecasts are based, are probably not very accurate, and the utilities making those forecasts do not have a great need for long-range forecasting. Some of these same arguments also apply to the regional forecasts. As we see in the following sections, by the time the National Power Surveys have been aggregated to the national level, the electrical energy forecasts do not coincide with forecasts based on historical trends in economic (GNP) growth, income and price elasticities, and per capita consumption.

Some utilities, architect-engineering firms, and other industry groups have electrical energy demand forecasts that are consistent with the latest FPC forecast. These may or may not be entirely independent of the FPC projections. For example, it has been noted[12] that a recent report by the National Academy of Engineering contains the projection of 10 trillion kwh for the year 2000, consistent with the FPC figures for that year. In fact, the electrical energy demand projections of the National Academy of Engineering[13] (NAE) are nothing more than the 1970 National Power Survey projections, extrapolated to 2000 just as the FPC had done.[14] Furthermore, the National Academy of Engineering notes, "In the postwar period, the trend of electric power generation, including industrial self-generation, has been an increase of about 3 kilowatt-hours for every dollar increase in GNP when GNP is expressed in 1958 dollars."[15] As will be shown in the following section, the 1970 National Power Survey projections (and therefore the FPC, AEC, and NAE projections) are inconsistent with this historical trend.

[12]K. A. Hub, Letter to the Editor, *Science*, 178 (Dec. 22, 1972), pp. 1240-1241, referring to National Academy of Engineering Committee on Power Plant Siting, *Engineering for the Resolution of the Energy-Environment Dilemma: A Summary* (Washington, D.C., 1972).

[13]Specifically, the working group on energy and economic growth of the Committee on Power Plant Siting.

[14]See, for example, Table 5 of NAE's *Engineering for the Resolution of the Energy-Environment Dilemma*, p. 326; and Table 2 of *Engineering for the Resolution of the Energy-Environment Dilemma*, p. 43.

[15]Ibid.

FORECAST BASED ON U.S. GROSS
NATIONAL PRODUCT GROWTH

Edwin Vennard of the Edison Electric Institute (EEI)[16] shows
that historical correlations between U.S. electrical energy demand
and U.S. GNP have been highly accurate. Milton Searl (of
Resources for the Future) has updated the EEI analysis described
by Vennard, using data from 1947 to 1969. He found that the total
U.S. electrical energy demand could be expressed as $k = -666 +$
$3.02G$, where k is the energy demand in billions of kwh, and G
is real GNP in billions of constant (1958) dollars.

The forecast of total electrical energy demand using Searl's
expression and constant GNP growth rates of 3.0, 3.5, and 4.0 percent are shown in Figure 16, alongside the AEC/FPC estimates,
which are discussed later. Even at a sustained compounded GNP
growth rate of 4.0 percent, the estimated total electrical energy
demand in the year 2000 would be only 6.5 trillion kwh, according
to Searl. At a GNP growth rate of 3.5 percent, a value apparently
more realistic to most economists, the estimated electrical energy
demand would be 5.5 trillion kwh. This is almost one-half of the
1970 FPC estimate for the same year. As seen from Figure 17,
it would very substantially reduce the net benefits of an early commitment to the breeder, virtually to zero.

In Figure 18, one notes that the data points for 1970 and 1971
fall above the regression line, and the deviations of these points
are greater than those at previous years. This does not necessarily
suggest a break from the historical trend. As can be seen from the
figure, the data tend to oscillate about the trend line. Searl has
shown that the deviations can be further reduced by also including
previous years' GNP into the correlation. However, this does not
change the projections significantly; it only improves the fit of the
curve. Also, it should be noted that, as the GNP and the electrical
energy demand continue to grow, one expects the absolute deviations to grow, while the relative deviations remain fairly constant.

The change in the ratio of *total* energy to gross national product
in recent years has been the source of some concern. For example,
in 1971 congressional hearings Commissioner Johnson stated:

---

[16]See Edwin Vennard, *The Electric Power Business*. Those unfamiliar with energy
forecasts based on GNP growth may find the review in Appendix F, based on Vennard's book, helpful.

In reviewing energy requirements, we find that the average annual increase in the rate of energy consumption was 3.4 percent for the 30-year period ending in 1970; 3.6 percent between 1960 and 1965; and a surprising 5 percent for the 5-year period between 1965 and 1970.

The increase in energy consumption since 1965 has not yet been fully explained. . . . Bearing on this point is the trend of energy use in relation to gross national product. For example, in the decade beginning in 1956 there was a progressive and rather substantial decrease in the ratio of energy to gross national product. However, beginning in 1966 this ratio

FIGURE 16. Annual U.S. Electrical Energy Demand

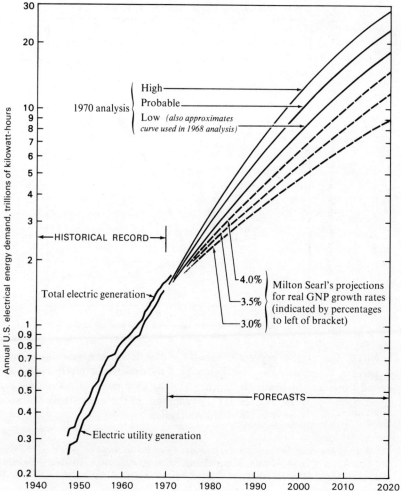

has gone sharply upward and presently is above the 1956 level. The important question is whether this increase in the energy consumption rate represents a long-term historic trend, which will be reflected in higher growth
rates over the future. Obviously, if this higher rate persists then all energy
requirements would have to be adjusted dramatically upward.[17]

I do not agree that the total U.S. electrical energy demand would
have to be adjusted dramatically upward. Most of the acceleration
in the growth of total energy consumption (from all sources includ-

FIGURE 17. Sensitivity of Present Value (mid-1971)
Net Benefits to Electrical Energy Demand

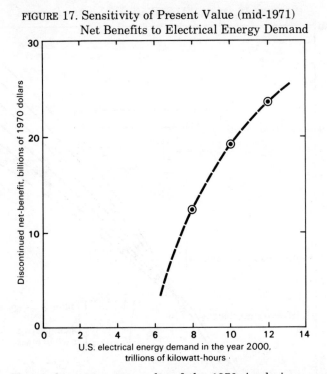

U.S. electrical energy demand in the year 2000,
trillions of kilowatt-hours ·

NOTE: The circles represent results of the 1970 Analysis assuming a
7 percent discount rate (see Table 7). The uppermost circle represents
case 13 results; the lower circle, case 11. The data point in the middle represents case 3, reflecting the AEC's judgment of the most likely values of
the parameters varied in the 1970 Analysis.

[17]Wilfrid Johnson, *Defense Production Act Progress Report–No. 50 (Vol. 2) Potential Shortages of Ores, Metals, Minerals, and Energy Resources*, in Hearings before
the Joint Committee on Defense Production, 92 Cong. 1 sess. (Sept. 22 and 23,
1971), p. 351.

FIGURE 18. Correlation Between U.S. Electrical Energy Demand and Gross National Product, in Constant Dollars

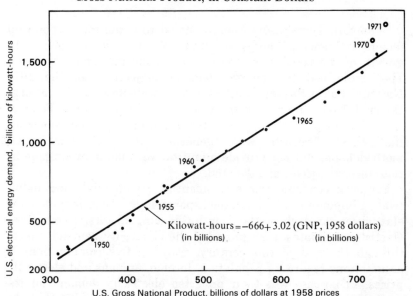

SOURCE: Milton Searl, private communication.

ing electricity) that occurred in the latter part of the 1960s was due to increases in the use of fossil fuels for transportation and thermal losses associated with electricity conversion at power plants.[18] Less than 10 percent of the acceleration was due to factors which might influence the long-term growth of electrical energy demand.[19] It is perhaps worth noting that the National Petroleum Council's Committee on U.S. Energy Outlook does not project the recent trend in the ratio of total U.S. energy consumption to GNP (constant dollars) to continue. Their projection of the ratio of total energy to GNP through 1985 remains fairly constant at approximately the 1970 value, 91,000 Btu per 1958 dollar.[20]

[18]Resources for the Future, Inc., "Energy Research Needs," Report to the National Science Foundation, in cooperation with M.I.T. Environmental Laboratory (Oct. 1971), pp. I-22–I-24.

[19]This would not be true if a large shift is made toward electric transportation. See also ibid.

[20]National Petroleum Council, "U.S. Energy Outlook, An Initial Appraisal, 1971-1985."

FORECAST BASED ON ELASTICITIES OF ELECTRICITY PRICE,
POPULATION GROWTH, INCOME, AND GAS PRICES

Chapman, Tyrrell, and Mount[21] noted that the most important
factors influencing energy demand appear to be its price, the
growth of the population, the growth of income, and gas prices.
They examined the energy demand projections of the 1970
National Power Survey, the National Petroleum Council's Energy
Demand Task Group, and the Cornell–National Science Foundation Workshop on Energy and the Environment, and concluded
that these forecasts were generally incorrect since their
methodologies did not provide quantitative links between population, income, prices, and demand.

For each consumer class (residential, commercial, and industrial), Chapman et al. estimated separately the electricity demand
elasticities for each of the four influencing factors. Using these
elasticity estimates, they projected the electricity demand growth
through the rest of this century, utilizing five combinations of
assumptions regarding population, income, and gas and electricity
prices. In no case was their projected electricity demand for the
year 2000 greater than 5 trillion kwh. They concluded that the
near future—say, 1975—is not much affected. All projections show
about 2 trillion kwh of generation in 1975. Supply problems in the
next few years will not be eased by likely rate increases and population trends.

They also found that the population assumption is unimportant
for demand growth in the next twenty to thirty years. In addition,
they constrained their solution to meet the FPC projection of 10
trillion kwh in 2000 and found that, using Bureau of Economic
Analysis projections of population and income, electricity prices
would have to decline 24 percent from 1970 to 1980, and 12 percent
each ten years thereafter until 2000. This, they noted, is inconsistent with FPC's rising price assumptions.

OTHER ELECTRICAL ENERGY DEMAND FORECASTS

I have also examined forecasts of electrical energy demand based
on Gompertz curves fitted to per capita demand, together with pro-

[21]Duane Chapman, Timothy Tyrrell, and Timothy Mount, "Energy Demand
Growth."

jections of the U.S. population. Because the Gompertz projections are not very reliable, the analysis of this forecasting technique is relegated to Appendix F. One additional forecast, that of Richard Salter, is also presented in this appendix.

Were it shown in Figure 16, the projection of U.S. electrical energy demand, using the Gompertz per capita electrical energy demand together with the Census Bureau Series E population projection (corresponding to the replacement fertility rate of 2.1 children per family), would lie between Searl's projections for GNP growth rates of 3 percent and 3.5 percent; that is, 3.5 trillion kwh in 2000. With the higher Series B projection (abandoned by the Bureau of Census in its 1972 projections), the U.S. electrical energy demand would correspond roughly to Searl's projection for 4 percent GNP growth—6.4 trillion kwh in 2000. Richard Salter's 1971 estimate for the same year was 4.5 trillion kwh.[22]

AEC ANALYSIS ESTIMATES

The estimates of the total U.S. electrical energy demand used in the AEC's 1970 Analysis are presented in Table 15 and Figure 16. The "probable" demand was obtained by extrapolating, to the year 2020, Federal Power Commission estimates through the year 2000.[23] The "low" and "high" electrical energy demands were selected to be 20 percent lower and 20 percent higher than the FPC estimates for the year 2000. The "low" estimate of demand is approximately equivalent to the base electrical demand in the 1968 Analysis, which in turn was based on the FPC's 1964 National Power Survey[24] projections through 1980. The "low" estimate provides a ready reference for comparing the 1968 Analysis with the 1970 Analysis.

[22]Richard G. Salter, "A Probabilistic Forecasting Methodology Applied to Electrical Energy Consumption," RAND No. R-993-NSF (Draft, Feb. 1972).

[23]The FPC forecast was obtained from the 1970 National Power Survey forecast by simple extrapolation, based on a graphic projection of its growth rate forecast through 2000. An exponential growth rate of 5.54 percent per year between 1990 and 2000 was used.

[24]FPC, Power Requirements Special Technical Committee, "Forecast of Electrical Utility Power Requirements to the Year 1980," in *National Power Survey, Part II–Advisory Reports* (1964).

TABLE 15.   1970 Electrical Energy Demand and AEC Estimates for Decades to 2020

(trillions of kwh/yr)

Year	Low	Probable	High
1970	1.52	1.52	1.52
1980	2.7	3.1	3.4
1990	4.8	5.8	6.8
2000	8	10	12
2010	12.5	16	19.5
2020	18	23	28

SOURCE: U.S. Atomic Energy Commission, Division of Reactor Development and Technology, *Updated (1970) Cost-Benefit Analysis of the U.S. Breeder Reactor Program,* WASH 1184 (Jan. 1972), p. 45.

In order to show the sensitivity of the net discounted dollar benefits of the breeder program to the projected total electrical energy demand in the United States, each demand curve is represented by a single value, the electrical energy demand in the year 2000. The results (i.e., net benefits for cases 3, 11, and 13 in Table 6 versus demand in 2000) plotted in Figure 17 show that the net benefits of the LMFBR program are very sensitive to electrical energy demand. For example, if the electrical energy demand were 40 percent less than the FPC projection, i.e., 6 trillion kwh in 2000 as Searl's figures suggest, and there were corresponding values for the other years (Figure 16), then the net benefits of the LMFBR program would be close to, if not less than, zero, all other assumptions unchanged. If the Chapman et al. figures of 5 trillion kwh were used, the negative effect would be even greater.

SUMMARY

The fifty-year electrical energy demand projections used in the 1970 Analysis are based on a simple exponential extrapolation of a twenty-year forecast of the Federal Power Commission's 1970 National Power Survey. The electrical energy demand projection of the 1970 Survey (actually, a 1969 estimate) is not very reliable beyond about ten years because all long-range energy forecasts are inaccurate due to the manner in which they are generated and because population and economic growth projections are not very accurate on a utility, or even regional, basis. Current long-range electrical energy demand projections, using independent forecasting techniques that are based on historical national trends in GNP growth, income, gas and electricity price elasticities, and per capita consumption, suggest that the 1970 Survey, and in turn the 1970 Analysis, projections overestimate the electrical energy demand. The true demand could easily be 25 percent, and possibly 50 percent, below the "probable" projection in the 1970 Analysis for the year 2000. If these projections are more correct than the 1970 Survey, the projected discounted net benefits of the LMFBR program—without changing the remaining economic and technologic projections from the most probable estimates in the 1970 Analysis—could vanish, due only to the reduction in energy demand.

5

Other Economic Considerations

ALTERNATIVE REACTOR PROGRAMS

The High Temperature Gas-Cooled Reactor

In determining the sensitivity of the 1970 Analysis results to HTGR market penetration, Whitman et al. reported:

Removal of the HTGR from the computational model increases the 7% discounted benefits of the breeder almost 100% from $21.5 billion to $42.3 billion. This is attributable to the fact that, without the HTGR, the base cost of producing power using only fossil plants and the LWR, is markedly increased.[1]

The $21.5 billion is the difference between the cumulative discounted energy cost using the plants shown in Figure 19(a) and the equivalent cost using the plants in Figure 19(b). Similarly, the $42.3 billion is the difference between the energy costs using the plants in Figures 19(c) and 19(d).

The 1970 Analysis, except in the last two cases where the HTGR was omitted, assumed 2000 Mw of HTGR capacity would be introduced in the 1978-79 biennium. Based on the performance to date of Gulf General Atomics Co. (GGA) (the only HTGR vendor in the country), it appears that this market entry date is quite reasonable, and that HTGRs will be introduced into the market

---

[1]M. J. Whitman, A. N. Tardiff, and P. L. Hofmann, "U.S. Civilian Nuclear Power Cost-Benefit Analysis" (presented at the Fourth United Nations International Conference on the Peaceful Uses of Atomic Energy, Geneva, Sept. 6-16, 1971).

FIGURE 19. Projected Generating Capacity in the United States

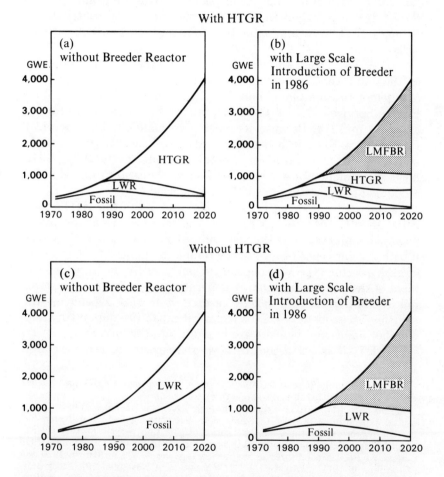

SOURCE: M.J. Whitman, A.N. Tardiff, and P.L. Hofmann, "U.S. Civilian Nuclear Power Cost-Benefit Analysis" (presented at the Fourth United Nations International Conference on the Peaceful Uses of Atomic Energy, Geneva, Sept. 6-16, 1971).

NOTE: Illustrations assume 1970 Analysis, case A uranium reserves and probable energy demand.

in significant numbers. In this regard, GGA anticipates selling about fifty HTGRs over the next eight years.[2]

GGA has developed the HTGR in cooperation with the electric utility industry and the AEC. Approximately $500 million of public and private funds has been spent on this program through 1972.[3] The federal government and electric utility contributions through 1971 were approximately $115 million and $90 million, respectively.

The 40-Mw Peach Bottom experimental HTGR was completed in 1965 and went into commercial operation in June 1967. A 330-Mw demonstration plant (Fort St. Vrain) has been constructed for Public Services Co. of Colorado, and commercial operation is expected in 1974. Because its small size makes it uneconomical, Philadelphia Electric has announced that Peach Bottom will be shut down at the end of its present core life (early 1974). GGA has commitments for six commercial-size plants, totaling 540 Mw, scheduled for operation in the 1980-83 period.[4]

As seen by comparing Figures 19(a) and 19(b), the HTGR competes directly with the LMFBR for the major share of the power generation market after the year 2000. This is, of course, only true if both reactor types penetrate the commercial market. The success of each reactor type will depend, in part, on the utilities' assessment of their respective energy generating costs, including operating reliability. In the HTGR case, it will also depend on the utilities' assessment of GGA's technical capability and, ultimately, whether additional vendors are brought into the picture.

The HTGR is attractive in several respects. It achieves high

[2]"Utility Group to Support GGA Gas Turbine Development for HTGRs," *Nuclear Industry*, 19 (April 1972), p. 38. (No author indicated.)

[3]Based on a $450 million estimate through 1971, that includes Fort St. Vrain capital expenditures through the same year, but does not include waivered fuel use charges or expenditures for the Thorium Utilization Recycle Facility (TURF) at ORNL that have been channeled through the Naval Reactor Program. Gulf Oil Company's R&D expenditures in the nuclear area were $30 million in 1970 and $50 million in 1971, mostly for the HTGR program. A November 1972 stock prospectus indicated total expenditures by Gulf in the nuclear area were $209 million, again mostly directed toward HTGR development.

[4]Philadelphia Electric Co. has agreed to purchase two 1160-Mw HTGR plants, scheduled to go into operation in 1981 and 1983. Delmarva Power and Light in Wilmington, Delaware, announced its intentions to purchase two 770-Mw HTGR plants (scaled-down versions of the Philadelphia Electric plants) for delivery in 1980 and 1982. Southern California Edison has signed a letter of intent for two 770-Mw HTGRs to be placed in the eastern California desert. The first unit is scheduled to go into operation in 1981.

steam temperatures and pressures, comparable to those of modern fossil-fueled plants and the LMFBR, and shares the same potential radioactive pollution control advantages that have been forecast for the LMFBR.[5] Some of the more attractive features of the HTGR are related to the use of helium as a coolant. Because helium is chemically inert, the fuel-coolant interaction is not a significant consideration in HTGR design basis accidents, as it is in LMFBR safety designs. Helium absorbs essentially no neutrons and does not contribute to the reactivity of the system. Thus, there is no mechanism for introducing large amounts of reactivity due to coolant voiding, as is the case with LMFBRs. In reactors using liquid coolants, a liquid-to-gas phase change provides a mechanism for converting large amounts of thermal energy into mechanical work. This factor is of particular significance in LWR loss-of-coolant accidents, but has no significance in HTGR safety design since the helium is already a gas.

The HTGR is not without its disadvantages. For example, with helium, natural convection cooling is insignificant, so there must be very reliable and redundant means to provide forced circulation of the gas coolant during all normal and emergency conditions. With pressurized gas, a failure in the pressure envelope can result in a rapid drop in pressure, with a corresponding need to provide continued forced cooling. The possibility of a sudden loss of coolant such as could occur with a massive rupture of the prestressed concrete containment vessel must be considered extremely remote.

GGA suggests that a rapid depressurization of the containment vessel is not a particularly severe accident relative to the loss-of-coolant accident in LWRs. This is primarily because the helium coolant does not change phase, and the graphite structure has a high heat capacity and a higher melting point than the metal clad used in LWRs.

The HTGR is not a breeder. However, like the LMFBR, the HTGR has the potential for improving fuel utilization over the LWRs, when and if the HTGR fuel recycle is established. During normal operation, the LWR, the HTGR, and LMFBR all convert nonfissionable material into fissionable material. LWRs and fast breeders, such as the LMFBR, convert nonfissile U-238 into fissile Pu-239. The HTGR and thermal breeders convert nonfissile thorium into fissile U-233. The conversion ratio of today's LWRs is approximately 0.5 to 0.6.[6] Present HTGR designs, when initially operated on U-235, have a conversion ratio of 0.7.[7] In the absence of recycle of bred U-233, this figure falls, over about a ten-year period, to an equilibrium level of about 0.6,[8] comparable to that of LWRs.

Several years after the development of a U-233 fuel recycle capability, some HTGRs can be fueled initially with U-233 instead of U-235 as now designed. The conversion ratio of these HTGRs should be approximately 0.8. Their fuel "amplification factor" should be twice that of today's LWRs.

LWRs can burn, or convert into fissile plutonium, only about 1 percent of the natural uranium. Over the lifetime of the plant an HTGR, due to its higher conversion ratio and because it converts thorium rather than uranium-238 into fissile material, requires roughly 40 percent less uranium than an equivalent-size LWR.

The LMFBR can, in theory, utilize about 40 to 50 percent of the uranium fuel—not 100 percent because of the small losses which occur each time the fuel is reprocessed and recycled, and because roughly 30 percent of the plutonium produced is not fissile.

While HTGRs are better utilizers of uranium fuel than LWRs, it does not necessarily follow that large-scale utilization of HTGRs in the civilian power economy will reduce our domestic uranium commitment during the next fifty years. The AEC's 1970 Analysis predicts that, whether or not the LMFBR is introduced, the U_3O_8 required to the year 2020 is virtually the same with and without the introduction of the HTGR (compare cases 1 and 15 and cases 3 and 16 in Table 13). The principal reason for this is that the power economy model predicts that the nuclear fraction of the total generating capacity will be larger if the HTGR is introduced. This can be seen by comparing Figure 19(a) with 19(c), and 19(b) with 19(d).

---

[6]The ratio of fuel bred to fuel burned is called the conversion ratio, if it is less than one, and the breeding ratio, if greater than one. The simple fuel doubling time for a breeder is proportional to 1/(breeding ratio − 1). Converter reactors, such as the LWRs and HTGR, may be regarded as devices that amplify the effectiveness of available fissile material by the factor 1/(1 − conversion ratio). Analogous with simple doubling time, this is simply an expression of the fact that a total of these many fissions is eventually produced for each net atom of fissile feed, when the fuel is ideally recycled.

[7]Peter Fortescue, "A Reactor Strategy: FBR's and HTGR's," *Nuclear News*, 15, No. 4 (April 1972), pp. 36-39.

[8]Ibid.

These figures are results from the 1970 Analysis showing the relative base load capacity generated by each power source when the demand is met with fossil-fueled and light-water reactor plants, with and without the addition of the HTGR and LMFBR. Large-scale utilization of HTGRs or fast breeders could substantially reduce our fossil fuel commitment.

In the 1970 Analysis the LMFBR wins out over the HTGR because the optimistic GE LMFBR design is introduced in 1990, at a cost of only $20/kw greater than the HTGR. As indicated earlier, however, with more likely capital cost differentials, LMFBR performance data, and fuel cycle costs, the LMFBR probably would not be competitive until uranium prices are higher than they are today by a factor of 3 or more.

According to the 1970 Analysis (see Table 7), introducing the HTGR in the absence of the LMFBR reduces the total undiscounted energy cost from $3,466 billion to $2,704 billion, i.e., a 22 percent reduction. Introducing the LMFBR in 1986 further reduces the cost to $2,346 billion, i.e., an additional 19 percent reduction. This suggests that about two-thirds of the projected gross benefits between now and 2020 can be realized by successfully developing and marketing the HTGR.

One final point—a significant reduction in HTGR plant capital costs, not included in the 1970 Analysis, could be achieved by the successful development of an associated closed-cycle gas turbine. GGA's Peter Fortescue suggests that such a development could yield a 15 percent total plant cost reduction initially, and additional benefits with later development of higher temperatures.[9] An additional merit of the gas turbine is that, as a result of the high mean temperature of the rejected heat, such a plant is readily adaptable to dry air cooling. Fortescue quotes preliminary HTGR plant studies indicating that the application of dry cooling to gas turbines costs some $25/kwh less than applying it to the equivalent steam plant.[10]

Kasten, Bennett, and Thomas reported that the 1970 Analysis did not consider the possibility of plutonium makeup for the HTGR.[11] Plutonium, as they noted, has a higher fuel value in the

[9]Fortescue, "A Reactor Strategy."
[10]Ibid.
[11]Paul R. Kasten, Leonard L. Bennett, and William E. Thomas, "An Evaluation of Plutonium Use in High-Temperature Gas-Cooled Reactors," Oak Ridge National Laboratory paper (no date given).

HTGR than in LWRs, and development of a plutonium recycle capability inherently develops the ability to fabricate plutonium-fueled HTGR fuel elements. They point out that, if the plutonium recycle capability were made available to the HTGR, the 1970 Analysis would have predicted that, between 1970 and 2015, more than twice as many HTGRs would be built, only 37 percent as many LWRs, and 5 percent fewer LMFBRs.[12]

The Gas-Cooled Fast Breeder Reactor

Beyond a discussion of parallel breeder costs, the AEC did not include the GCFBR in either the 1968 or 1970 Analysis. However, in their initial evaluation of the civilian nuclear power program, the AEC considered the GCFBR the logical follow-on to the HTGR. The GCFBR is less well-developed than the LMFBR, since no units have been built; the principal effort has consisted of engineering studies and a demonstration plant proposal submitted to the AEC by GGA. GGA is, at present, the only U.S. supplier showing a strong interest in developing the GCFBR, undoubtedly because the GCFBR represents a relatively small step beyond the HTGR in terms of coolant technology, and because the design and testing of the fuel for the GCFBR have much in common with (and GGA would profit by) the work on fuel for the LMFBR. Other U.S. reactor vendors were probably less interested because they had made early commitments to the LMFBR, due at least in part to the AEC's promotion of this reactor since the mid-1960s.

The AEC has officially spent about $9 million on the GCFBR through fiscal 1972, and has been supporting the program at an annual level between $1 million and $2 million over the years since 1968. The authorization for fiscal 1973 was $2 million; however, OMB held back half of this amount.

The 1970 Analysis examines the cost of a parallel gas-cooled fast breeder program to be introduced in 1994, eight years after the LMFBR (see case B-5, Table 2). From Table 2 it is seen that the AEC's estimate of the added cost of a GCFBR program is $2.2 billion, or $1.2 billion when discounted to mid-1971 at 7 percent. GGA estimates the federal contribution through one demonstration

---

[12]Although they reported results through 2015 rather than 2020, their program and input data were essentially the same as those used in the AEC's 1970 Analysis.

plant at about $190 million (no escalation), a factor of 6 less than the AEC estimate. Neither the AEC nor GGA have published an itemized list of their respective cost estimates. The AEC figure is probably based on several demonstration plants and a competitive GCFBR industry. GGA believes the eight-year difference between the LMFBR and GCFBR introduction dates is high—that two years is more reasonable. A third estimate of the most probable GCFBR entry date, that in the report of the EEI Reactor Assessment Panel, shows the GCFBR available in 1990, five years after the LMFBR entry date.

While it is beyond the scope of this study to analyze the GCFBR in the same detail that has been given the LMFBR, it can be said, first, that it has most of the desirable and undesirable characteristics of the HTGR cooling system and the LMFBR fuel and breeding potential. To elaborate, I rely on brief discussions derived from a 1970 article by former AEC Chairman Glenn Seaborg and his associate Justin Bloom, and the congressional testimony of Manson Benedict, one of the "deans" of the nuclear community. According to Seaborg and Bloom:

The essential difference between the two fast breeders [GCFBR and LMFBR] is that the gas-cooled one uses helium gas at a pressure of from 70 to 100 atmospheres rather than molten sodium to transport the heat from the reactor core to the steam generators. Since the gas does not become radioactive and cannot react chemically with the water in the steam generator, there is no need for an intermediate heat exchanger. The resulting simplification of the system is a helpful offset against the need to design for a higher coolant pressure with gas.

The use of helium as a coolant has other special advantages for a fast breeder reactor. Helium does not interact with the fast neutrons in the reactor core, resulting in both simplified control of the reactor and enhanced breeding of new fissionable fuel from fertile material. In addition helium is transparent and chemically inert, providing visibility during refueling and maintenance operations, a simpler engineering design and freedom from corrosion problems.

In a gas-cooled fast breeder the reactor core, helium circulators and steam generators are all contained in a prestressed-concrete reactor pressure vessel. These major components and their arrangement are almost the same as in a thermal gas-cooled reactor.

The development of a gas-cooled fast breeder reactor could result in substantial additional savings beyond those that would be achieved by liquid-metal fast breeders. Neutrons are moderated, or slowed, less in helium than they are in sodium. Hence the doubling time is short. It is also possible to foresee the development of a gas-cooled fast breeder with a direct power cycle wherein the gas coolant flows from the reactor directly to a gas turbine that drives the electrical generator. Such a cycle should help to reduce the capital cost of fast breeder reactors.[13]

Benedict noted that the major disadvantage of the GCFBR results from the poor heat transfer characteristics of helium and its low heat capacity, resulting in the need for high operating pressure. As with the HTGR, in the event of a rapid loss of coolant, the fuel could overheat, melt, and release the more volatile fission products. Benedict adds that:

> Engineering studies suggest that such a disastrous accident can be pre-vented by proper design of the prestressed concrete pressure vessel and by surrounding the vessel with secondary containment to maintain the pressure after a leak high enough to prevent fuel melting. Further engineering studies and extensive tests under simulated accident condi-tions will be required before these factors can be fully evaluated. Because of the many advantages of this reactor type, these safety investigations and other development problems of the GCFBR should be attacked vigor-ously and merit substantially increased funding.
>
> Both fast breeder reactors [LMFBR and GCFBR] have problems con-nected with mechanical deterioration of fuel and construction materials when exposed for long times to fast neutrons [e.g., the stainless steel swell-ing and creep phenomena].[14]

The model used by the AEC in its initial evaluation[15] predicts that the GCFBR, due to its lower estimated capital cost, will be the only breeder built once it becomes commercially available. However, this prediction is highly sensitive to capital cost differen-ces; arbitrarily adding $20/kw to the GCFBR capital cost makes it uncompetitive. Paul MacAvoy, formerly a member of the staff of the President's Council of Economic Advisers, concluded that a GCFBR program would be more economical than an LMFBR program.[16]

On paper at least, the LMFBR cannot compete with the GCFBR due to the latter's lower estimated capital cost and better projected performance (e.g., breeding ratio). On the basis of case 3 assump-tions, had the GCFBR been introduced as late as the year 2000, the LMFBR generating capacity projected by the 1970 Analysis

[13]Glenn T. Seaborg and Justin L. Bloom, "Fast Breeder Reactors," *Scientific American*, 223 (Nov. 1970), pp. 13-21.

[14]Manson Benedict in Hearings before the Committee on Science and Astronau-tics, Subcommittee on Science, Research and Development, 92 Cong. 2 sess. (May 1972), p. 40.

[15]U.S. AEC, *Potential Nuclear Power Growth Patterns*, p. 6-52.

[16]Paul MacAvoy, *Economic Strategy*, p. 94.

would have been limited to the amount introduced prior to 2000, or about 20 percent of that projected without GCFBRs.

A 1972 evaluation of the GCFBR by the AEC noted that:

The consistent conclusion reached in the cost-benefit studies (WASH-1126 and -1184), viz., sufficient information is available to indicate that the projected benefits from the LMFBR program can support a parallel breeder program, is highly sensitive to the assumptions on plant capital costs. With the recognition that even for ongoing concepts on which ample experience exists, capital costs and especially small estimated differences in costs are highly speculative for plants to be built 15 or 20 years from now, it is questionable whether analyses based upon such costs should constitute a major basis for decision making relative to the desirability of a parallel breeder effort.[17]

This conclusion applies equally to the AEC's cost-benefit analyses as a basis for decision making relative to the desirability of the LMFBR program.

ECONOMIC CONSIDERATIONS EXCLUDED FROM THE LMFBR COST-BENEFIT ANALYSES

There are several topics directly bearing on the question of whether the United States should pursue the currently proposed LMFBR program plan that were not addressed in either the 1970 Analysis or the earlier 1968 Analysis. Three of these topics having economic implications are discussed below.

Alternative Energy R&D Programs

Other than in the context of choosing the appropriate discount rate, neither the 1970 Analysis nor the AEC's Demonstration Plant Environmental Statement discussed the potential benefits forgone by investing in the LMFBR program on a priority basis (40-45 percent of federal energy R&D funds). In response to the request of the President in his energy message of June 4, 1971, the Office of Science and Technology (OST), which has since been abolished, began extensive assessment of new energy technologies, *except the LMFBR and coal gasification to produce pipeline-quality gas.* These were not assessed because "they have already received

---

[17]*AEC Authorizing Legislation Fiscal Year 1974*, Hearings before the Joint Committee on Atomic Energy, 93 Cong. 1 sess., on Civilian Reactor Development, March 14, 1973, Part 3. Washington, D.C.: Government Printing Office, 1973.

priority commitments," and because "they are sufficiently far advanced and are well enough defined to permit their introduction with some degree of confidence into descriptions of the future energy systems."[18]

A case can be made for the argument that the *total* federal energy R&D expenditures are too low. For example, the federal energy R&D funding for fiscal 1973 ($622 million) represents only 3.4 percent of the 1971 revenues of the electric utility industry ($21 billion). Energy is such an important component of our society, both as a factor input to production and consumption and because of the substantial externalities produced as a result of its generation, that increased funding in this area appears to be justified. Recognizing this, the Administration recently proposed spending $10 billion in five years on energy research.

It has been argued, and is presumably the position of the AEC and OST, that the government should continue LMFBR funding at the currently proposed level, at the same time increasing the funding to other energy programs. While some nuclear programs have benefited from increased funding in the past—for example, the expenditures for fusion have doubled since fiscal 1969—it is clear that other programs have suffered because of the priority given the LMFBR. Funding for the enormous backlog of unfinished research and unanswered questions regarding LWR safety, as well as funding for the gas-cooled fast breeder and molten salt breeder reactors, are good examples here. According to an estimate by Ralph Lapp, a noted nuclear energy consultant,[19] cumulative federal expenditures for light water reactor safety research through fiscal 1973 totaled $205 million, that is, less than one-third of the proposed LMFBR program budget for fiscal 1974 alone. As indicated earlier, the OMB held back the additional funding for nuclear programs, appropriated by Congress in fiscal 1973 but not included in the original budget.

[18]Associated Universities, Inc., *Reference Energy Systems and Resource Data for Use in the Assessment of Energy Technologies* (Upton, New York, April 1972), p. 4. In order to facilitate intercomparison of the net benefits that would accrue from the development of those technologies being assessed, and to justify R&D priorities, in this report, Associated Universities prepared a common set of economic ground rules, assumptions regarding future energy systems, and characteristics of existing technologies. (While it is emphasized that the descriptions of the major components of the U.S. energy systems are not to be construed as predictions, it is interesting that the reference electrical energy demand for the year 2000 is 8 trillion kwh, equivalent to the "low" demand used in the 1970 Analysis.)

[19]In a private communication.

Likewise, funding for nonnuclear energy programs has suffered. This is due largely to the lack of strong industrial, congressional, and executive agency support, as well as a strong federal R&D base comparable to the AEC's. It seems likely that energy R&D will have similar budget constraints in the future. On the assumption that this will be true, the following are a few examples of programs that might benefit from increased funding:

1. Improved methods for recovery of domestic oil and natural gas. For example, cumulative U.S. discoveries of oil in place in the ground are over 400 billion barrels. On the average, about 31 percent of the oil in place has been recovered. Total 1972 domestic consumption of oil was around 5 billion barrels per year and production from domestic sources less than 4 billion barrels. There appear to be significant opportunities to increase the amount of oil in place recovered through R&D. Each increase of 1 percent (e.g., from 31 percent to 32 percent) in recovery provides an amount of oil roughly equal to current domestic production without the need for any new discovery.

2. Stack gas cleaning for fossil fuel, particularly coal-fired power plants.

3. Coal gasification to produce low-Btu (producer) gas to be used in electrical power generation.

4. Magneto-hydrodynamic conversion of coal (60 percent thermal efficiency versus 40 percent today).

5. Gas turbine development for the HTGR (discussed earlier).

6. LWR safety research.

7. Long-term management of high-level radioactive waste.

8. Development techniques for deep geothermal energy.

9. Solar space heating and air conditioning.

10. Nuclear fusion—funding here may be adequate today but has tended to be low in the past. With continued breakthroughs and corresponding requirements for larger machines in the near future, this energy source may compete more strongly for R&D funds.

Some of these R&D efforts—for example, oil and gas recovery—have potential short-term benefits, and, because of the discount rate factor, the net benefits from R&D in these areas may exceed the projected net benefits of the LMFBR program. With others, such as fusion, the benefits are unlikely to accrue until after the projected commercial availability of the LMFBR.

Nevertheless, these new technologies, if successfully introduced before about 2010, could significantly reduce the projected benefits of the LMFBR program. Some of the program—for example, stack gas cleaning and coal gasification—would provide significant environmental benefits in the short term. The LWR safety research, fusion, and the nonnuclear programs, all have the advantage of reducing the risk of catastrophic nuclear accidents.

Considering the questionable economics of the LMFBR program, there appear to be no adequate grounds for excluding the LMFBR from any future assessment of new energy technologies.

Averch-Johnson Effect

One of the more interesting aspects of the LMFBR program is that, even if these reactors are not competitive, the utilities may still buy them. The basis for this assumption, often referred to as the Averch-Johnson effect,[20] is described by MacAvoy as follows:

... there is a difference in the input purchase patterns between a regulated electricity generating company and another company not under a profit constraint. More is used of capital relative to fuel in the regulated firm; in fact, the producing facilities are capital using and fuel saving, even if the total costs of generation are increased by changing the capital-fuel ratio. With equipment as the favored input, those components promising lower fuel costs in the future would be most favored of all.[21]

There is also evidence demonstrating that the Averch-Johnson effect does not always prevail. One offsetting force is that a certain amount of competition occurs among utilities. Another offsetting factor is the difficulty in financing what must be regarded as very expensive installations, i.e., $500 million nuclear plants and cooling towers costing tens of millions of dollars. Some, therefore, argue forcefully that the Averch-Johnson effect will not prevail when commercial LMFBRs come to be considered by the electric utilities. It has been argued that electric utilities are subject to adequate governmental and public pressure (through state regulatory commissions) to prevent them from buying uneconomical

---

[20]Harvey Averch and Leland L. Johnson, "Behavior of the Firm Under Regulatory Constraint," *American Economic Review*, Vol. LII (Dec. 1962), pp. 1052-69.

[21]Paul MacAvoy, *Economic Strategy*, pp. 54-55. See also Alfred E. Kahn, *The Economics of Regulation: Principles and Institutions, Vol. II—Institutional Issues* (New York: John Wiley & Sons, Inc., 1971), pp. 49-59 and 106-108.

power plants, and (through the AEC reactor licensing process) to ensure adequate plant safety.

On the other hand, MacAvoy notes that

. . . companies have departed from an exclusive interest in adding the largest and lowest cost plant. The nonbreeder nuclear reactors purchased in the early and mid-1960's, at the demonstration or postdemonstration stage, required net expenditures per kilowatt hour far greater than those in alternative fossil fueled facilities. The companies have not only purchased "high cost" advanced systems, but have engaged in outright research where the specific company research gains were not obvious and where the public explanation was couched in terms of "the good of the industry."[22]

If this same experience is evidenced when the fast breeders become available, and if they are not competitive initially (recall Bertram Wolfe's suggestion that subsidization may be required), then the economic loss to society may not be limited to government LMFBR program expenditures. Society may also suffer from higher power generation costs until the LMFBR electrical energy generating costs are competitive.

Economic Losses from Accidents and Environmental Discharges

The AEC has not included in its cost-benefit studies the cumulative cost of small accidents and effects of low-level radioactive releases. Of course it is also true that the AEC has not charged fossil-fueled plants with their environmental pollution costs, which are likely to be higher. Even if one accepts this trade-off, the potential of the catastrophic nuclear accident is unique to nuclear plants and cannot be balanced by any comparable potential environmental costs associated with fossil-fueled plants. A comprehensive environmental assessment should consider such an eventuality.

The discussion here is more germane to the question of whether the United States should continue in the direction it is taking—that is, relying heavily on fission as an energy source—than it is to the question of whether the LMFBR should be introduced as scheduled rather than relying further on existing reactor types. However, in light of the potentially hazardous features of LMFBRs (and a plutonium economy)—features which are severely accentuated as one demands greater performance in terms of both economics and doubling time—the possibility of accidents cannot

[22]Paul MacAvoy, *Economic Strategy*, p. 53.

be ignored even when addressing the question of introducing the LMFBR.

Several authors, notably Starr, Greenfield, and Hausknecht,[23] have examined the relative hazards of fossil-fueled and nuclear plants. These studies are examined later (see Chapter 7). It should be noted here, however, that the conclusions reached in these studies depend on assumptions related to the probabilities of occurrence of the more severe classes of reactor accidents. Ignoring for the moment the potential health risk to the public, due to the exposure to radioactivity following these accidents, it is interesting to examine the additional discounted costs by arbitrarily assuming the occurrence of such an accident at, say, ten, twenty, or thirty years after the commercial introduction of the LMFBR. If one arbitrarily assumes an economic loss of $10 billion—due to the loss of the power plant facility, radioactivity decontamination costs, reductions in property value, medical expenses over the lifetime of the survivors, uncompensated decrease in business activity following the incident, personnel losses in the labor force, etc.—then the present (1972) value of such a loss would be:

Year of $10 billion loss	Present value (billions of dollars) assuming a discount value of:	
	7 percent	10 percent
2000	1.5	0.63
2010	0.76	0.27
2020	0.39	0.10

It is clear that the projected benefits of the LMFBR program are less sensitive to an economic loss of this magnitude ($10 billion), that far in the future, than to some of the variables discussed previously, e.g., capital cost, reactor performance data, etc. (By the same token, additional LMFBR benefits of this magnitude would have a similar impact.) This conclusion could easily be reversed if all LMFBRs (if not all nuclear plants) were shut down after such an accident, or if these plants were forced to operate at reduced power levels. Furthermore, the arbitrarily assigned cost of $10 bil-

[23]C. Starr, M. A. Greenfield, and D. F. Hausknecht, "A Comparison of Public Health Risks: Nuclear vs Oil-Fired Power Plants," *Nuclear News* (Oct. 1972), pp. 37-45.

lion may not accurately reflect the cost of human life and suffering. A counterargument is that none of these costs is relevant if the probability of such an accident is remote, as is maintained by the AEC. Again, this question will be addressed in the chapter on reactor safety.

The conclusion here is that catastrophic nuclear accidents cannot be measured using cost–benefit techniques. As has been well stated by Kneese:

It is my belief that benefit-cost analysis cannot answer the most important policy questions associated with the desirability of developing a large-scale, fission-based economy. To expect it to do so is to ask it to bear a burden it cannot sustain. This is so because these questions are of a deep *ethical* character. Benefit-cost analyses certainly cannot solve such questions and may well obscure them.

The advantages of fission are much more readily quantified in the format of a benefit-cost analysis than are the associated hazards. Therefore, there exists the danger that the benefits may seem more real. Furthermore, the conceptual basis of benefit-cost analysis requires that the redistributional effects of the action be, for one or another reason, inconsequential. Here we are speaking of hazards that may affect humanity many generations hence and equity questions that can neither be neglected as inconsequential nor evaluated on any known theoretical or empirical basis. This means that technical people, be they physicists or economists, cannot legitimately make the decision to generate such hazards.[24]

NONQUANTIFIABLE CONSIDERATIONS

The 1968 and 1970 Analyses list a number of benefits which "would accrue from an early introduction of the breeder" and which "are not readily susceptible to quantitative analysis but are of substantial consequence." Some of these are discussed in other chapters. The remainder are mentioned briefly below, but not discussed in detail because they have in common the fact that *they do not become benefits until the LMFBR becomes competitive.*

1. *Introduction of the LMFBR will reduce separative work capacity*[25] *required to sustain the U.S. power economy.*

Because the LMFBR program could not have an appreciable impact on separative work before the mid-1990s at the earliest,

[24]Allen V. Kneese, "The Faustian Bargain," RFF *Resources* (Sept. 1973) pp. 1-2.
[25]See Glossary for definition of separative work.

and possibly not until after 2000, the question of enrichment strategy is not germane to LMFBR development strategy. Enrichment strategy must be considered independently. If it is more economical to postpone the LMFBR entry, then it is more economical to increase separative work capacity.

2. *The LMFBR will provide a premium market for plutonium production in light water reactors.*

Plutonium and electricity are joint products of LWRs and fast breeder reactors. As described in Appendix A, the AEC's Power Economy Model treats all electricity-generating companies, or utilities, as a single firm, and plutonium as an intermediate product. The plutonium price is calculated as a shadow price. If, with realistic input assumptions, the model predicts that the LMFBR will not be competitive, then, in effect, it says other costs offset the advantages the LMFBR offers with respect to plutonium utilization. The goal here is minimizing energy costs, not plutonium utilization.

3. *The LMFBR will provide an ample supply of low-cost electricity to areas which have been denied low-cost energy, and the use of low-cost electricity in energy-intensive applications.*

This argument was used in support of the LWR program. During the initial stages of development when LWR costs were expected to be high, it was argued that the LWRs could compete favorably with fossil plants in geographic areas where fossil-fuel costs were high. There are no geographic areas favorable to the LMFBR over other nuclear plants. Thus, we are back to the economic argument. If the LMFBR cannot compete with either the HTGR or the LWR, then it cannot supply lower-cost energy to areas which do not have low-cost energy or provide lower-cost energy for energy-intensive applications.

4. *The LMFBR will stimulate improvements in other energy-producing industries, including those associated with the production, transportation, and utilization of fossil fuels.*

If the LMFBRs have higher electrical energy-generating costs, then they will not provide competition to stimulate improvements in other energy-producing industries. Moreover, in the case of LWRs it appears that their development inhibited the development of coal resources and may have delayed the development of technology for using coal in an environmentally acceptable manner. One of the opportunity costs of investing in the LMFBR program is that these funds will not be available for improvements in other energy-producing industries.

5. *The resources committed to the breeder program in the AEC national laboratories, in U.S. industry, and in U.S. utilities will be used more efficiently.*

Just because facilities have been constructed does not mean it is economically rational to use them. Even in the private sector, a facility that is constructed may or may not be used, depending on the economic assessment of the cost of all alternatives.

6. *The LMFBR would provide increased use of technical and economic ties as a principal vehicle for international cooperation and as a means for promoting peace and for assisting industrial development in other countries.*

If the LMFBR program does not increase national economic efficiency, it would be difficult to justify the program for the above reasons. Since the less-developed countries do not have the same resources of highly trained and experienced personnel in the nuclear field, since they are unlikely to provide the same degree of quality assurance and safety review as the United States in constructing and licensing nuclear facilities, and since management and operation of their facilities, including safeguarding fissile material, may not be as effective as in the United States, using the LMFBR as a vehicle for assisting development in these countries could have dire consequences.

It is not at all clear how the LMFBR would promote peace.

7. *The preeminence of the United States in its leadership role in nuclear power will be continued.*

A first answer to this is that a number of Western European countries, as well as the Soviet Union, are already ahead of the United States in LMFBR development. Many of these invested in the LMFBR at the same time as the United States, for essentially the same reasons, although the pressures of uranium scarcity or lack of enrichment capacity made this reactor more attractive both economically and politically to some of these nations than it would be to the United States.

At any rate, I would suggest that, if the United States were the first to recognize the economic realities of the LMFBR, it could possibly accomplish a real coup by investing in other promising (nonfission) means of generating electricity. In fact, it is conceivable that the United States could bypass fast breeders altogether.

II

Environmental Considerations

Introduction to Part II

If, as the analysis to this point suggests, the economic arguments, both quantifiable and nonquantifiable, do not support an early (1986) commitment to the LMFBR, what about the environmental arguments which have been raised in support of the program? Some of these have already been discussed in connection with uranium demand. Those discussed in the chapters that follow have been compiled from a variety of sources.[1]

The first chapter examines the environmental effects of routine releases at the reactor and its support facilities. First, routine releases of residuals from the power plant sites are examined. The primary purpose here is to compare the routine releases from the LMFBR with those from alternative nuclear plants. In the remainder of the chapter, discussion is limited to the environmental impacts associated with routine releases from nuclear fuel reprocessing plants. The most important releases are the radioactive gaseous residuals. There are two important points noted here. First, the gaseous releases are strongly dependent on the waste decay time before reprocessing the spent fuel. Second, when considering the entire fuel cycle—principally, the power plant and the

---

[1] U.S. AEC, *Cost-Benefit Analysis,* WASH 1126; U.S. AEC, *LMFBR Demonstration Plant Environmental Statement;* William Doub, "The Future of the Breeder, Its Impact on the Environment, and Its Regulatory Aspects," AEC News Release (Dec. 15, 1971); Whitman, Tyrrell, and Mount, "U.S. Civilian Nuclear Power."

reprocessing plant—with respect to routine radioactive releases, no reactor has a significant advantage over the others.[2]

The principal environmental impacts associated with radioactive solid wastes result from: (1) accidents transporting these wastes; (2) the destruction or the loss of coolant (or management) of the proposed above-ground engineered storage facility for high-level radioactive waste; and (3) the transport of fission products from their place of burial to the biosphere, for example, by erosion or ground water circulation.

The solid waste transportation hazard is of secondary importance compared with the spent-fuel transportation hazard discussed earlier in connection with the fuel cycle. The management of high-level radioactive waste and the transport of fission products after burial are subjects important to the question of whether the United States should continue to rely on fission as a source of energy; they are less germane to LMFBR development strategy once the choice has been made in favor of nuclear energy development. As seen from Table 16, the volumes of material to be managed are not significantly different for the LMFBR and LWR. Actually, these data, while having economic significance, e.g., for estimating transportation or storage costs, are not by themselves good measures of the environmental costs. For example, to some extent dilution of fission products in a larger volume of inert material can be an advantage in terms of reducing some hazards associated with transportation and burial of these materials. A complete assessment of the environmental hazards should address not only the quantities of radioactive material produced but also the probabilities that some of it will be released, the transport mechanisms in the environment, and the hazard of the released material in terms of its radioactivity (i.e., the radiation type and energy and the radioactive and biological lives of the material). These and other factors bear on the probability that quantities of damaging radiation will be absorbed by man and other living things. When comparing the hazards associated with radioactive waste from LWRs and LMFBRs, many of these factors can be neglected since their values, or contributions, would be roughly the same.

In my view, the most critical environmental problems or risks associated with the nuclear power industry are not due to routine

---

[2]Except, perhaps, the molten-salt breeder, which is not examined in this analysis.

releases of residuals from the nuclear plants and their support facilities, rather they are risks related to unscheduled events: (1) severe nuclear reactor accidents; (2) unauthorized utilization of nuclear weapons (or plutonium dispersal devices) constructed from highly enriched nuclear fuel; (3) loss of management of the proposed engineered facility for interim storage of high-level waste; (4) sabotage at any number of locations in the fuel cycle—the reactor, fuel preparation, fabrication and reprocessing plants, and the transportation sector; and (5) release of very hazardous long-lived isotopes, e.g., plutonium-238 and -239, into the environment.

The position taken by the AEC and a number of responsible individuals in the nuclear community is that, while the possibility of the occurrence of these events cannot be ruled out, it is of such low probability that it falls into the negligible risk category. I can-

TABLE 16. Quantities of Solid Wastes Containing Fission Products, Annual Rate Based on AEC Estimate

Site and type of waste	1000-Mw LWR	1000-Mw LMFBR
Produced at reactor site		
Low-level solid		
cubic feet/year	2000—4000	1000—2000
kilograms/year	60,000—100,000	30,000—50,000
Produced at reprocessing plant site		
High-level solid		
cubic feet/year	90	70
kilograms/year	5000	4000
Cladding hulls		
cubic feet/year	60	170
kilograms/year	15	45
Other solids		
cubic feet/year	600—4000	2000—12,000
kilograms/year	30,000—65,000	100,000—200,000
Produced at fabrication plant site		
Pu contaminated waste		
cubic feet/year	12,000[a]	8000

SOURCE: U.S. Atomic Energy Commission, *Liquid Metal Fast Breeder Reactor Demonstration Plant Environmental Statement,* WASH 1509 (April 1972), pp. 194–95.

[a]Assumes Pu recycle.

not agree with this evaluation of the problem.[3]

For this reason, following the discussion on routine releases, the remainder of the environmental part of this study is an attempt to place in perspective the risks associated with some of the unscheduled events listed above. Considerable attention is given to severe nuclear reactor accidents (discussed in Chapter 7). After a review of the consequences, if a severe reactor accident ever occurs, Chapter 7 contains a general discussion of the inadequacies in the methods currently used to evaluate whether these reactors can be operated without undue risk to public health and safety. Next, some of the basic differences between the safety characteristics of the various reactors are reviewed. This is followed by a more detailed discussion of some of the uncertainties related to evaluating the explosive potential of an LMFBR.

The implication that these uncertainties have on the containment of the plutonium fuel and the fission products is discussed in connection with the Fast Flux Test Facility (FFTF). The FFTF is essentially a small LMFBR, except that without the U-238 blanket material it is incapable of breeding more fuel than it burns. It was chosen because there is considerable data available on this reactor. The FFTF is currently the object of an AEC safety analysis comparable to the safety analysis performed on a commercial reactor prior to the issuance of an operating license.

A discussion of LMFBR safety would not be complete without an appreciation of the extreme toxicity of plutonium, and the paucity of data and concomitant uncertainties related to the plutonium health risk.

The cumulative health risk over the generations, associated with plutonium releases to the environment from all sources, is discussed in the section, "Overall Health Hazards of a Plutonium Economy." Here, the significant point is the almost total absence of any realistic means for evaluating this risk.

The chapter concludes with a discussion of the risks associated with the unauthorized use of fissile material.[4]

---

[3]The assessment of these risks contains what Alvin Weinberg calls a "transscientific" element, i.e., "matters that simply do not admit of the same order of scientific certainty as when we say it is incredible for heat to flow against a temperature gradient." See Alvin Weinberg, *Science* 177 (July 7, 1972), p. 34.

[4]An exhaustive analysis of the risk of nuclear violence using material diverted from the nuclear power industry has been written by Mason Willrich and Theodore B. Taylor in "Nuclear Diversion: Risks and Safeguards," prepared for the Energy Policy Project of the Ford Foundation (to be published).

6

Environmental Impact at the Reactor and Its Support Facilities

IMPACT AT THE NUCLEAR PLANT SITE

Waste Heat

The percentage of the heat generated at the power plant that is converted to electricity is equal to the thermal efficiency of the plant. The remainder, the waste heat, is released to the environment.

The 1000-Mw AI and GE follow-on designs for the LMFBR each have thermal efficiencies of 41 percent. As noted in the *LMFBR Demonstration Plant Environmental Statement:*

> The waste heat discharge from a 1000-Mw LMFBR with an expected efficiency of around 41 percent will be about 5 billion Btu/hr when the plant is operating at full load. This is comparable to the heat rejection rate of a modern fossil plant [and the projected efficiency of a 1000-Mw HTGR] but is less than that from a 1000-Mw LWR because of the LWR's lower thermal efficiency [i.e., 32.5 percent].[1]

It should be noted that since roughly 10 percent of the waste heat from fossil-fueled plants goes up the stack, these plants require roughly 10 percent less cooling water than nuclear plants of comparable efficiency.

The 39 percent design thermal efficiency of both the HTGR demonstration plant (Fort St. Vrain) and the HTGR follow-on

---

[1] U.S. Atomic Energy Commission, *Liquid Metal Fast Breeder Reactor Demonstration Plant Environmental Statement,* WASH 1509 (April 1972), pp. 186-87.

143

plants is less than the 43 percent efficiency assumed in the 1970 Analysis. The net thermal efficiency of Westinghouse's LMFBR demonstration plant is 38 percent; less than the 41 to 42 percent assumed for the follow-on plants. Based on HTGR experience, the initial LMFBR follow-on plants may not achieve thermal efficiencies higher than the demonstration plant. The efficiency will be determined by optimizing total energy generating costs within the constraint of providing adequate safety margins.

With respect to waste heat rejection and the conservation of fresh water, the gas-cooled reactors, i.e., the HTGR and the GCFBR, offer potential advantages over the other reactor concepts, ·including the LMFBR. These advantages would occur through the development of the closed-cycle gas turbine, and, looking further into the future, through the development and application of magnetohydrodynamic conversion to gas-cooled reactors.

As can be seen by comparing Figures 19(a) with 19(b), the 1970 Analysis predicts that, if HTGRs are available, then LWRs are produced in greater numbers if LMFBRs are built than if LMFBRs are not built. One might conclude that with LMFBRs built the total amount of waste heat rejected to *all* condenser cooling systems will be more, not less. This of course may not be the case. The success of the HTGR will depend in part on the utilities' assessment of the HTGR's reliability and GGA's technical capability, and ultimately on whether additional vendors are brought into the picture. Furthermore, as indicated earlier, the 1970 Analysis did not include an HTGR plutonium recycle capability.

In summary, while the LMFBR offers an improvement over LWRs with respect to waste heat rejection, it has about the same thermal efficiency as other plant types: fossil-fueled, HTGR, and GCFBR. At a specific power plant site where waste heat rejection is a critical factor, the HTGR represents a good nuclear plant alternative to the LMFBR. Furthermore, in the long run, the gas-cooled reactors offer potential advantages over the LMFBR in terms of total thermal efficiency and water use.

Gaseous and Liquid Residuals

There are two comparisons that are useful to make concerning discharges to the atmosphere other than waste heat: LMFBRs with fossil-fueled plants and LMFBRs with other nuclear plants.

LMFBRs Compared with Fossil-Fueled Plants. In contrast to fossil-fueled plants, the LMFBR, like other nuclear plants, will not discharge SO_2, nitrogen oxides, particulates, etc., to the atmosphere. Environmental costs of air pollutants from fossil-fueled plants are important to discussions of whether the United States should rely heavily on nuclear fission as an energy source, but they affect LMFBR development strategy only to the extent to which LMFBRs would displace fossil-fueled plants in the market. Unfortunately, the 1970 Analysis is of little benefit in assessing this possibility, since the AEC was primarily concerned with the trade-offs among nuclear plants. Nevertheless, it may be useful to examine the predictions of the 1970 Analysis with respect to fossil-fueled plant capacity placed in operation after the proposed LMFBR market entry date.

Due to their relatively high capital costs and low operating costs, nuclear plants are expected to be purchased to meet base load electrical energy demand. The 1970 Analysis predicts that, without introducing LMFBRs, 277,000 Mw (or 9 percent) of the base load generating capacity placed in operation between 1990 and 2020 would be fossil(coal)-fueled capacity. LMFBR introduction in 1986 or 1990 would decrease this percentage to 0.4 percent, or 2 percent, respectively—a small overall percentage reduction in either case. According to this analysis, between 1990 and 2020 the LMFBR's major competition will come from other nuclear plants, namely, LWRs and HTGRs (compare Figures 19[a] and 19[b]). While roughly equivalent to today's total fossil-fueled plant capacity, the 277,000 Mw of fossil capacity placed in operation after 1990 (assuming no LMFBRs) is a reflection of the 1970 Analysis assumption that uranium prices will rapidly rise to $50/lb before 2020, in which case nuclear plants other than LMFBRs would no longer be competitive with coal-fueled plants in many areas of the country. Under more realistic uranium supply assumptions, the model would project few, if any, fossil-fueled plants added after 1990, even without the LMFBR. Any differences in additional fossil-fueled capacity with introduction of LMFBRs would be lost in the uncertainties in the model. Furthermore, it is reasonable to assume that, by 1990, improvements will be made in stack gas cleaning, and that unit air pollutant discharges from fossil-fueled plants will be less than they are today. Thus, assuming that the United States continues to rely on nuclear fission as a source of electrical energy, any purported reduction in environmental costs associated with fossil-fueled plants resulting from LMFBR introduction in the foreseeable future is not significant compared with other possible costs, for example, the health risks associated with large-scale utilization of LMFBRs.

LMFBRs Compared with Other Nuclear Reactors. In the nuclear fuel cycle, the principal routine releases of radioactivity to the environment occur at the reactor and at the fuel reprocessing plant. The releases of interest are the gaseous and liquid effluents, since radioactive solid wastes, i.e., the spent-ion exchange resins, laboratory wastes, spent-air filters, etc., can be contained, packaged, and shipped off-site for permanent storage or burial. It is the AEC's contention that the LMFBR is far superior to other reactors in regard to routine release of these effluents.

One finds in the literature statements such as:

The [LMFBR] benefits include: . . . . The virtual elimination of air pollution from electric power plants.[2]

The LMFBR will be designed for negligible emission of gaseous and liquid effluents, whereas the current LWR is designed to release controlled amounts of effluents well within the bounds set by strict regulations.[3]

. . . it would be difficult to improve upon the LMFBR from an environmental standpoint, since its design will not permit any planned radiological release to the environment.[4]

As indicated in the analysis that follows, these positive statements are based on a comparison of the design characteristics of the LMFBR with the historical performance of the LWRs; the comparison does not reflect the planned performance of new LWRs or other reactor types.

Liquid Effluents Other than Tritium

In the LWR, the HTGR, and the LMFBR, the principal sources of radioactive liquid wastes, except tritium, at the reactor are personnel shower drains and decontamination activities—principally during refueling operations.[5]

---

[2]U.S. Atomic Energy Commission, Division of Reactor Development and Technology, *Updated (1970) Cost-Benefit Analysis of the U.S. Breeder Reactor Program*, WASH 1184 (Jan. 1972), p. 6.
[3]U.S. AEC, *LMFBR Demonstration Plant Environmental Statement*, p. 219.
[4]Ibid., p. A-25.
[5]For example, GGA estimates that a 1160-Mw HTGR would generate about

In addition, all reactor types will have small quantities of radioactive liquid effluents resulting from routine laboratory operations, spills, and such minor leaks from reactor systems as those from valve seals. (Here, the HTGR and LMFBR offer an advantage over the LWRs because they do not utilize water as a coolant.)

While the LWRs now in operation also release small amounts of radionuclides from activation of reactor components other than fuel, in the newer LWRs and those planned for the future, these sources of radioactivity are small compared with the others mentioned above.

The newer LWRs, including some of those planned for the near future, have estimated releases of radioactivity in liquid effluents, other than tritium, on the order of a few to about 50 curies per year. In order to reduce the liquid releases even further, one can anticipate that utilities in the future will be recycling as much as possible all LWR liquids containing tritium and other low-level liquid wastes, and will be providing systems for processing steam generator blowdown. TVA is incorporating such systems on its three 1065-Mw Browns Ferry BWR plants and two 1124-Mw Sequoyah PWR plants. The quantity of liquid radioactive waste, other than tritium, released to the environment is estimated to be less than 0.5 Ci/yr from the Sequoyah plants.[6] This level of release represents what one might reasonably expect from HTGRs and LMFBRs in actual operation, thus eliminating any purported advantage of the LMFBR with respect to radioactive liquid effluents.

Gaseous Effluents Other than Tritium

In the past, discharges of radioactive gases have constituted a major source of external radiation from reactors. Early LWR plants were operated with basic gaseous effluent treatment systems consisting of filtration, a holdup period to allow for short-lived fission product decay, and elevated stack release. BWRs delay the release of the gas about thirty minutes while PWRs provide storage tanks

---

75,000 gallons per year containing 70 curies of radioactivity from these sources. All but 0.1 curies per year of this is in about 4,000 gallons per year of water from decontamination activities. See M. Gitterman and A. J. Goodjohn, "Radioactive Waste Management System for High Temperature Gas-Cooled Reactors," Gulf General Atomic, San Diego, Calif., No. Gulf-GA-A12023 (March 10, 1972).

[6]American Nuclear Society, *Transactions*, Vol. 15, No. 2 (November 1972), p. 661.

to hold up the radioactive gases for thirty days or more, the difference being due to the differences in their respective steam cycles.

In both types of LWRs, the radioactive gaseous discharges consist mainly of noble gas fission products that enter the coolant from the fuel. At present a very small portion of these gases is discharged at the reactor site; the remainder is released during fuel reprocessing. Even so, in 1970, BWRs in the United States released between 700 curies and 914,000 curies of noble gases, and PWRs, with their longer holdup times, released between 17 curies and 10,000 curies.[7] The calculated doses to hypothetical unshielded individuals at the site boundaries of these plants, based on noble gases discharged in 1969, ranged from 5×10^{-3} mrem to 150 mrem for the BWRs, and 5×10^{-3} mrem to 5 mrem for the PWRs.[8]

In order to meet the proposed limits (10 CFR 50 Appendix I) and keep the releases as low as practicable, LWRs are extending gaseous effluent holdup times and incorporating additional off-gas treatment systems, e.g., cryogenic charcoal absorption or distillation processes, and catalytic recombiners.

The proposed standard limits the total radioactive material from all LWRs at a specific site. With respect to radioactive noble gases and iodines and radioactive material in particulate form, it limits to 5 mrem[9] the annual exposures from these sources to the whole body (or any organ of an individual).

In a PWR, a large volume reduction of gaseous effluent from the primary coolant system is possible.[10] As with the LMFBR, it is possible to contain the accumulated fission gases in a large storage tank indefinitely, or to purify and bottle the concentrated noble gases for permanent storage. In addition, the more advanced PWRs, and other reactors as well, will treat all of the vent gases and ventilation systems.

The radioactive waste treatment system currently being offered for processing the coolant off-gas in the BWR provides for additional decay times,[11] and will limit the off-plant dose to about 0.1

---

[7]United Nations, "Ionizing Radiation: Levels and Effect," Vol. 1, UN Publication No. E.72.IX.17 (New York, 1972), p. 102.

[8]Ibid., p. 105.

[9]Radioactive iodines are restricted by an additional factor of 1000, due to reconcentration effects in the grass-cow-milk food chain.

[10]In the primary coolant system the nitrogen dilutant cover gas is replaced by hydrogen and a catalytic recombiner.

[11]Fifteen to forty days for xenon and sixteen to forty-six hours for krypton.

mrem per year or less from this source.[12] While it may be difficult
to justify a further reduction in the dose from BWR gaseous
effluents on a cost-benefit basis, particularly in light of the fact
that the actual maximum dose to an individual off-site from these
sources is probably five to ten times less than the theoretical site
boundary dose,[13] nevertheless, when noble gas storage systems
become available for LMFBRs, they could equally well be used for
the BWR cryogenic system. Therefore, any advantages the LMFBR
might offer over LWRs with respect to control of radioactive gaseous effluents, other than tritium, is insignificant.

Three sources of radioactive waste gas, other than tritium, that
might arise during normal HTGR operations are instrumentation
effluent, gas evacuated from fuel handling equipment during
annual refueling, and gas resulting from regeneration of adsorp-
tion beds in the helium purification system. According to GGA,
radioactive gaseous effluents (principally Kr-85), from a 1160-Mw
HTGR will be about 22 percent of the proposed 10 CFR 50
Appendix I limits. With a gas recovery system the plant would
release less than 0.02 curies per year, 7 percent of the proposed
limits.[14]

The LMFBR will have sources of radioactive gaseous waste
similar to the HTGR. The LMFBR employs inert gas blankets over
all liquid sodium surfaces. In Westinghouse's demonstration plant
design helium is used in the primary sodium system, argon in the
intermediate sodium system, and nitrogen in the fuel storage
tanks. All will require purification systems. The LMFBR will probably offer essentially no advantages over the HTGR with regard
to these sources, since the HTGRs can be equipped with the same
gas storage systems that will be required of LMFBRs.

Tritium

Tritium is produced as a fission product and by neutron activation of elements in the reactor coolant (i.e., hydrogen in LWRs and

---

[12]J. M. Smith and J. D. Kjemtrup of General Electric Co., "BWR Development
in Nuclear Plant Effluent Management," paper presented at the American Power
Conference, 34th Annual Meeting (April 1972), p. 6.

[13]The theoretical exposure estimates are (a) uncorrected for shielding that would
be provided by clothing and buildings, (b) uncorrected for occupancy time in the
area, and (c) they assume that a child ingests milk contaminated with radioiodine
from a family cow that grazes at the site boundary.

[14]Gitterman and Goodjohn, "Radioactive Waste Management System," pp. 8, 17.

helium in the HTGR) and reactor components (e.g., boron and lithium). As with the noble gases, most of the tritium produced in reactors remains with the fuel and is eventually shipped to the reprocessing plant. This is not necessarily true with respect to breeders. The first generation of LMFBRs will use sealed fuel the way LWR fuel is sealed today. But later, they may vent the tritium and gaseous fission products directly to the sodium coolant and remove most of the gaseous fission products at the reactor rather than the reprocessing plant.

Estimates of tritium released to the environment from LWRs, HTGRs, and LMFBRs are compared in Table 17. Tritium release is higher in PWRs than BWRs, primarily because of the use of dissolved boron in PWRs, which gives considerably more tritium in the coolant. About 90 to 95 percent of the tritium released dur-

TABLE 17. Tritium in Liquid Waste Discharged
from Selected Nuclear Power Plants

Reactor	Power level (Mw)	Annual discharge (Ci)	
		1970	Projected
BWR			
Oyster Creek	515	22[a]	
Nine Mile Point	500	20[a]	
Projected (GE estimate)	1000		9[b]
PWR			
San Onofre[c]	430	4800[a]	
Conn. Yankee[c]	575	4700[a]	
Ginna	420	110[a]	
Projected	1000	∼1000	
HTGR (GGA estimate)	1160		640[d]
LMFBR (AEC estimate)	1000		"negligible"[e]

[a]Data from United Nations, "Ionizing Radiation: Levels and Effects, Vol. 1—Levels," UN Publication No. E. 72.IX.17 (New York, 1972), p. 100.

[b]Estimate from J. M. Smith, "Power Reactors and Tritium," General Electric Company (June 1970). About one-third of this would be released to the atmosphere as stack gas.

[c]Stainless steel cladding used on fuel elements in these reactors allows greater diffusion of fission product tritium into the coolant than the zircalloy cladding used in the Ginna plant.

[d]Estimated from M. Gitterman and A. J. Goodjohn, "Radioactive Waste Management System for High Temperature Gas-Cooled Reactors," Gulf General Atomic, San Diego, Calif., No. Gulf-GA-A12023 (March 10, 1972), p. 15.

[e]U.S. Atomic Energy Commission, *Liquid Metal Fast Breeder Reactor Demo Plant Environmental Statement,* WASH 1509 (April 1972), p. 213.

ing HTGR operations is from tritium gas produced by neutron activation of He-3 in the coolant; the remainder is fission product tritium that leaks from, or fuses through, the fuel particles.[15]

Simply comparing the tritium activity (measured in curies) from these plants is misleading. Tritium is several orders of magnitude less hazardous than some of the other radionuclides released to the environment.[16] A more appropriate measure is to examine the maximum off-site dose rate to individuals at the site boundary.

The site boundary tritium dose from a BWR (or LMFBR) is simply not a problem compared with other radioactive releases, since the dose is several orders of magnitude below background levels. The tritium dose to an individual at a site boundary of a PWR (or BWR) is limited by the proposed 10 CFR 50 Appendix I to 5 mrem per year, the dose from all liquid effluents. In Table 17 the 1000 curies per year projected for 1000-Mw PWRs is a conservative upper limit designed to meet the Appendix I limit.[17] As noted previously with respect to liquid releases, the actual maximum dose to an individual beyond the site boundary is likely to be one to two orders of magnitude below the dose calculated using the more conservative assumptions, i.e., 1000 curies/yr release corresponds to 0.05 to 0.5 rem/yr rather than 5 rem/yr at the site boundary. As noted previously, utilities are moving toward recycling as much as possible all liquids containing tritium and other activity. Almost all tritium produced by the TVA's Sequoyah plant will be retained in the primary system by recycling.[18] Hence, before LMFBRs become commercially available, one can expect that routine tritium releases from PWRs will be reduced even further.[19]

---

[15]Helium-3 is an isotope of helium and represents a naturally occurring impurity present in helium-4 at a concentration of less than 2×10^{-5} percent.

[16]Comparing the maximum permissible concentrations, one curie of iodine-131 is one to four orders of magnitude more hazardous than one curie of tritium. Similarly, one curie of plutonium-239 is two to six orders of magnitude more hazardous than one curie of tritium. The range of the differences in the hazard is due to differences in maximum permissible concentrations, depending on whether the element is in a liquid or gaseous state and whether the element is soluble or insoluble.

[17]Based on present experience, the actual tritium release rate from the newer PWRs is about 20 percent of this level (cf. the release from Ginna in Table 17).

[18]American Nuclear Society, *Transactions* (1972), p. 661.

[19]Even with maximum recycle there still may be something like 40,000 gallons per year of excess tritiated water from PWR operations. If one wished to have essentially zero-release PWRs, comparable to LMFBRs, this tritiated water could be readily stored and shipped off-site for burial in about four railroad tank cars per year.

GGA projects that the tritium release from a 1160-Mw HTGR would result in a maximum off-site dose rate of about 3.2 mrem per year initially, dropping to less than 1 mrem per year after about ten years.[20] The latter is less than 1 percent of the dose from natural background radiation. Again these are conservative estimates, with the actual dose probably being one or two orders of magnitude less.[21]

Summary

At the reactor site, the proposed routine radioactive effluents from LMFBRs represent a significant improvement over *historical* releases from LWRs. This is the comparison that is made in the *LMFBR Demonstration Plant Environmental Statement* (pp. 212-13). The proposed routine releases from LMFBRs represent a slight improvement over estimated releases from LWRs now being designed to meet 10 CFR 50 Appendix I standards, and over HTGRs that do not remove the helium-3 from the coolant or bottle the noble gases.

When comparing the *proposed* routine radioactive effluents from LMFBRs with what can be expected (economically and with the same technology) from LWRs and HTGRs built during the same time period, the LMFBR represents no significant improvement environmentally over the other reactors. For these plants at these low levels of releases, one can anticipate that variations in the amount of activity released among plants having the same type of reactor will be greater than the variability among the different types of plants.

Furthermore, as will be evident after examining routine releases from fuel reprocessing plants (discussed in the following section), and reactor safety considerations (Chapter 7), at 10 CFR 50 Appendix I release levels, routine radioactive releases from reactors are no longer central to the question of whether LMFBRs rep-

[20]Gitterman and Goodjohn, "Radioactive Waste Management System," p. 4.

[21]The tritium dose from an HTGR could be reduced, perhaps by an order of magnitude, by cryogenic distillation to remove the He-3 before the helium is shipped to the reactor. An HTGR requires a helium inventory of about 1000 scf/Mw, and leakage losses have been quoted at 10 percent per year (see Gitterman and Goodjohn, ibid.). Assuming distillation costs are no more than $50 per 1000 scf, this would add only about $25,000 per year to HTGR energy costs, or about 0.003 mills/kwh.

resent an improvement, environmentally, over other types of reactors.

IMPACTS AT THE FUEL REPROCESSING PLANT

The AEC's *Environmental Survey of the Nuclear Fuel Cycle* (November 1972)[22] contains a thorough discussion of the contribution to the radioactive effluents from routine operations of LWR fuel reprocessing plants due to the average annual fuel requirements of a model 1000-Mw LWR. In this analysis, the model fuel cycle facilities were selected to be representative of the industry today and to lead to conservative or pessimistic assessments of the environmental considerations associated with routine releases. With respect to solid and high-level liquid wastes from the reprocessing plant, the *Environmental Survey* is consistent with the *LMFBR Demonstration Plant Environmental Statement,* which states:

> There will be essentially no high-level liquid wastes released as a result of reprocessing LWR and LMFBR fuel since all high-level liquid wastes generated will be converted to solid form . . . kept on site for 5 to 10 years and then shipped to a Federal Repository for permanent storage. These wastes will contain about 6 to 8 magacuries of radioactivity per year from 1000 Mwe LMFBRs and LWRs at the time of shipment.[23]

This summary applies to the HTGR as well.

The *Environmental Survey* analyzes the radioactive liquid and gaseous effluents from a model fuel reprocessing plant representing the collective operation of the three commercial fuel reprocessing plants that will be in operation in the United States in the mid-1970s, normalized to an annual capacity of 900 metric tons of fuel per year.[24] According to this model, reprocessing the annual fuel discharge from each model 1000-Mw LWR contributes 2500

---

[22]Hereafter termed the *Environmental Survey.*

[23]U.S. AEC, *LMFBR Demonstration Plant Environmental Statement,* p. 215.

[24]Nuclear Fuel Services in West Valley, N.Y., has a capacity of 1 metric ton of uranium (MTU)/day. It is now shut down in order to expand the plant's capacity to 3 MTU/day, or 900 MTU/year by 1973. The Midwest Fuel Recovery Plant in Morris, Ill., scheduled for operation in 1974, also has a design capacity of 300 MTU/year (1 MTU/day). Barnwell Nuclear Fuel Plant, scheduled for late 1974 or 1975 operation, has a design capacity of 1500 MTU/year (5 MTU/day). It is the first commercial reprocessing plant of truly significant size.

TABLE 18.   Irradiated Fuel Reprocessing Plants, Gaseous Radioactive Effluents

Radionuclide	Exposure mode	Annual release[a] (Ci/yr)	Exposure[b] (mrem/yr)
Kr-85	External irradiation of whole body	9,000,000	0.2
	Irradiation of skin		13.5
H-3	Internal irradiation of whole body	400,000	0.65
I-129	Irradiation of thyroid	0.06	8.7
I-131	Irradiation of thyroid	0.60	6.0
Other fission products	Irradiation of body	25	<0.10
Transuranics	Irradiation of bone	0.10	0.15

SOURCE: U.S. Atomic Energy Commission, *Environmental Survey of the Nuclear Fuel Cycle* (Nov. 1972), p. F-24.

[a]Normalized to the annual 900 MTU/yr capacity of the model plant.

[b]Estimated maximum exposure at the site boundaries of the three plants comprising the industry.

curies of tritium and 4 curies of ruthenium-106 to the annual low-level liquid effluents from the LWR fuel reprocessing plants. At the site of Nuclear Fuel Services, the first commercial reprocessing plant,

... the concentrations of H-3 [tritium] and Ru-106 at the point of release from the holding pond exceed the maximum permissible concentrations given by 10 CFR 20 and require dilution in receiving streams, which pass through the site. Receiving stream measurements in 1971 indicated that the concentration of tritium never exceeded $10^{-4}\mu$ Ci/ml and that the maximum concentration of Ru-106 was $4 \times 10^{-7}\mu$ Ci/ml. These maximum levels are less than $4 of the limits in 10 CFR 20.[25]

The newer plants will store on site in tanks, or convert to salt cake, most or all of the low-level liquid waste. In any event, as will be evident from the discussion below, the low-level liquid effluents are of secondary importance compared with the gaseous effluents. Furthermore, considering advances in waste management techniques, it is unlikely that any reactor type will offer significant advantages over the other types with respect to routine releases of low-level liquid effluents from their respective fuel reprocessing plants.

With respect to the principal radioactive gaseous effluents, Table 18 summarizes the releases from the model fuel reprocessing plant.

[25]U.S. AEC, *Environmental Survey*, p. F-26.

As seen from the table, the principal activity in gaseous effluents are the noble gases, tritium, and iodines. The model assumes that none of the noble gases (e.g., krypton) or the tritium is bottled for permanent storage.

As a result of reprocessing spent fuel from a single 1000 Mw LWR, about 0.3 megacuries of radioactivity will be released in gaseous effluents annually to the atmosphere, as opposed to about 0.2 megacuries from the LMFBR fuel cycle. It is expected that these emissions will be reduced to 1 percent of the above figures with the introduction of advanced techniques now under development.[26]

The 0.3 megacuries of activity is consistent with the contribution due to reprocessing the annual fuel requirements of the model 1000-Mw LWR in the *Environmental Survey,* namely:

Effluent	*Curies*
Tritium	15,700
Kr-85	350,000
I-129	0.0024
I-131	0.024
Fission products	1.0

The 0.3 megacuries is also consistent with the assumption that the waste decay time is ninety days or more.[27] Finally, the 0.2 megacuries of activity due to reprocessing fuel from a 1000-Mw LMFBR is consistent with the assumption of ninety days or more spent-fuel cooling time.[28]

The important point here is that the ninety-day, or longer, waste decay time before reprocessing LMFBR spent fuel, consistent with the radioactive releases used in the *LMFBR Demonstration Plant Environmental Statement,* is not consistent with the thirty-day assumption used in the 1970 Analysis.[29] This is one of several examples where the ground rules used in the 1970 Analysis to pro-

---

[26]U.S. AEC, *LMFBR Demonstration Plant Environmental Statement,* p. 214. Advanced techniques refer principally to the technology for removal and storage of noble gases.

[27]ORNL-4451, *Siting of Fuel Reprocessing Plants,* pp. 3-15 to 3-20.

[28]Ibid., pp. 3-23 to 3-39.

[29]See Chapter 2, section on fuel cycle costs.

TABLE 19. Tritium, Noble Gas, and Iodine Contributions to the Total Activity in the Annual Fuel Discharged from a 1000-Mw LWR and a 1000-Mw LMFBR

(curies)

Reactor[a]	Radioactive releases	Waste decay time			
		30 days	90 days	150 days	365 days
LWR	Tritium	19,000	19,000	19,000	18,000
	Krypton	310,000	310,000	310,000	300,000
	Xenon	1,100,000[b]	3200	90	3.0×10^{-4}
	Iodine	1,900,000[b]	10,000	60	1.0
LMFBR	Tritium	17,000	17,000	17,000	16,000
	Krypton	190,000	190,000	180,000	180,000
	Xenon	1,500,000	4000[b]	100[b]	4.5×10^{-4}
	Iodine	2,600,000	14,000[b]	82[b]	1.0

SOURCE: Based on data in Tables 3.10 and 3.34 in U.S. Atomic Energy Commission, *Siting of Fuel Reprocessing Plants and Waste Management Facilities,* compiled and edited by the staff of Oak Ridge National Laboratory, ORNL-4451 (July 1971).
  [a]Annual fuel discharged: LWR = 27 metric tons of uranium; LMFBR = 18 metric tons.
  [b]Author's estimate, source data not available.

ject economic benefits of the LMFBR program are different from the ground rules used to assess the environmental effects of an LMFBR economy.

Table 19 gives the tritium, noble gas, and iodine contributions to the total activity in the annual spent fuel discharged from a 1000-Mw LWR (of the Diablo Canyon PWR type) and the AI reference oxide LMFBR, discussed above.

According to the *LMFBR Demonstration Plant Environmental Statement,* "it is expected that a reasonable extrapolation of current technology will yield retention factors (input concentration/release concentration) for tritium, krypton-85, and iodine-131 of 10, 100, and 10,000,000 respectively."[30] At present one can achieve iodine retention factors in the range of 10^{-2} to 10^{-5}. While no single system now exists for achieving 10^{-7}, it is probably reasonable to assume that it can be achieved by 1985 or 1990. Likewise, the technology for removal and storage of krypton-85 is several years away.

Assuming the retention factors above and the data in Table 19, the contributions to the reprocessing plant routine releases due to processing the annual fuel discharges from the reference LWR and LMFBR are easily calculated, and are given in Table 20.

[30]U.S. AEC, *LMFBR Demonstration Plant Environmental Statement,* p. 185.

TABLE 20. Contributions to the Routine Radioactive Releases of Reprocessing Plants Due to Processing the Annual Fuel Discharges from LWRs and LMFBRs

(curies)

Radioactive releases	Assured retention factor	LWR 150-day waste decay time	LMFBR (AI-design) waste decay time	
			30 days	150 days
Tritium	10	1900	1700	1700
Noble gases	100	3100	13,000	1800
Iodines	10^7	6×10^{-5}	0.26	8×10^{-5}

It should be noted that the contributions to the routine releases at future fuel reprocessing plants (i.e., the activity levels in Table 20), even at the 150-day decay times, are higher than the projected routine radioactive releases from the reactors themselves, regardless of reactor type. This assumes that similar radioactive gaseous effluent treatment systems having equivalent retention factors are incorporated in the reactor radioactive systems.

In order to compare the environmental effects of each reactor, LWR, HTGR, and LMFBR, due to routine radioactive releases, one should examine the entire fuel cycle, including reactor plus reprocessing plant, and compare the total man-rem dose per unit of electrical energy generated. To do this, one must postulate plant sizes, population densities, and meteorological conditions around future reactors, fuel reprocessing plants, and other facilities. Considering the order-of-magnitude uncertainties in these variables, plus the uncertainties in the retention factors and LMFBR spent-fuel cooling periods, it is clear that one cannot say that any reactor type has an advantage over the others.

Downwind consequences resulting from the routine release of radionuclides from a plant processing LWR and FBR fuel are estimated to be controlled by the release of noble gases and iodine.[31] As Table 21 shows, if the larger fast breeder fuel reprocessing plants are to meet the 10 CFR 20 standards for iodine and the noble gases, they require larger sites in order to process FBR fuel after a thirty-day decay period. The data in Table 21 are based on the release of all the noble gases and one part in 10^7 of the iodine. Judging by these data, one should not look for an appreciable reduction in the limits to routine radioactive release at fast breeder fuel reprocessing plants similar to those at the reactor site

[31]U.S. AEC, *Siting of Fuel Reprocessing Plants*, p. S-2.

TABLE 21.   Fraction of Maximum Permissible Average Annual Air Concentrations Resulting from the Routine Release of Radionuclides (Noble Gases and Iodine) at the Site Boundaries of Commercial Fuel Processing Plants

(260 days of operation per year)

Plant	Plant capacity (metric tons/day)	Fuel characteristics			Distance to site boundary (km)	Fraction of concentrations at site boundary[a]	
		Average burnup (Mwd/ton)	Specific power (Mw/ton)	Decay period (days)		^{85}Kr-$_{133}Xe$	^{129}I-$_{131}I$
LWR	1	33,000	30	150	<0.6	0.58 (2.9 × 10⁶)	0.15 (0.56)
LWR	6	33,000	30	150	0.5—6	1.0 (1.7 × 10⁷)	0.25 (3.4)
LWR	36	33,000	30	150	5—29	1.0 (1.0 × 10⁸)	0.25 (20)
FBR	1	33,000	58	30	<0.6	0.92 (4.6 × 10⁶)	0.52 (3.6)
FBR	6	33,000	58	30	1.5—10	1.0 (2.8 × 10⁷)	0.56 (22)
FBR	36	33,000	58	30	7—42	1.0 (1.7 × 10⁸)	0.56 (130)

SOURCE: U.S. Atomic Energy Commission, *Siting of Fuel Reprocessing Plants and Waste Management Facilities* (compiled and edited by the staff of the Oak Ridge National Laboratory), ORNL-4451 (July 1971), pp. 2–24.

NOTE: Release rates, in curies per year, are given in parentheses.

[a]The reference values selected are one-third of the concentrations found in 10CFR20, Appendix B, Table II, Column 1. The 10CFR20 value for ^{85}Kr-$_{133}Xe$ is 1×10^{-7}. The 10CFR20 value for ^{131}I was reduced by a factor of 700, resulting in a reference concentration of 1.4×10^{-13}. The 10CFR20 value for ^{129}I was reduced by a factor of 7000, resulting in a reference concentration of 3×10^{-15}.

unless (a) further improvements are made in the noble gas and iodine retention factors beyond those that have been postulated; and (b) the spent-fuel decay period is extended beyond thirty days, or site boundaries are extended even further.

7

Safety Aspects

REACTOR SAFETY

Health effects associated with routine releases of radioactivity from operating nuclear power plants represent only part of the overall risk to public health from these plants. Clearly, some risk of accidental release of radioactivity exists, both at the reactor and in other sectors of the nuclear fuel cycle. In this section, I will attempt to place in perspective the health risk associated with accidental releases from the reactor itself. Since most of the studies in this area are based on LWRs, the health risk associated with these reactors will be discussed as a means of introducing the hazards associated with LMFBRs.

Light Water Reactors

The cumulative fission product inventory of a typical 1000-Mw LWR with a thermal efficiency of 32 percent after three years of operation is shown in Table 22. There are other fission products as well, but generally because they are either less volatile, less hazardous, or produced in smaller quantities, they can be ignored in assessing the health hazard associated with reactor accidents. Since roughly one-third of the fuel is replaced each year, for practical purposes the fission product inventory reaches equilibrium by the third year.

In order to detail the consequences of reactor accidents, I rely

TABLE 22. Fission Product Inventory

Isotope		Half-life		Megacuries present in 1000-Mwc plant[a]		Elemental boiling point (°F)	Health considerations
				At shutdown	1 day after release[b]		
Tritium	(H-3)	12.4	yr.	0.020	0.020	212 (As HTO)	Internal hazard
Krypton	83m	1.86	hr.	5.7	0	−243 (Gaseous)	External radiation
	85m	4.4	hr.	17	0.33		
	85	10.76	yr.	0.60	0.60		
	87	76	min.	34	0		
	88	2.8	hr.	50	0.10		
	89	3.18	min.	61	0		
	90	33	sec.	68	0		
Strontium	89	52.7	days	72	71	2490 (Nonvolatile)	Internal hazard to bone and lung
	90	27.7	yr.	5.2	5.2		
Iodine	131	8.05	days	72	66	333 (Highly volatile)	External radiation plus internal irradiation of thyroid gland due to concentration
	132	2.26	hr.	103	0.050		
	133	20.3	hr.	137	58		
	134	52.0	min.	156	0		
	135	6.68	hr.	123	9.23		
	136	83	sec.	54	0		
Xenon	131m	11.8	days	0.58	0.55	−162 (Gaseous)	External radiation
	133m	2.26	days	3.3	2.43		
	133	5.27	days	137	120		
	135m	15.6	min.	37	0		
	135	9.14	hr.	26	3.9		
	137	3.9	min.	132	0		
	138	17.5	min.	128	0		
	139	43	sec.	107	0		
Cesium	134	2.046	yr.	14	14	1238	Internal hazard and concentration in muscle tissue
	137	30.0	yr.	6.6	6.6		
Total fission products				1.2×10^4	2.6×10^3		

SOURCE: Thomas H. Pigford, "Protection of the Public from Radioactivity Produced in Nuclear Power Reactors," *IEEE Transactions on Nuclear Science*, Vol. NS-19, No. 1 (Feb. 1972), p. 23. A more complete table can be found in T. H. Pigford, M. J. Keaton, B. J. Mann, "Fuel Cycles for Electrical Power Generation," Report for EPA No. 68-01-0561, Teknekron EEED 101 (Jan. 1973).

[a]Calculated for a thermal efficiency of 32%. Assumes 3-year exposure of 3.3% enrichment water-reactor fuel at a specific power of 30×10^6 watts (thermal) per metric ton, includes all fission sources, assumes 1/3 of the fuel is replaced each year.

[b]Calculated on assumption that radioactive precursors are not present after release.

on a 1972 assessment by F. R. Farmer, Safety and Reliability Directorate, United Kingdom Atomic Energy Agency.[1] Farmer's analysis is based on a 480-Mw reactor (1500-Mw thermal) containing 4×10^9 curies of volatile and gaseous fission products, of which the I-131 component is 5×10^7 curies. First, Farmer discusses and dismisses accidents releasing 5,000 curies or less as having relatively small consequences. He bases his example on accidents that release from 10 to 100 times this amount—that is, about 10 percent of the gaseous and volatile fission products of the reactor. Farmer postulates average weather conditions and what he and others consider a typical site, namely, "a town of a few thousand people a few miles from the reactor, and one million people in the range twenty-thirty miles, with rural population between (density 250 per square mile)."

Under these conditions, Farmer concludes:

The fission product release ... would contain 5×10^6 curies I-131 and 5×10^5 curies Cs-137. The dose to the child thyroid would be about 10 rads at 60 miles and within this radius there is a likelihood of up to 1,000 cases of thyroid cancer appearing within 20 years. Whole body radiation from the fission product cloud and through inhalation of Cs-137 would give about 50 cases of leukemia and other cancers, and a similar number of cases of lung cancer might arise through the inhalation of ruthenium if this is taken as only 10% as volatile as iodine or caesium. The dose level from the contamination of ground, and particularly the caesium, could affect the reoccupation of land evacuated at the time of the incident. In terms of a limit of 0.5r per year, this delayed return could extend to 10 miles.

The most notable contaminant, that of I-131, on pasture land could require control on the consumption of milk to a distance of 100 miles or over an area of 2,000 square miles.

The effect on people has been described as though the wind carried the fission products through the nearby town and then to the more distant town and, of course, the wind may not do this, although there may be other towns at other distances. We have a more general way of describing the effect, taking into account the probability of wind direction and probability of weather pattern. We apply this to real sites with their varied location of towns. For a coastal site for which the wind has a 50% probability of blowing to sea, I can then say that for the accident I am discussing, there would be a 30% probability of generating between 100 and 1,000 cases of thyroid and other cancers, and a 20% chance that the number

[1]F. R. Farmer, "How Safe is Safe Enough and Why?" remarks to Special Session at the International Conference on Nuclear Solutions to World Energy Problems, sponsored by the American Nuclear Society, Nov. 12-17, 1972, Washington, D.C.

would lie between 1,000 and 10,000—these cases appearing progressively over ten or more years.[2]

To extrapolate these casualty estimates, based on a 480-Mw reactor, to today's 1000-Mw reactors, the number of casualties should be slightly less than twice the figures presented by Farmer.[3] To extrapolate Farmer's result to the 2000- to 3000-Mw unit sizes predicted by the 1970 Analysis to be available from about 1990 onward (Figure 6), the number of casualties should be multiplied by roughly 5 to 8. Accidents considerably more severe than these can be envisioned by considering sabotage and warfare, where power plants are prime targets. In these cases a large fraction of the plutonium and nonvolatile fission products could be released in addition to the gaseous and volatile fission products.

The 1970 Analysis, using case 3 assumptions (LMFBR introduced in 1986), projects the following generation capacity (in 1000 Mw) placed in operation by the indicated year.[4]

Year	LWR	HTGR	LMFBR
2000	385	126	593
2020	1008	568	2948

[2]F. R. Farmer, "How Safe is Safe Enough?" There is insufficient data to support a conclusion that there is a radiation dose or dose rate above which the probability of resultant damage is zero. Therefore, Farmer's estimates of leukemias and other cancers are based on the prudent assumption that a non-threshold linear relationship for dose versus effect exists in the region of low dose. To the extent that threshold effect may exist, estimates based on the linear dose-effect relationship should be regarded as estimates of maximum possible effects. On the other hand, Farmer's estimates are not necessarily the most pessimistic estimates based on the linear dose-effect assumption. For example, estimates of cancer risk by Gofman and Tamplin, based on a doubling dose concept, are several times larger than ICRP estimates. See T. H. Pigford, "Protection of the Public from Radioactivity Produced in Nuclear Power Reactors," *Nuclear Science,* Vol. NS-19, No. 1 (Feb. 1972), p. 20. Also, Farmer has not included possible genetic effects, which are even less certain. Based on a linear dose-effect relationship and mouse data for estimating the mutation rate doubling dose, the risk from chronic radiation at low doses, relative to the spontaneous mutation, has been estimated to be 0.005 to 0.05 per rem. See National Academy of Sciences, "The Effects on Populations of Exposure to Low Levels of Ionizing Radiation," Report of the Advisory Committee on the Biological Effects of Ionizing Radiations (Washington, D.C., 1972), p. 129. These data suggest that the genetic risk could be significant compared with the total risk of cancer.

[3]This assumes that only a small fraction of Farmer's casualties are persons receiving relatively large radiation doses due to their close proximity to the reactor. At doses above about 200 rem, the individual risk-dose curves clearly are not linear.

[4]U.S. Atomic Energy Commission, Division of Reactor Development and Technology, *Updated (1970) Cost-Benefit Analysis of the U.S. Breeder Reactor Program,* WASH 1184 (Jan. 1972), p. 34.

The total number of plants will depend on their unit size (1000-Mw to 3000-Mw) and the accuracy of the model predictions. The plant lifetimes are expected to be approximately thirty years. Given these data and the consequences of the more severe, often referred to as "catastrophic," accidents described above, what constitutes an acceptable risk, or probability of occurrence of such an accident? Farmer asks:

Should we endeavour to keep the risk of the accident at less than 1 in 10? My own feeling is that a risk of 1 in 10 that this event could occur is not very palatable and I would prefer to propose that, as far as our competence allows, the risk of the event should be less than 1 in 100.[5]

Considering only the 500 reactors now existing, or under construction, Farmer's acceptable risk rate for the severe accident implies a risk rate per reactor of less than 10^{-6} per year. Using his criteria and the projected nuclear capacity in the United States through 2000 or 2020, the probability would be almost an order-of-magnitude lower. For the sake of argument, I will assume 10^{-6} per reactor year is acceptable. The exact figure is unimportant to my discussion.

For well-established systems—for example, fossil-fueled plants —the public health risk can be estimated from historical records. With respect to nuclear power, however, there have been no accidents involving civilian plants that have resulted in significant releases of radioactivity to the environment. But the cumulative operating experience with civilian nuclear plants is less than 100 reactor-years in the United States, and 300 reactor-years worldwide, and this mostly in small reactors. As many authors have noted, this history by itself is inadequate to demonstrate that nuclear plants can be operated for 10,000 to 100,000 plant-years with the required degree of safety.

Two other approaches to safety analysis are mentioned in the literature—the judgmental review by experienced professionals to determine if adequate design precautions have been taken and the use of probability analysis techniques, whereby the estimation of system risk is derived from the reliability of individual components and their interaction.[6]

[5] F. R. Farmer, "How Safe is Safe Enough and Why?"

[6] C. Starr, M. A. Greenfield, and D. F. Hausknecht, "A Comparison of Public Health Risks." This article is an abridged version of their report "Public Health Risks of Thermal Power Plants," prepared for The Resources Agency of California (UCLA School of Engineering and Applied Science, May 1972).

To assure the public that each nuclear plant can be operated without undue risk to public health and safety, the AEC relies on the judgmental review procedure before issuing a construction permit or operating license, and also on plant inspections during construction and operation. Through engineering and licensing review and quality assurance programs, the AEC hopes to confirm that codes, standards, and other criteria are met and maintained. The details of the technical and administrative review procedures, and the content of the required nuclear plant safety analysis reports are reviewed in the *LMFBR Demonstration Plant Environmental Statement* (pp. 114-125) and other AEC reports.

Despite this extensive review procedure, based on the judgmental approach, the short operating history of nuclear plants has been less than satisfactory with respect to plant safety. This is a controversial issue, and my view does not necessarily reflect that of others, some of whom are more knowledgeable in this area. To support it, I refer the reader to the ORNL summaries of abnormal reactor operating experiences,[7] the AEC reports on *Reactor Operating Experience*,[8] and Ralph Lapp's "Report to the Illinois Commerce Commission".[9]

The ORNL Report for 1969-71 includes the following cases:

1. During reactor shutdown following a second electrical fire at one PWR, "Safe operation of the plant was compromised since cooldown was initiated and partially completed prior to verifying the reactor shutdown margin. Unawareness by the operator of his inability to adjust operating parameters and misinterpretation of control room instrumentation intelligence resulted in a decrease in the reactor shutdown margin. Although the reactor shutdown margin remained within permissible limits, if dilution had continued for sufficient time the reactor could have become critical." (p. 9).

2. Following repair of the damage above, a control rod was miswired and as a result it "drifted" into the core where it remained undetected for 19 days. The plant's maloperation was attributed to a combination of "failure to observe proper maintenance practices, inadequate system checkout and testing, non-adherence to plant operating procedures, and failure to recognize an abnormal operating condition." (p. 11).

[7]*Abnormal Reactor Operating Experiences,* ORNL-NSIC-17; *Abnormal Operating Experiences, 1966-1968,* ORNL-NSIC-64; and *Abnormal Operating Experiences, 1969-1971,* ORNL-NSIC-103, are available from National Technical Information Service, U.S. Dept. of Commerce, Springfield, Va. 22151.

[8]See, for example, ROE 71-2, ROE 71-3, and ROE 71-22.

[9]Ralph E. Lapp, "Report to the Illinois Commerce Commission," Springfield, Ill., December 1972.

3. Contamination of the drinking water resulted from cross-connecting the well water tap to a radioactive waste tank. (p. 26).

4. A complete loss of off-site electrical power was experienced. "In this case, no actual safety problem resulted, because the on-site emergency power source operated in accordance with design and assumed the electrical load for shutting down and cooling the reactor safely." (p. 45).

5. ". . . there have been a number of FAILURES OF EMERGENCY POWER SOURCES to respond properly when called upon. In no case did a serious radiation hazard result from the failure. In many instances, the source of the failure was human error. . . . Sources of on-site emergency power are considered to be essential components of engineered safety features for reactors. The reliability of such sources should approach 100%." (p. 51).

6. "During power operation of a BOILING WATER REACTOR, a MALFUNCTION in the PRESSURE CONTROL system, coupled with a DESIGN ERROR in the direction of DISCHARGE of a SAFETY VALVE, resulted in a partial BLOWDOWN of the PRIMARY COOLANT system to containment. Damage within the containment vessel was limited to overheating of electrical cables for flux monitoring instrumentation and water impact damage to thermal insulation. No measurable radioactivity was released to the site or the environs." (p. 122).

In this case, "Although written emergency procedures call for initiation of containment sprays whenever the pressure inside containment is above 2 psig, two licensed senior reactor operators concurred in the decision not to activate this system because of concern for damage that might be caused by the thermal shock and other drywell damage which might result from use of the sprays.

In retrospect, this decision may not have been warranted in view of the lack of available information on conditions of leakage, temperature, pressure and radioactivity inside containment. The desirability of making actuation of containment sprays an automatic rather than a manual function is under consideration." (p. 126).[10]

A more recent case occurred at a New Jersey Plant, where, "An operator mistake . . . shut the plant down for 10 days and caused some 50,000 gal of radioactive water from the reactor core to be released over a 2½-hr period when a safety valve failed to close. The water was contained in the reactor building, and utility officials are trying to decide how to dispose of it. A large fish kill

---

[10]This last incident occurred June 5, 1970, at Dresden Unit-2 while operating at 75 percent rated power (623 Mw). A detailed investigation of this and two other abnormal incidents at Dresden has been made by Ralph Lapp, a highly regarded nuclear consultant, and can be found in his "Report to the Illinois Commerce Commission." The reader is urged to review this report for insight into safety problems associated with the operation of light water reactors.

is also attributed to a sudden drop in discharge-water temperature. The error occurred when the operator mistakenly opened a door to an instrument cabinet controlling the plant's transformers. This act caused a safety fuse to blow, de-energizing the cabinet. The plant's automatic monitoring system interpreted the fuse blowing as a signal that the generators had stopped, and shut down the reactor and opened a valve to vent excess steam. Only 100 gal would have been vented had not the safety valve failed to close."[11]

The above cases represent only a relatively small sample of those that have been reviewed. In addition, there has been at least one serious act of sabotage at a nuclear plant, which resulted in several million dollars worth of damage to electrical equipment.

In addition, AEC experiments related to emergency core cooling systems (ECCS) have caused concern with regard to the adequacy of the design and operating criteria of current nuclear plants in the event of an accident involving loss of coolant. Extensive public hearings on the adequacy of ECCS have prompted the AEC's Directorate of Licensing to tighten its ECCS criteria.[12] Hearings on this issue by the JCAE are anticipated in 1974.

As discussed in Chapter 2 (section on performance data), the fuel failures in the first core of the Peach Bottom HTGR and the recent unanticipated fuel degradation problems in PWRs with unpressurized fuel elements are examples of incidents that raise questions about the adequacy of both earlier and recent safety review procedures.

In its review of some of the cases reported here, the ORNL 1966-71 report indicates that, while no serious threat to public health and safety has occurred, "The absence of serious effect is largely the result of good luck." (p. 22)

One must assume that continued improvements will be made in the area of nuclear reactor safety before large numbers of reactors become operational, and that the safety criteria will be strengthened with additional operating experience. Clearly, none of the older nuclear plants would have met today's licensing criteria. If reactors are not now safe enough, will future improve-

[11]*Electrical World,* February 15, 1973, pp. 19-20.
[12]U.S. Atomic Energy Commission, Draft Environmental Statement concerning Proposed Rule Making Action: Acceptance Criteria for Emergency Core Cooling Systems for Light-Water-Cooled Nuclear Power Reactors (December 1972).

ments be sufficient and made in time? Assumptions that they will, in the absence of any hard evidence, are not very comforting.

The "deductive process" for assessing reactor safety, referred to earlier, is the approach taken by Otway and Erdmann,[13] who present a method for evaluating the sum of all biological risks from all conceivable accidents weighted by the respective accident probabilities. They divide accidents into two categories: those due to random independent failures of reactor systems; and those due to the simultaneous, related failures of systems due to an outside source such as an earthquake or a tornado.

To demonstrate the first case, where they assume independence of reactor systems, the accident probability is approximated by

$$P_a \cong P_p \prod_1^n P_i(\tau),$$

where

P_a = probability of the postulated accident per year,
P_p = probability of a primary system failure (i.e., coolant pipe rupture) per year,
$P_i(\tau)$ = probability of the ith safeguard system failing to start or spontaneously failing during the time interval (τ) when the failure would affect the accident outcome.[14]

The radiation dose received and the estimated mortality as functions of the downwind distance from a postulated release corresponding to each accident are calculated by established methods.

Using estimated system failure rates, Otway and Erdmann demonstrated their procedure by applying it to a 1000-Mw PWR. For the severe nuclear accident—the type described by Farmer—Otway and Erdmann calculated an accident probability of 10^{-14} per reactor-year, and therefore very low individual mortality risks downwind from the reactor.

In their example calculation, Otway and Erdmann did not consider: (1) sabotage, (2) operator error, maintenance error, and other human factor considerations, (3) possible inadequacy of ECCS, and

[13]Harry J. Otway and Robert C. Erdmann, "Reactor Siting and Design from a Risk Viewpoint," *Nuclear Engineering and Design,* 13 (1970), pp. 365-76.
[14]Ibid., p. 369.

(4) common mode failures (i.e., the possibility that reactor systems are not independent). There is limited historical data, some of which is cited above, that forces consideration of these factors. The assumption that reactor systems fail independently—a fundamental assumption in this model—is simply not true. The system failure rates used by Otway and Erdmann are based on data not available in the published literature. Furthermore, their assumption that the accidents analyzed represent a sample of a complete spectrum of accidents is open to question.

Using the technique of Otway and Erdmann, but considering the factors above, one can just as easily calculate a severe nuclear accident probability less than 10^{-6}, an unacceptable risk. Again, by "severe" I mean the release of fission products equivalent to 5×10^6 curies, or more, of I-131—the type of accident described by Farmer. For example, assume the United States will acquire 10,000 reactor-years of operating experience during the next thirty years. One successful act of sabotage by a terrorist group during this period places the severe nuclear accident probability at 10^{-4}, or greater. Of course, one does not need to go through this simple calculation to realize that, if a successful act of sabotage is highly probable, a fission energy economy constitutes an unacceptable public risk.

There have been other assessments in which probability theory has been applied to LWRs,[15] including an attempt to account more accurately for common mode failure.[16] However, as some investigators have noted, all of these estimates "are of questionable validity because of the lack of meaningful and reliable input data on failure mechanisms and failure rates, because of the very limited extent to which real and possible failure mechanisms have been considered, and because of idealized and optimistic assumptions of uncorrelated failure modes made in calculating probabilities of multi-event accidents."[17]

[15]For example, K.H. Lindackers and W. Stoebel, "Probability Analysis Applied to Light-Water Reactors: Loss-of-Coolant Accidents," *Nuclear Safety*, 14 (Jan.-Feb. 1973), pp. 14-20.
[16]Harry J. Otway, Ronald K. Lohrding, and Morris E. Battat, "A Risk Estimate for an Urban-Sited Reactor," *Nuclear Technology*, 12 (Oct. 1971), pp. 173-184. This risk estimate was made for an 8-Mw(t) research reactor.
[17]Thomas H. Pigford, Michael J. Keaton, and Bruce J. Mann, "Fuel Cycles for Electrical Power Generation," prepared for EPA by Teknekron, Inc., Berkeley, Calif. (January 1973), p. 51.

The main point is, we do not know the probabilities associated with the factors above—principally human factors and common mode failure—and, therefore, we do not know, and probably will never be able to calculate, whether a nuclear power economy (including power plant, fuel shipping and reprocessing and waste disposal) constitutes an acceptable public risk.[18]

Before moving to LMFBR safety considerations, one further problem should be noted. The health risk from a severe 1000-Mw LWR accident as a function of the distance downwind from the reactor has been calculated by Pigford.[19] Pigford's hypothetical accident corresponded to the release of 2.4×10^8 curies of the fission product iodine (roughly 25 percent of the inventory) released over a twenty-four hour period, i.e., no containment. It is two to three times more severe than the accident described by Farmer. Pigford compared the health risk of this accident with the risk from routine radioactive effluents from the same plant, assuming it meets the proposed 10 CFR 50 Appendix I standard—the maximum dose rate at the site boundary equal to 5 mrem/yr. The results of this comparison are reproduced in Figure 20.

For the severe accident, the health risk depends not only on the assumed release conditions but also on the accident probability. The two dashed curves in Figure 20 correspond to arbitrarily assumed probabilities of 10^{-5} and 10^{-9} accidents of this severity per reactor per year. Interpolation between these curves suggests that, if the probability of this severe accident is *greater* than about 10^{-7} per reactor per year, the health risk from the severe nuclear accident is greater than the risk from routine releases from the same plant.

In summary, it has been assumed that roughly 10^{-6} per reactor per year is the largest acceptable probability of a severe nuclear accident, if large-scale use of nuclear plants is to constitute an acceptable health risk. Perhaps the number should be lower. But because of sabotage, operator and maintenance error, other human factor considerations, common mode failures, and the possibility that emergency systems do not operate as designed, one will prob-

---

[18]Despite this, several authors have used the results of Otway and Erdmann in their own assessments of the health risk due to reactor operations. See, for example, L.A. Sagan, "Human Costs of Nuclear Power," *Science,* 177 (August 11, 1972), pp. 487-93; and Starr et al., "A Comparison of Public Health Risks," p. 45.

[19]Thomas H. Pigford, "Protection of the Public from Radioactivity Produced in Nuclear Power Reactors," *Nuclear Science,* Vol. NS-19, No. 1 (Feb. 1972).

FIGURE 20. Individual Risks for Normal and Accidental Releases

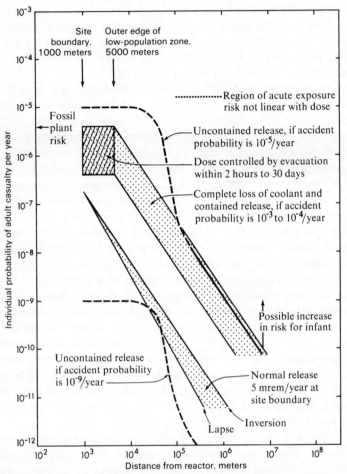

SOURCE: Thomas H. Pigford, "Protection of the Public from Radioactivity Produced in Nuclear Power Reactors," *IEEE Transactions on Nuclear Science*, Vol. NS-19, No. 1 (Feb. 1972), p. 26.

ably never be able to demonstrate (until after the fact), or even realistically estimate whether the probability is indeed this small. This is aside from similar uncertainties regarding the perpetual management of the high-level radioactive waste and the safeguarding of highly enriched fissile material generated by these plants.

LMFBR Safety

During normal operations the LMFBRs, HTGRs, and LWRs behave in much the same way. Because they also share the same uncertainties regarding sabotage, operator and maintenance error, other human factor elements, common mode failure, etc., the LMFBR, at best, faces the same uncertainty as the others with regard to public health risk. But this has not been a principal LMFBR safety issue in discussions to date. The areas of greatest concern center on the behavior of the reactor after the initiation of an accident—a focal point of current LMFBR safety research—and the potential for releasing large quantities of plutonium to the environment. Before discussing specifics of these issues, it is perhaps worth reviewing a few of the general safety characteristics of the reactors of interest that differ because of factors inherent in their designs.

Differences exist among the various reactor types, and each has safety advantages and disadvantages. The LWRs and HTGRs operate with a high-pressure coolant and thus are subject to accidents involving depressurization. As reviewed above, the consequences of a loss-of-coolant accident in LWRs can be particularly severe. The LMFBR uses a low-pressure coolant (1–10 atmospheres) with more favorable heat transfer properties and heat storage capacity. Under normal operations the sodium coolant temperature is well below the boiling point, 1640°F, but the coolant must be kept above its melting point of 210°F. Because the sodium coolant is at a lower pressure than the LWR coolant, the sodium should be lost less rapidly following a primary pipe rupture. The low pressure, good heat transfer characteristics, and single phase of the sodium coolant during normal operations make the LMFBR appear safer immediately after shutdown.

The use of sodium as a coolant has additional advantages and disadvantages. Sodium is extremely active chemically. This makes it very efficient in retaining many fission products, an advantage should an accident occur. However, the LMFBR molten-fuel–coolant interaction, important to safety assessments, is not well understood. For various postulated initial conditions, it is not clear what fraction of the thermal energy in the fuel is converted to mechanical work capable of damaging the reactor core and breaching the containment vessel. When exposed to air, sodium oxidizes rapidly, if it is in the solid state; and if liquid, it burns spontaneously, releasing a caustic smoke. The fast reactor coolant circuits operate at temperatures above the spontaneous ignition temperature of sodium in air. Fortunately, liquid sodium burns at a controlled rate (2 to 4 pounds per hour per square foot of exposed surface). But this advantage is lost in the case of spray fires, due to explosive introduction of sodium into the surrounding atmosphere. When exposed to water, sodium reacts violently resulting in the release of heat, hydrogen, and several very corrosive reaction products. The hydrogen, in turn, can combine with oxygen and increase the reaction energy. Interactions between sodium and water in steam generators are expected in the event of leakage of water or steam into the sodium. Steam generator leaks are common in LWRs; and one or more, requiring reactor shutdown and maintenance, are expected in the lifetime of an LMFBR. According to an unpublished AEC assessment (WASH 1100), as of about 1970, "The state of the art for detecting, locating, and containing sodium leaks and for fighting sodium-air or sodium-water reactions is rudimentary." While some improvements in this area have been made since 1970, the steam generator may yet be the Achilles heel of the LMFBR.

Sodium becomes intensely radioactive when exposed to neutrons. Shielding must be used to protect workers who are near sodium that has been through the core and blanket of an operating reactor. Since sodium is opaque, provisions must be made for refueling the reactor without benefit of visual observation, thereby increasing the possibility of refueling accidents. Fuel handling systems are probably the most complex feature of an LMFBR.

The reliability of sodium hardware—valves, pumps, etc.—is still an area of major concern. All of the factors above make sodium technology one of the most critical areas of the LMFBR program.

For economic reasons the LMFBR and other fast reactors are operated at power densities an order-of-magnitude greater than commercially available thermal reactors.[20] The active core volume is therefore much less, in fact only a few cubic meters in volume. The higher power density means that core meltdown occurs more vigorously should adequate cooling be lost. Consequently, to avoid center fuel melting in an LMFBR, the fuel is divided into more pins (roughly 60,000 to 90,000 in the core of a 1000-Mw LMFBR) each smaller in diameter, and there is a need for a coolant having

---

[20]Power density is the amount of heat generated in a given volume of the reactor per unit time. The power density in an LMFBR core is roughly 0.5 to 1.0 Mw(t)/liter.

good heat transfer characteristics, e.g., sodium. The advantage of a coolant with good heat transfer characteristics is necessarily sacrificed in the GCFBR.

The fast breeder reactors (i.e., LMFBR and GCFBR) use highly enriched fuel, as opposed to the less than 4 percent fuel enrichment in LWRs.[21] In the event of a fuel meltdown in these reactors, assuming the fuel could rearrange itself into a more dense configuration, less fuel is required to form a critical mass.[22] This secondary criticality would provide additional energy and fission products to the accident in progress.

Contrary to thermal reactors, the geometrical arrangement of the core of a fast reactor does not correspond to the most reactive configuration. The enrichment of the fuel in LMFBRs is high enough to provide a potential for large reactivity insertion rates from coherent motion of the fuel, e.g., collapse of the core. Thus, the operation of a fast reactor is extremely sensitive to fuel motion during an accident. It takes only a slight compaction (about 2 percent volume reduction of a core) to trigger an explosive nuclear runaway. Similarly, a slight expansion of the reactor core would have a strong shutdown effect on any accident in progress.

The fraction of delayed neutrons[23] produced by fission of plutonium-239 and uranium-233 is 0.003, compared with 0.0065 for uranium-235. Under normal operating conditions the delayed neutrons increase the reactor period, i.e., slow down the reactor reaction rate or power rise, and enable one to control the reactor. The smaller fraction of delayed neutrons present in the LMFBR and HTGR increase the sensitivity of these reactors to adjustments of control rods and to other inputs that affect reactivity, such as temperature variations in the core.

In a major accident, if sufficient reactivity has been added such

---

[21]The HTGR uses highly (90-95%) enriched uranium. However, as reactor fuel the uranium is highly diluted with thorium and this mixture in turn is distributed in a graphite structure. Likewise, in LWRs operating on recycled plutonium, the highly enriched plutonium is diluted with uranium to low (3-5%) enrichment.

[22]A homogeneous mixture of LMFBR fuel and stainless steel (47 volume percent steel) in the shape of a cylinder 72 cm in radius and 40 cm in height would be sufficient. D. L. Hunt and J. G. Moore, "Problems Associated with Molten Fuel," in United Kingdom Atomic Energy Authority, *An Appreciation of Fast Reactor Safety* (1970), NP-18487, Ch. 4, p. C.2.9.

[23]Delayed neutrons are released on the average 10 to 20 seconds after the prompt neutrons, which are released at the time of the fission. The delayed neutrons are released from the fission products as they undergo radioactive decay.

that the chain reaction is maintained by means of the prompt neutrons alone, the reactor is said to be prompt critical, or undergoing a prompt critical excursion. Under these conditions the reactor period is more a function of the neutron lifetime than the delayed neutron fraction. The average neutron lifetime in thermal reactors is on the order of one thousand times longer than in fast reactors, because the neutrons are slowed down before they are captured.[24] It is even longer in HTGRs than in LWRs because, on the average, the HTGR neutrons lose less energy per collision in the slowing down process. While both thermal and fast reactors have rather similar reactor periods in the range of delayed criticality (normal conditions), when exceeding prompt criticality the period of a fast reactor drops to about 10^{-4} to 10^{-5} seconds, as compared with 10^{-1} to 10^{-2} seconds in the thermal reactor. If sufficient reactivity has been added to reach or exceed prompt criticality, the power level can rise so rapidly that the ordinary safety controls would not have time to operate before damage has occurred to the reactor as a result of high temperature and neutron flux. One of the principal fast reactor safety problems remaining is to make failure to shut down the reactor "incredible." In this regard, the reader is referred to the discussion of the "doppler effect" in Appendix C.

For reasons of safety it is unlikely that commercial LMFBRs will be designed with average positive power coefficients under normal operating conditions (see Appendix C). On the other hand, all 1000-Mw LMFBR designs now under consideration have positive sodium void coefficients over significant regions of the reactor cores. Current design conditions are such that boiling is generally unstable, and, if there is void formation, the void is expected to propagate rapidly through the coolant channel with subsequent overheating of the fuel, which in turn could lead to an explosive disruption of the core. In contrast to other reactors (including small LMFBRs), the region of positive void coefficient in large LMFBRs can be very extensive, and the amount of reactivity added through such voiding can be very large. Moreover, the small prompt neutron lifetime of the fast reactor emphasizes the effects of the rate of reactivity insertion.[25]

[24]In fast reactors, such as the LMFBR, the average neutron lifetime is on the order of 10^{-7} seconds as compared with 10^{-3} to 10^{-4} seconds for thermal reactors.
[25]C. N. Kelber et al., "Safety Problems of Liquid-Metal-Cooled Fast Breeder Reactors," Argonne National Laboratory, ANL-7657, *Reactor Technology* (Feb. 1970), p. 12.

In large LMFBRs, because of their size, propagation of fuel failure due to sodium voiding represents an important new dimension to fast reactor safety considerations. Experience with smaller sodium-cooled fast reactors has little relevance to this problem.

The safety disadvantages have led some critics of the LMFBR program to conclude that LMFBRs generically are less safe than the commercially available LWRs. Others disagree, including many whose research is in the field of LMFBR safety. Because of the differences in reactor characteristics—some good, some bad—and because the accidents of greatest concern are different for each reactor type (e.g., pipe rupture followed by loss of coolant and core meltdown in LWRs versus large reactivity insertion followed by explosive disruption of the core in LMFBRs), many believe it is impossible to conclude that commercial LMFBRs will be more, or less, safe than alternative reactors. Some believe that there has been excessive preoccupation with the apparent differences between reactors; the task, they believe, is to develop reactors that are adequately safe. This is the approach being taken by the AEC and the international fast-reactor community.

There are two fundamental questions associated with reactor safety research. First, what are the probabilities of the occurrence of conditions that initiate reactor accidents? Second, what are the possible sequences of events following initiating conditions, and the probabilities associated with these sequences? "The major United States [LMFBR] safety development emphasis is on technology related to off-normal operating conditions which have previously been postulated as potentially leading to major accidents. Emphasis is also placed on the accommodation of hypothetical consequences of undefined events."[26] In other words, LMFBR safety research is directed primarily toward answering the second question and devising the necessary steps to reduce the associated probabilities to acceptable levels. If there is a single word characterizing this research, it is "uncertainty." Below are reviewed a few important unanswered questions which remain subjects of intensive research. The review is by no means complete. To do justice to this subject would require more time and discussion than has been allocated to the entire report.

[26]A. J. Pressesky et al., "Recent Developments in the United States Liquid-Metal Fast Breeder Reactor Safety Program" (paper presented at the Fourth United Nations International Conference on Peaceful Uses of Atomic Energy, Geneva, Sept. 6-16, 1971).

To facilitate the review, discussion is divided among several overlapping areas of research:

1. Reactor shutdown capability.
2. Local coolant blockage and fuel faults.
3. The molten-fuel–coolant interaction.
4. Validity of accident analysis models.
5. Containment design and plutonium release fraction.
6. Biological significance of plutonium radiation dose.

1. Reactor shutdown capability—In the United States, commercial reactors are generally designed with two independent emergency shutdown systems. In contrast to thermal reactors, both LMFBR shutdown systems are fast acting. This is because of the shorter reactor period of fast reactors when they reach, or exceed, prompt criticality. There is general agreement that failure to shut down the LMFBR should be made "incredible" by providing sufficient redundancy and diversity in the control and safety rod systems and designing against common mode failures. However, there is no general consensus on criteria for establishing required reliability of fast reactor shutdown systems. Furthermore, it is not clear whether failure to shut down can be made "incredible," while at the same time preserving the economics of the system. With respect to U.S. designs, it is noted that the emergency shutdown systems in the FFTF are electrically independent and separated physically but are not of diverse design.[27]

2. Local coolant blockage and fuel faults—Can local blockage of coolant channels in the reactor core occur in future LMFBR designs? Coolant flow blockage can lead to local fuel pin melting, or, as occurred in the Enrico Fermi fast breeder reactor, partial meltdown of the reactor core. With concomitant failure of the emergency shutdown systems (failure to scram), this can lead to power excursion, complete core melting, and nuclear explosion. If local coolant blockages or local fuel melting occur, how quickly can they be detected? Can they be detected with acceptably low probabilities of instrument failure and spurious signals?

3. The molten-fuel–coolant interaction—Assuming molten or vaporized fuel breaches the fuel pin cladding (e.g., melts through the cladding), what is the nature of the molten-fuel–coolant interaction? Consider, for example, the following sequence of events. After

[27]U.S. Atomic Energy Commission, Directorate of Licensing, *Safety Evaluation of the Fast Flux Test Facility*, Project No. 448 (Oct. 31, 1972), pp. 63-67.

breaching the cladding, the molten (or vaporized) fuel, fission product, and cladding materials rapidly superheat the sodium coolant
upon contact. The sodium in a localized area of the coolant channel
is vaporized (i.e., boils). The bubbles of vaporized sodium, fuel, etc.,
in the coolant channel expand toward equilibrium in the manner
of vapor bubbles in boiling water. The vapor bubbles or voids move
up the channel with the flowing coolant. Except at the periphery
of the core, these voids have a positive reactivity contribution
(positive sodium void coefficient). If the cladding breach occurs
below the midplane of the reactor, the movement of the fuel debris
up the coolant toward the midplane has an additional positive reactivity contribution. Positive reactivity contributions can in turn
lead to increased fisson densities, power densities, and temperatures, and possible further fuel melting, more cladding breaches,
etc. The question here is whether in this manner local faults can
rapidly propagate to other areas of the fast reactor core, possibly
leading to an explosive disruption of the core. The answer depends
in part on: (1) whether individual pin breaches with attendant coolant pressure pulses, reactivity effects, etc., occur randomly, or
coherently; and (2) the efficiency with which thermal energy in
the molten or vaporized fuel is transferred to work energy in the
form of expanding voids and attendant pressure pulses in the coolant. A high efficiency and coherent voiding is tantamount to a
vapor explosion.

Is a vapor explosion possible, highly unlikely, or impossible? If
even a localized vapor explosion is possible, to what extent will
this fault propagate rapidly through the reactor core? The nature
and extent of the fuel-coolant interaction appear to be strongly
affected by initial conditions associated with the accident; for
example, the distribution and state of the fuel and coolant, quantity and disposition of fission product gas and coolant vapor, the
degree of fuel fragmentation, rate of mixing, and the configuration
of the system.

To better understand the molten-fuel-coolant interaction, experiments have been performed in the TREAT reactor,[28] where, under
controlled conditions, small amounts of LMFBR fuel were driven

[28]See, for example, R. W. Wright et al., "Fuel-Coolant Interaction Effects During
Transient Meltdown of LMFBR Oxide Fuel in a Sodium-Filled Piston Autoclave:
TREAT TESTS S-2 to S-6," ANL/RAS 71-32, Argonne National Laboratory (Sept.
1971).

rapidly to very high power levels and temperatures. The fuel was clad in short fuel pins and immersed in liquid sodium heated in an effort to simulate LMFBR conditions. The sodium, however, was not flowing, and only one or a few fuel pins were used in the tests. The sodium boundary included a mechanical piston used to record pressure pulses resulting from the fuel–coolant interaction. The device was used to calculate the efficiency with which the thermal energy of the fuel is converted into work energy during the fuel-coolant interaction. In tests performed to date, only noncoherent individual pressure pulses that did little mechanical work have been recorded. The calculated conversion ratios ranged from 0.2 percent to 0.002 percent.[29] This is two to four orders of magnitude below the upper thermodynamic limit on the conversion efficiency, which is about 20 percent.

Calculation of the conversion efficiency is difficult because of the difficulty in inferring the mechanical energy due to ejected fuel particle-sodium debris as a result of the molten-fuel–coolant interaction. Furthermore, to date there have been less than a dozen TREAT tests designed to measure the conversion efficiency, not all of which have been useful to the conversion efficiency calculation. There is also the question of whether one can infer from these results the conversion efficiencies for other initial conditions. Finally, the TREAT period is slow relative to the transient period in an LMFBR hypothetical core disruptive accident.[30] Therefore, the TREAT analyses to date are considered insufficient to reach any definitive conclusion about the efficiency for converting the thermal energy to mechanical energy. Gilby of the UK AEA Safety and Reliability Directorate, concludes,

... There has been some success in theoretical analyses in interpreting these experiments on the basis of an assumed fine dispersion of particles typical of the debris found in the experiments. This process is useful in understanding mechanisms but in all models a wide range of severity can be predicted for plausible combinations of parameters. In other experiments attempts have been made to simulate conditions in the reactor fault but can these simulations ever be accurate enough? Many people would already agree that efficiencies of interaction will almost certainly be less than 10% and will probably be 1% or less [efficiencies of about 20% are thermodynamically possible]. To improve on this it is necessary to identify some physical parameter or some feature of the fault development which

[29]Ibid.
[30]U.S. AEC-DL, *Safety Evaluation of the FFTF*, Appendix D, p. 45.

can be counted upon under practically all circumstances to limit the extent of any interaction.[31]

One such theory of fault development suggests that a large-scale coherent vapor explosion between UO_2-Na is not possible in LMFBRs.[32] Referring to this theory, Gilby has noted that ". . . experimental evidence has always been found to contradict such theories in the past. . . ."[33] An excellent review of the adequacy of such theories has been presented by Anderson and Armstrong.[34] Comparing two vapor explosion models and recent experiment results, they conclude, "Each model was based on a set of experimental measurements which it adequately explained. However, each model was incapable of correctly predicting the trends in the alternate experimental data.[35]

Summarizing only the fast reactor safety problems concerning local faults in the core, Gilby concludes,

In summary, development of a sub-assembly fault depends upon a sequence of unlikely events but it is difficult to see how any one link in the chain will be shown to be incredible. An alternative which is being explored is that the probability of individual links might be shown to be in the range 10^{-2} to 10^{-3} so that the overall probability could then be very small $(< 10^{-7})$. Is it sufficient that blockages are unlikely to occur, that detection is almost sure to work, that the undetected blockage will very probably not cause serious damage to the rest of the core?[36]

A number of mechanisms by which local faults might propagate through the reactor core have been mentioned: (a) pressure pulses from fuel-cladding breaches; (b) fuel-movement reactivity effects; and (c) coolant reactivity effects, i.e., sodium voiding. It is the goal of LMFBR safety research to devise means to minimize and, where possible, obviate these mechanisms, for these and others may lead to prompt critical power excursions involving the entire reactor

[31]E. V. Gilby, "Fast Reactor Safety—Problems and Solutions" (paper presented at the International Conference on Nuclear Solutions to World Energy Problems, sponsored by the American Nuclear Society, Washington, D.C., Nov. 12-17, 1972.)

[32]Hans K. Fauske, "The Role of Nucleation in Vapor Explosions," paper presented at the International Conference cited above.

[33]E. V. Gilby, "Fast Reactor Safety."

[34]R. P. Anderson and D. R. Armstrong, "Comparison between Vapor Explosion Models and Recent Experimental Results" (paper presented at the Fourteenth National Heat Transfer Conference, AIChE-ASME, Atlanta, Georgia, August 5-8, 1973), AIChE Preprint 16.

[35]Ibid., p. 42.

[36]Ibid.

core, resulting in a severe explosion with a sizable portion of the core being vaporized. The implications of this are discussed below.

4. Validity of accident analysis models—There are two parts to this discussion. First, how accurate are LMFBR accident analysis models, with respect to critical power excursions involving the entire reactor core, for the accident sequences that are currently being analyzed? Can the utilization of these models place realistic bounds on the explosive potential of these accidents, i.e., the size and shape of the first power pulse of the fast reactor nuclear excursion under analysis? In this regard, when the PAD (Pajarito Dynamic) computer code was compared, after the fact, against the experimental data from Kiwi-TNT, Godiva, and Snaptran experiments, the predicted thermal energy releases were within 80 percent, and explosive (or kinetic) energies were only within a factor of 2.[37] It is not known to what extent the power pulse shapes could be reproduced. Will VENUS and other LMFBR disassembly codes be similarly compared against experimental data? To what extent is this practical in view of the many initial conditions that would have to be tested? Positive reactivity feedback mechanisms which lead to hypothetical disassembly accidents in LMFBRs were not present in the Kiwi-TNT, Godiva, and Snaptran experiments.

The second part of this discussion is related to the fact that the calculative methods for determining the maximum explosive potential of LMFBRs have not been developed to include all possibilities, and their combinations, for autocatalytic phenomena during and after an initial nuclear runaway. That is, there are conceivable mechanisms by which reactivity can or might be "inserted" due to the motion of fuel material resulting from an initial core explosion or meltdown event. Here, an initial event, or series of events, might cause the reactor to feed itself a massive dose of "reactivity," which would amplify the initial runaway or cause a very severe secondary runaway, either of which might lead to a severe explosion. Can probabilities realistically be assigned to these event sequences? In this regard, do the current codes provide

[37]Godiva was a 2.9 liter sphere of highly enriched uranium. Kiwi-TNT was the explosive disassembly of a propulsion reactor (819 liter core). Snap is a small (10.3 liter) reactor fueled with enriched UH_3 in ZrH_2. See W. R. Stratton, D. M. Peterson, and L. B. Engle, "The Pajarito Dynamics Code with Application to Reactor Experiments," paper presented at the International Conference on Nuclear Solutions cited above.

a valid calculative method for determining the explosive potential of LMFBRs? To what extent will the possibility, or impossibility, of these event sequences be experimentally confirmed?[38]

5. Containment design and plutonium release fraction—Each reactor safety analysis generally contains an assessment of one or more hypothetical design basis accidents (DBAs), each of which analyzes the sequence of events as the accident progresses. These DBAs are used to assess the safety margins provided by the reactor containment system. For example, in safety assessments of the FFTF, two arbitrary postulated sets of initial conditions which lead to hypothetical core-disruptive accidents have been examined: (1) an overpower accident beginning with an arbitrary reactivity insertion, concurrent with total failure of two reactor shutdown systems; (2) a loss of flow with flow decay corresponding to a pump coastdown, concurrent with total failure of the two shutdown systems.[39] It is important to understand that these initial conditions and the subsequent sequences of events in the hypothetical accidents analyzed by the AEC are not representative of the most severe nuclear accidents that one can envisage. Therefore the maximum available work energy estimates in the following discussion are applicable to hypothetical accidents only and not to the entire spectrum of possible accidents involving liquid metal fast breeder reactors.

Depending on assumptions regarding numerous events and reactions (for example, the efficiency of transferring the thermal energy of the molten fuel to mechanical energy, the properties of liquid sodium, and the degree to which the accident develops coherently, for a hypothetical accident of the type analyzed by the AEC), estimates of the maximum energy available in the form of work in the reactor vessel of a large LMFBR may be several thousands

[38]Richard E. Webb in *Liquid Metal Fast Breeder Reactor (LMFBR) Demonstration Plant,* Hearings before the Joint Committee on Atomic Energy of the U.S. Congress, 92 Cong. 2 sess. (Sept. 7, 8, 12, 1972), p. 180. These questions merit examination in more detail. In this regard the reader is urged to review the statement by Dr. Richard Webb, cited above, and an AEC Staff Review of Webb's statement. Portions of these statements pertaining to the questions addressed here are reproduced in Appendix G of this report. Dr. Webb had extensive training in nuclear reactor operations before receiving his Ph.D. in Nuclear Engineering at Ohio State University. His dissertation concerned the explosive potential of LMFBRs. Webb has prepared a response to the AEC Staff Review of his statement.

[39]*FFTF Preliminary Safety Analysis Report,* Westinghouse Hanford Company (Sept. 1970).

of Mw-sec or only a few tens of Mw-sec.[40] One arrives at the higher value, several thousands of Mw-sec, by compounding conservative assumptions regarding the numerous factors involved. The lower value, a few tens of Mw-sec, is an estimate of the AEC Division of Reactor Development and Technology (DRDT).

A value of 150 Mw-sec of available work energy was originally selected as a basis for the containment design of the FFTF, a 400-Mw(t) liquid metal fast reactor.[41] This value was based on the conservative assumption of instantaneous fragmentation and uniform dispersal of molten fuel in the sodium coolant and a thermal energy conversion efficiency of about 5 percent. The AEC's DRDT now suggests that 150 Mw-sec is conservative by about two orders of magnitude, on the basis of their interpretation of the limited TREAT data (and perhaps belief in theories suggesting that large-scale coherent vapor explosions are not possible),[42] and the belief that the locations, sequence, and time histories of local fault developments are predictable. A summary of the safety analyses supporting this thesis is presented in "Fast Flux Test Facility Design Safety Assessment," prepared by Hanford Engineering Development Laboratory (HEDL) for AEC-DRDT.[43]

The AEC's Directorate of Licensing (DL) has conducted its own independent FFTF safety analyses and reviewed DRDT-HEDL's evaluation of FFTF hypothetical DBAs. The Directorate's results are presented in the AEC's *Safety Evaluation of the Fast Flux Test Facility*. On the basis of independent analyses, based primarily on the same analytical tools and accident modes used by DRDT for the analysis presented in the *FFTF PSAR*, but using more conservative assumptions, DL concluded:

... it appears possible that an appropriately conservative maximum theoretical work energy estimate [for the FFTF] might be somewhat higher than 150 Mw-sec. It can be concluded, however, that it will be less

---

[40]Mw-sec = megawatt-second, or megajoule. The energy released by exploding one pound of TNT is approximately two Mw-sec.

[41]*FFTF Preliminary Safety Analysis Report*. (Hereafter referred to as PSAR.) The 400-Mw(t) FFTF would be equivalent to a 160-Mw LMFBR designed for electrical power production. Recall, the LMFBR demonstration plant is 300-Mw to 400-Mw and the smallest LMFBR unit size assumed in the 1970 Analysis is 1500-Mw (∿3800-Mw(t)). The plutonium content of the reactor cores of the FFTF, the LMFBR demonstration plant, and a 1000-Mw LMFBR (AI design) will be roughly 540 kg, 970 kg, and 2300 kg, respectively.

[42]H. K. Fauske, "The Role of Nucleation in Vapor Explosions."

[43]HEDL-TME 72-92, July 1972.

than 500 Mw-sec with an estimated value of about 300 Mw-sec. This lower value is based on our preliminary evaluation of the effects of analytical refinements to the early models to account for incoherence in sodium voiding and fuel motion, and molten fuel-coolant mixing dynamics. These refinements, of course, are not as extensive as those being made in DRDT's new models. . . .[44]

With respect to the new models, DL concluded,

. . . the more recent [DRDT] models require further development and experimental verification in a number of respects before final conclusions are reached through their use.[45]

The significance of the uncertainties in the more important input variables (and assumptions) used in LMFBR safety analyses and the variation in assumptions used in estimating the explosive potential of LMFBRs should become more apparent in the following discussions of LMFBR containment designs and the potential for fuel and fission product release.

A hypothetical release of energy in the core would cause a pressure loading on the surrounding structures and also could cause a slug of sodium overlying the reactor core to be accelerated upward. Should this occur, not all of the available work energy would be imparted to the sodium slug. In the *FFTF PSAR* it was estimated that the sodium slug received 30 of the 150 Mw-sec of kinetic energy available.[46] The sodium slug could impact the reactor vessel cover, resulting in a lift of the head and the absorption of energy by strain in the holddown bolts and a small radial strain in the upper part of the reactor vessel.[47]

There are two ways to view the containment problem. The first is with respect to complete failure of both the reactor vessel and its concrete enclosure. This is not very likely since the reactors are now designed so that work energies equivalent to a few hundred pounds of TNT will be absorbed by strain in vessel head holddown bolts and by radial strain in the vessel itself. The containments of two of the 1000-Mw LMFBR follow-on designs were intended to withstand an available work energy up to 1000 Mw-sec and 2000 Mw-sec. The latter is equivalent to 1000 lbs of TNT. It has been noted that an accidental "hypothetical" energy release

[44]U.S. AEC, *Safety Evaluation of the FFTR*, p. 100.
[45]Ibid., p. 95.
[46]HEDL, "FFTF Design Safety Assessment," p. 3.4-7.
[47]Ibid., p. 1-23.

equivalent to the detonation of 1000 lbs of TNT in a sodium-filled reactor would propel a 143-ton shield plug 100 feet above its rest position, with only 2 percent of the TNT blast energy imparted to the plug.[48] From discussions in Chapter 2 (section on reactor performance data), it may be recalled that the GE follow-on LMFBR design, the basic LMFBR design in the 1970 Analysis, could not contain its estimated maximum explosive potential; rather, accidents of this type would have to be shown to be "incredible" by further development work.

The second way to view the containment problem is with respect to the probability of fuel and fission product leakage, which may occur in the absence of complete failure. The extent of the leakage as a function of available work energy for large commercial-size LMFBRs is unknown. There is considerable uncertainty even for the smaller FFTF.

It has been calculated that the 150 Mw-sec accident would lift the FFTF reactor vessel head 5 inches, which is below the expected 10-inch strain capability of the holddown bolts.[49] Under these circumstances the *FFTF PSAR* assumed that all containment vessel seals (around control rod drives, the vessel head, etc.) remain intact. However, in the energy range from 350 Mw-sec to 500 Mw-sec, DL expects major seals for the FFTF reactor vessel to be lost.[50]

As stated earlier (Chapter 2), there are significant uncertainties in the plutonium and fission product transport from the reactor vessel to the environment. Not only are there uncertainties related to the work energy available from a core disruptive accident, as discussed above, but there are also uncertainties about the following:

1. The motion and fate of sodium-fuel vapor bubbles which may be formed in a severe nuclear disassembly accident.

2. Various fuel and fission product depletion and removal mechanisms within the reactor vessel.

3. The integrity of welds, vessel head closure seals, and seals about control rods and other vessel penetrations, as a

[48]N.J.M. Rees, "Structural Model Experiments to Evaluate the Explosion Containment Potential," in U.K. Atomic Energy Authority, *An Appreciation of Fast Reactor Safety*, NP-18487 (1970), Ch. 5, p. C.5.2. Here it is assumed that the shield plug is not bolted down.

[49]HEDL, "FFTF Design Safety Assessment," pp. 3.4-5 to 3.4-7.

[50]U.S. AEC, *Safety Evaluation of the FFTF*, p. 107.

function of available work energy and shock front movement during the disassembly accident.

4. Sodium vapor-fuel aerosol leakage paths through the broken seals, as a function of aerosol particle size.

5. Aerosol leakage, fallout, plateout, settling, agglomeration during transport from the reactor vessel cavity to the secondary containment building and to the environment, as a function of time and reactor cavity and containment temperature and pressure.

The combined effect of these and related uncertainties implies uncertainties of at least two orders of magnitude in the plutonium leakage fraction under hypothetical accident conditions. Is the potential plutonium release fraction from the reactor vessel to the containment building 10^{-4}, as suggested by DRDT's radiological evaluation[51], and discussed below, or is it one, two, or more orders of magnitude greater?

In the radiological evaluation of a hypothetical core-disruptive accident for the 400-Mw(t) FFTF, AEC's DRDT assumed that, in addition to the noble gases and 1 percent fission products, 0.1 kilograms of plutonium are released from the reactor vessel.[52] The 100 g of plutonium (actually PuO_2) correspond approximately to 1.6×10^{-4} of the FFTF plutonium inventory.[53]

As of mid-1972, detail models had not yet been developed by AEC's DRDT to determine what release fractions to use in the analysis of radiological consequences of FFTF hypothetical DBAs.[54] In selecting the release fractions, however, consideration was given to the fact that sodium is more active chemically. Therefore, all other things being equal, it should retain more fuel and fission products debris than other coolants.

AEC's DL also evaluated the potential radiological consequences of FFTF hypothetical DBAs. This AEC division ". . . selected 100

---

[51]HEDL, "FFTF Design Safety Assessment," pp. 3.6-1 to 3.6-11.

[52]Ibid., p. 3.6-3.

[53]While the above release fractions are somewhat arbitrary and should be viewed as reference values for containment design and assessment purposes, AEC guidelines (10 CFR 100) require that: "This fission product release assumed for these calculations should be based upon a major accident, hypothesized for purposes of site analysis or postulated from considerations of possible accidental events, that would result in potential hazards not exceeded by those from any accident considered credible" (see 10 CFR 100.11 [a], footnote 1).

[54]HEDL, "FFTF Design Safety Assessment," p. 3.6-1.

TABLE 23.   Radiological Consequences of Hypothetical Core
Disassembly Accidents for FFTF

(30-day exposure at 4.5 miles, rem^a)

(a) AEC–DRDT Results

Body organ dose	Guideline values^b	Case 1^c	Case 2^d
Whole body (total)	25	0.007	0.025
Thyroid (total)	300	0.04	0.31
Lung^e	75	0.035	0.5
Bone^e	150	0.014	0.2

(b) AEC–DL Results

	Single containment^f	Double containment^g
Whole body	0.9	0.03
Thyroid dose^h	54	0.6—1.6
Bone^i	197	1.8—10

SOURCE: Part (a): "Fast Flux Test Facility Design Safety Assessment," HEDL-
TME 72-92 (July 1972), prepared by Hanford Engineering Development Laboratory
for the AEC, p. 3.6–6.

Part (b): U.S. AEC, Directorate of Licensing, *Safety Evaluation of the Fast
Flux Test Facility,* Project No. 448 (Oct. 31, 1972), p. 111.

^{a}Rem is the unit of dose equivalent (or simply "dose"). One rem is the quantity
of radiation that is equivalent—in biological damage of a specific sort—to one rad
of X rays at a given energy. A rad is a unit of absorbed dose equal to 100 ergs
per gram. It is a measure of the energy imparted to matter by radiation per unit
mass of irradiated material at the place of interest. See discussion in text.

^{b}The guideline values for whole body and thyroid dose represent specific criteria,
adopted by the AEC in 10 CFR 100.11(a), for purpose of evaluating sites for nuclear
reactors, establishing site boundaries, and preparing safety analysis reports. The
guideline values given for lung and bone doses are values currently being used by
the AEC staff for FFTF evaluation in the absence of any established AEC criteria
(see discussion in text).

^{c}Case 1 assumes the reactor head seals are effective in delaying release of fission
products and sodium-fuel aerosol from the reactor and the processes of agglomeration, and fallout would be an effective force for minimizing releases to the outer
containment. A leak rate corresponding to 1000 vol % per day at 35 psig is assumed.
See HEDL, "FFTF Design Safety Assessment," pp. 3.6-3 and 3.6-4.

^{d}Case 2 assumes fission gases and fuel-sodium aerosols pass through the seals,
without depletion, into the containment atmosphere. See HEDL, "FFTF Design
Safety Assessment," p. 3.6-4. Halogen, solid fission product, and fuel fallout occur
as shown for no-sodium case in Figure 3.6-2 of source for Part (a) above.

^{e}Plutonium exposure calculated from model of ICRP Task Group on Lung
Dynamics. See "Deposition and Retention Models for Internal Dosimetry of the
Human Respiratory Tract," *Health Physics Journal,* Vol. 12, No. 2 (Feb. 1966).

^{f}The single containment model assumes that the head cavity region is not sealed
and inerted and that the head lifts and gross venting of sodium and core material
occurs through the head cavity region into the reactor containment building. See
U.S. AEC, *Safety Evaluation of the FFTF,* p. 109.

(Notes to Table 23 continued)

[g]The double containment model assumes that either the seals between the reactor vessel and the head cavity region remain functional or that the reactor head seals fail but that the head cavity region is sealed and inerted. See U.S. AEC, *Safety Evaluation of the FFTF*, p. 109.

[h]Assumes 25% of I_2 inventory released in aerosol form.

[i]Assumes 25 kg of fuel initially available for leakage as an aerosol.

kg as a reasonable estimate of the mass of fuel that could be vaporized and theoretically be available for transport from the reactor. The arbitrary and conservative assumption is made that 25 percent of this vaporized fuel could be transported out of the reactor vessel in a form that could produce an aerosol in the containment space."[55] The 25 kg of PuO_2-UO_2 corresponds to a plutonium release fraction of 10^{-2} (1 percent). This is approximately two orders of magnitude greater than the release fraction assumed by DRDT. By the same token, DL's iodine release fraction is about 25 times higher than DRDT's.

There have been no scale model experimental tests, or even detailed analytic models, to determine leakage rates as a function of available work energy for large LMFBRs.

Doses to a hypothetical person downwind at the FFTF site boundary, about 4.5 miles distant,[56] were calculated both by DRDT and DL. The DRDT results are presented in part (a) of Table 23. The DL dose calculations for thirty-day exposure at the site boundary are shown in Table 23(b). For all practical purposes the DL and DRDT fuel and fission product transport models are equivalent. Comparing the two, DL found that relatively small differences were due to meteorological and aerosol assumptions, and concluded, ". . . the major differences in the radiological dose calculations are the assumed quantity of radioisotopes released and the use of single containment versus a double containment."[57]

With respect to the radiological consequences of FFTF hypothetical core disassembly accidents, it is interesting that AEC's DRDT

[55]U.S. AEC, *Safety Evaluation of the FFTF*, pp. 115-16.

[56]The FFTF site boundary is the boundary of the AEC's Hanford reservation on which the FFTF is located. Typically, sites for commercial nuclear plants are several hundred acres, with boundaries less than a mile distant.

[57]U.S. AEC, *Safety Evaluation of the FFTF*, p. 113.

notes, "... the calculated doses [in Table 23(a)] from each con-
tributor are virtually insignificant in comparison with guideline
values,"[58] and concludes:

The evaluation ... indicates that exposure to the general public under
HCDA [hypothetical core disassembly accident] considerations are a small
fraction of the accepted site guideline values and that adequate protection
is being provided in the plant design for the protection of health and safety
of the public.[59]

Whereas AEC's DL concludes:

... that potential offsite doses from HCDA's would be well within 10 CFR
Part 100 guidelines if it can be demonstrated that gross ejection of core
materials into the head cavity cell cannot occur. If this cannot be demonstrated, there may be a potential for exceeding guideline doses. This potential could be removed by sealing and inerting the head cavity region or
possibly by making other changes in the design. It may also be possible
to show through the use of improved information and behavior of aerosols
that potential doses would be within guideline values with no alterations
in the design.[60]

In Table 23, the orders-of-magnitude differences among the
respective off-site dose calculations are a measure of the sensitivity
of the dose estimates to assumptions related to seal conditions and
fuel and fission product release fractions and removal mechanisms
during transport. These data also suggest that, in terms of
absorbed radiation doses to critical organs of persons immediately
downwind, the release of between 1 percent and 10 percent of the
plutonium inventory (a release fraction between 10^{-1} and 10^{-2}) is
equivalent to the release of all the halogens and noble gases.[61] This
would also roughly be the case for commercial-size LMFBRs.[62]
LMFBRs have noble gas and halogen fission product inventories
comparable to LWRs. Recall that the severe LWR accident discussed by Farmer involved the release of 10 percent of the gaseous
and volatile fission product inventory (e.g., noble gases and
halogens) from a 1500-Mw(t) reactor, almost four times as large

---

[58]HEDL, "FFTF Design Safety Assessment," p. 3.6-6. See footnote 2, Table 23
for discussion of "guideline values."

[59]Ibid., p. 3.6-10.

[60]U.S. AEC, *Safety Evaluation of the FFTF*, pp. 117-18.

[61]The reader should be cautioned that the biological significance of a given
absorbed dose depends on the critical organ. The biological significance of
plutonium doses to critical organs is discussed in a later section of this chapter.

[62]The "equivalent" plutonium release fraction is probably less for smaller site
boundary distances.

as the FFTF but less than one-half the size of a 1000-Mw LMFBR. A plutonium release fraction on the order of 10^{-2} for the LMFBR demonstration plant and commercial-size LMFBRs can lead to radiation doses to the lung and skeleton of an individual at typical commercial-reactor site boundary distances that exceed dose level guidelines now used by the AEC staff in the FFTF safety analyses.[63]

The AEC (DRDT and DL) analyses of the radiological consequences of FFTF hypothetical core disassembly accidents are based on the explosive potential of the two hypothetical accidents which they examined, neither of which considers the possibility of complete failure of the FFTF containment systems. To the extent that not all possible autocatalytic (fuel motion) effects have been included, as Webb maintains, the explosive potential could be even higher than the DL analysis suggests. Core vaporization with complete failure of the containment can lead to plutonium release fractions much higher than 1 or 2 percent.

6. Biological significance of plutonium radiation dose— Plutonium is one of the deadliest substances known to man. As noted by the International Commission on Radiological Protection (ICRP), "in terms of amount available, projected usage, extent of anticipated accidental human exposure, and radiotoxicity, plutonium is the most formidable radionuclide in the periodic table.[64] The available useful data on human exposure to plutonium is meager. It consists primarily of accidental occupational exposures of twenty-seven persons during the early years of nuclear weapons programs. These persons accumulated plutonium burdens from 0.007 to 0.09 microcuries (μCi). Twelve of the twenty-seven had body burdens of 0.035 μCi or greater.[65] Most of these persons are still alive and none has shown symptoms or signs of radiation injury. However, because of the relatively small numbers of individuals, the relatively low level of their body burdens, and the short span of time compared with a seventy-year lifetime, direct information on the toxicity of plutonium is avail-

[63]See footnote 2, Table 23.

[64]ICRP, "The Metabolism of Compounds of Plutonium and Other Actinides," Publication 19 (May 1972), p. 1.

[65]Harsharay G. Gayankar, "Risks and Emergency Radiation Doses from Plutonium Dioxide Exposures," Ph.D. dissertation, University of California (June 1972), p. 55.

able only from animal studies, principally rats and dogs.[66] Indirect information is obtained by comparing plutonium-239 (and other plutonium isotopes) with radium-226 (and daughter products), both being radionuclides which emit highly energetic alpha particles.[67]

Early assessments of radiation dose to the critical organs were based on the assumption that lung-deposited plutonium would enter the circulatory system and redeposition would occur in the skeleton (90 percent) with a minor fraction (7 percent) in the liver.[68] More recent data based on dog studies make it clear that the fraction of inhaled plutonium (PuO_2) going to the liver has been severely underestimated, and concentrations in the lung can be greater or less than that in the liver.[69] The most sensitive organ is now generally taken to be the lung. Summarizing some of the specific concerns here, it is noted that: (1) under a number of probable circumstances plutonium forms aerosols; (2) the physical character of these aerosols is such that on inhalation by humans they are preferentially deposited in the deep respiratory tissue; (3) because of slow clearance and because of the insolubility of the aerosol, particles deposited in this tissue may experience long residence times (hundreds of days); (4) an appreciable mass fraction of the aerosol is associated with particles sufficiently large that significant volumes of lung tissue[70] will be exposed to intense

[66]From the limited human exposure experience, it appears that, in the distribution and retention of inhaled plutonium, humans behave more like dogs than rats (ICRP Publication 19, p. 5).

[67]Alpha particles (helium nuclei) emitted by radionuclides have ranges in tissue that are generally less than 50 microns, not enough to penetrate the skin. Here, the absorbed radiation doses that are of principal concern are from radionuclides that have been ingested, inhaled, or that enter through wounds. There are several categories of persons who have received significant internal burdens of radium. The most notable group were the radium dial painters, who, in the 1920s, licked their brushes as they painted numerals on watches, clocks, and instruments. Many of these people died with symptoms of radiation poisoning. This indirect information is of limited usefulness in assessing the health risk due to the inhalation of insoluble aerosols forming long-lived alpha-emitters, such as plutonium.

[68]Chapter 7 of early draft version of B. R. Fish et al., "Calculation of Doses Due to Accidental Released Plutonium from an LMFBR," ORNL-NSIC-74 (Nov. 1972), p. 126. This chapter was deleted from the final version at the direction of AEC-DRDT because it was judged to be not directly applicable to the objective of the study, and the information base from which it was developed was already available in other documents. The deletion of the chapter was not due to the quality of the work.

[69]Furthermore, equating maximum permissible body burdens, that is, equivalent to 0.1μ Ci of radium-226, implies that plutonium-239 is about five times as damaging as radium-226 per rad delivered to the total skeleton.

[70]Volumes equal to or greater than one alveolus (an air cell in the lung).

radiation exposure (greater than 1000 rem) within a meaningful physiological time.

Assessments of biological risk from plutonium (PuO_2) inhalation are extremely uncertain for several reasons: (a) deposition and retention in the lung are dependent on aerodynamic parameters of the plutonium aerosol; (b) the partition of insoluble plutonium into body organs is a complex process which is highly dependent on numerous physical, chemical, and biological factors; (c) radiation dose due to the action of intense point source alpha irradiation is not uniform; (d) uncertainties in the radiobiological information on PuO_2, such as the biological half-life of PuO_2 and modifying factors for calculating dose equivalent in rems, e.g., quality factors and dose distribution factors; (e) there is a lack of meaningful experimental data involving humans.

Current assessments of the lung cancer risk from plutonium (PuO_2) inhalation are made by first estimating the lung cancer response in dogs and then "extrapolating" these data to humans. It requires pathological optimism to find reassurance in the resulting estimates.

First, there is a paucity of data available for estimating the lung cancer risk in dogs.[71] Figure 21 summarizes the available survival data for exposed dogs (about sixty-five in number).[72] Presented in this manner these data suggest that initial depositions of less than about 1 nCi/g[73] of lung would not reduce the lifetime of the dog (normally about fifteen years). However, an exclusive interpretation of this crude correlation to mean a practical threshold of burden would be incorrect. At nine years after exposure the lung cancer response was virtually saturated, and some dogs had evidence of multiple tumor origins. The range of exposures (0.2 to 3.3 μCi or 3 to 45 nCi/g of lung tissue) may be interpreted as a region of saturated response, that is, a burden regime in which cancer induction in the dog population approaches 100 percent during normal life span. The time to death may be related to the burden through population depletion rather than through the latent

[71]Summarized in ICRP, Publication 19.

[72]J. F. Park, W. J. Blair, and R. H. Busch, "Progress in Beagle Dog Studies with Transuranium Elements," Health Physics, Vol. 22, No. 6 (June 1972), p. 805.

[73]A nanocurie (nCi) is 10^{-9} curies (one-billionth of a curie). The 1 nCi/g is the $^{239}PuO_2$ concentration in the bloodless mass of the lung.

FIGURE 21. Relationship Between the Quantity of $^{239}PuO_2$ Deposited and Survival Time of Dogs with Pulmonary Neoplasia and/or Pulmonary Fibrosis, Compared with Dogs that Showed Pulmonary Neoplasia

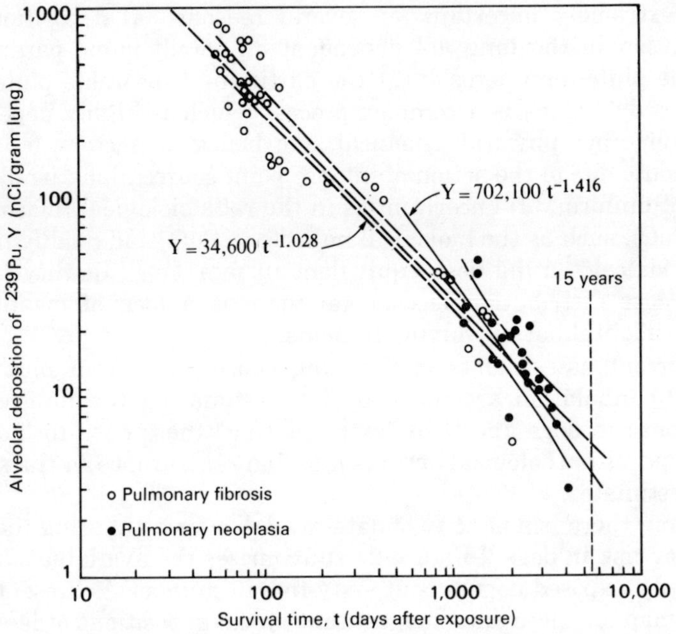

SOURCE: J.F. Park, W.J. Bair, and R.H. Busch, "Progress in Beagle Dog Studies with Transurmission Elements," *Health Physics*, Vol. 22, No. 6 (June 1972), p. 805.

period. In the former case, appreciable cancer incidence would be anticipated at lower lung burdens.[74]

To appreciate this possibility, recall that plutonium particles deposited in the lung irradiate small volumes of lung tissue at high dose rates. Many of the cells immediately surrounding these "hot spots" either are killed or are mitotically sterilized. Studies of the effects of intense local radiation on tissue suggest that an enhanced carcinogenic potential may exist, in the sense that energy dissipated in a limited volume may be far more carcinogenic than

[74]Letter from Donald P. Geesaman to Dr. Stanley M. Greenfield, July 8, 1971 (subject: AEC's Draft Environmental Statement, Rocky Flats Plant Plutonium Recovery Facility).

if the same radiation were to dissipate its energy over a larger volume.[75] The question is, then, whether larger particulates in a plutonium aerosol lead to associated alveolar exposures that have enhanced carcinogenic potential. If they do, then a correlation observed between initial burden and time to cancer death (Figure 21) cannot be used to infer the limit burden for no lifeshortening. Depending on the particle size distribution, appreciable cancer incidence could occur at initial lung depositions one or more orders of magnitude below the 1 nCi/g cited above.[76] If any threshold is relevant, it is not the dose threshold, since local exposures are large, but rather a structural or volumetric threshold that must be exceeded by the physical extent of the exposure.[77]

Efforts to predict potential carcinogenic effects in man from the dog studies involve making one or more assumptions relating the dose response from one species to the other. For example, one can assume that the induction of pulmonary tumors at low doses is related to plutonium concentration in tissue, total plutonium burden in the organ, the absolute number of irradiated foci in the lung (i.e., the number of plutonium aerosol particles), the number of cells at risk, or some combination of these (e.g., the number and size distribution of the plutonium aerosol particles). There are three models—threshold, dose rate, and life span—discussed in the literature, which are based on the assumption that a given concentration (μCi/g) of plutonium in the lung of a dog is biologically equivalent to the same concentration in the lung of man. The threshold model is generally not used because of the lack of evidence of a practical threshold for radiogenic cancer in humans. The dose-rate model assumes that the risk in man and dog is linearly proportional to the dose rates averaged over long exposure times. The life-span model assumes the susceptibility to cancer induction and the latent period for cancer induction relative to life span are the same for various mammalian species.

The choice of the assumptions, or model, used to predict, from observing dogs, the potential lung tumor risk in man is almost

[75]Donald P. Geesaman, "An Analysis of the Carcinogenic Risk from an Insoluble Alpha-Emitting Aerosol Deposited in Deep Respiratory Tissue: Addendum," Lawrence Radiation Laboratory, UCRL-50387 (October 9, 1968), and "Plutonium and Public Health," in *Underground Uses of Nuclear Energy*, Part 2, Hearings before the Subcommittee on Air and Water Pollution of the Committee on Public Works, United States Senate, 91 Cong. 2 sess. (August 5, 1970), p. 1524.

[76]UCRL-50387, pp. 6-7.

[77]Donald P. Geesaman letter to Stanley M. Greenfield, July 8, 1971.

completely arbitrary at this time. This is because the mechanisms by which ionizing radiation interacts with biological material and the mechanisms of disease end points caused by radiation (e.g., lung cancer) are not understood, and because mortality profiles are known to be species-specific. With this in mind, it is nevertheless useful to make estimates of the human health risk and to note their uncertainties.

On the basis of the dog experiments, Thompson et al., suggested 50 percent lung tumor incidence in beagles for 5 nCi/g initial concentration of plutonium in the lung.[78] Using this estimate together with the dose-rate model and a linear nonthreshold extrapolation of dose versus effect to low doses, the corresponding estimate for the human lung tumor risk is 0.2 per person per μCi of initial lung deposit.[79] With the alternate assumption, that the tumor risk is a function of the number of irradiated foci and the particle size distribution, Geesaman and others have noted that the lung tumor risk may be one or more orders of magnitude greater than the above estimate.[80]

These results give a rough measure of the health risk associated with plutonium releases to the environment and the uncertainty in this estimate. Considering that a 1000-Mw LMFBR (AI design) would contain roughly 2490 kg, or 1.5×10^{11} μCi, of plutonium-239, and the lung tumor risk is estimated to be 0.2 per person per μCi of initial lung deposit—a risk estimate could be several orders of magnitude too low—one can appreciate the need to prevent even small releases of plutonium to the environment.

In conclusion, given the unresolved LMFBR safety issues and the order-of-magnitude uncertainties in key safety-related variables, one might question whether the LMFBR program has reached the third development phase, that is, the utility commitment phase which includes the demonstration plant program. More importantly, these unresolved safety issues raise significant questions bearing on the success of the overall LMFBR program. What

[78]R. C. Thompson, J. F. Park, and W. J. Blair, "Some Speculative Extensions to Man of Animal Risk Data on Plutonium," in *Radiobiology of Plutonium*, Betsy J. Stover and Webster S. S. Jee, eds. (The J. W. Press, University of Utah, Salt Lake City, 1972), p. 225.

[79]Gavankar, "Risks and Emergency Radiation Doses from Plutonium Dioxide Exposures," p. 64.

[80]See Geesaman, "An Analysis of the Carcinogenic Risk," UCRL-50387; Fish et al., "Calculation of Doses," Ch. 7, p. 64; and A. B. Long, "Plutonium inhalation: The burden of negligible consequence," *Nuclear News* (June 1971), pp. 69-73.

funding does the AEC's projected LMFBR budget include for safety research? The Commission has never provided the public with a laundry list of proposed budget expenditures. Are there sufficient funds to experimentally verify, under various commercial-size LMFBR operating conditions, the mathematical model and numerous assumptions that are currently the basis of LMFBR safety assessments? Assuming companies such as Westinghouse and General Electric will seek profits from previous light water reactor development efforts, can they be expected to continue to invest heavily in LMFBR safety research beyond the demonstration plant phase?

How is the public to be informed of LMFBR safety issues and the progress or lack of progress in this area? The present policy of the AEC, as expressed by Commissioner Doub in December 1971, is that "... we are determined that discussions relative to breeder safety and the impact of the breeder on the environment be conducted in the public arena."[81] It would be helpful if the Commission would state explicitly how this policy is to be implemented. It is not clear that the public, or even the Congress, is receiving a balanced view of the Commission's thinking with respect to LMFBR safety issues at this time. For example, the JCAE requested that the Commission give serious consideration to testimony by Dr. Barry Smernoff with respect to undergrounding the LMFBR demonstration plant as an alternative to the currently proposed above-ground site plan. One of the comments in the Commission's written response says in part:

> In order to clarify a statement attributed to G. L. Weil used to support his thesis that LMFBRs are more hazardous than LWRs, i.e., "... plutonium, a very small fraction of which, in the event of a reactor core meltdown or deformation, might trigger a nuclear explosion ... commonly referred to as the 'criticality accident' ... ," use of the term "explosion" is misleading. The plutonium fuel is not in a form or concentration suitable for an "explosion" in the sense of a nuclear bomb. The maximum energy release available in the form of explosive energy *would most likely be* [italics added] the equivalent of tens of pounds of TNT. Nuclear reactors, LMFBRs as well as LWRs, are designed with pressure vessels and containment vessels sufficiently strong to adequately contain the consequences of hypothesized explosive releases of that magnitude.[82]

In view of the recent assessment of the FFTF by AEC's Directorate

---

[81]"The Future of the Breeder, Its Impact on the Environment, and Its Regulatory Aspects," AEC News Release (Dec. 15, 1971), p. 8.

[82]*LMFBR Demonstration Plant,* Hearings, p. 261.

of Licensing, and the LMFBR safety issues raised by Webb,[83] the above statement appears misleading. It would perhaps be useful if the JCAE requested comments related to reactor safety issues from the AEC's Director of Regulation and outside consultants rather than relying solely on AEC comments generated by DRDT.

Safety Aspects in Support Facilities

In other areas of the fuel cycle, the safety hazards associated with LMFBR fuels appear to be greater than the safety hazards with LWR or HTGR fuels. In the AEC's LMFBR Program Plan it is acknowledged that spent LMFBR fuels will present greater potential hazards to the public than spent LWR fuels.[84] This is due principally to the hazards associated with an inadvertent release of the noble gases and radioiodine in accidents involving the shipment of spent fuel after the short thirty-day cooling time (discussed earlier). The shorter cooling time also forces more stringent requirements at the fuel reprocessing plant, due to routine releases of the short-lived noble gases and iodines.

It is difficult to compare the seriousness of inadvertent criticality accidents, fires, etc., at fuel reprocessing and fabrication plants without a knowledge of the specific plant designs, equipment, processes, etc. Nevertheless, it is useful to examine an ORNL staff calculation of the additional radiation doses that would result from a "unit" nuclear excursion.[85] The calculations were based on the release of one kilogram of LWR or mixed LMFBR fuel from a 100-m stack under representative meteorological conditions. The results are reproduced in Table 24. For the purposes here, the absolute magnitudes of the numbers are unimportant. The ratios of the doses from the LWR fuel excursion to the comparable LMFBR fuel excursion roughly measure the relative severity of the corresponding releases. These data suggest that the LMFBR fuel accidents would be three to four times more hazardous than similar accidents involving LWR fuel, although one must keep in mind that the design of the plant and its equipment, and the processes performed on the materials, are also important in determining accident potential, as is the quantity of radioactivity in the material being reprocessed.

[83]*LMFBR Demonstration Plant*, Hearings.
[84]U.S. AEC, *LMFBR Program Plan*, Vol. 8, WASH 1108 (Nov. 1968) p. 8-39.
[85]U.S. AEC, *Siting of Fuel Reprocessing Plants*, ORNL-4451 (July 1971), p. 8-68.

TABLE 24. Summary of Maximum Inhalation Dose Commitments at 400 m Downwind Following the Release of 1 kg of LWR or Mixed LMFBR Fuel from a 100-m Stack

(rems)

	Whole body	Bone	Lungs	Liver	Thyroid
LWR fuel — first-year dose commitment					
Volatile fission products	0.00000039	—	0.000018	—	0.0000136
Semivolatile fission products	0.0695	0.0898	2.56	0.120	0.000303
Nonvolatile fission products	0.242	3.74	4.83	1.38	—
Plutonium	0.129	5.78	1.48	0.552	—
Transplutonic elements	0.215	3.22	3.17	3.37	—
Total	0.655	12.8	12.0	5.42	0.000318
LWR fuel — lifetime dose commitment					
Volatile fission products	0.00000039	—	0.0000317	—	0.0000136
Semivolatile fission products	0.0709	0.0983	2.76	0.126	0.000304
Nonvolatile fission products	0.839	13.7	5.13	1.64	—
Plutonium	3.51	151	2.94	16.0	—
Transplutonic elements	1.12	18.3	3.33	9.67	—
Total	5.54	183	14.2	27.4	0.000318
LMFBR core-blanket fuel — first-year dose commitment					
Volatile fission products	0.00156	—	0.0123	—	0.872
Semivolatile fission products	0.0194	0.169	6.98	0.0578	0.00621
Nonvolatile fission products	0.610	8.29	10.4	2.68	—
Plutonium	0.672	30.1	7.68	2.87	—
Transplutonic elements	0.791	11.8	11.7	12.3	—
Total	2.09	50.4	36.8	17.9	0.879
LMFBR core-blanket fuel — lifetime dose commitment					
Volatile fission products	0.00156	—	0.0123	—	0.873
Semivolatile fission products	0.0480	0.174	7.40	0.0604	0.00621
Nonvolatile fission products	1.01	15.4	10.9	3.14	—
Plutonium	18.6	806	15.3	85.0	—
Transplutonic elements	2.24	34.6	12.0	22.1	—
Total	21.9	856	45.6	110	0.879

SOURCE: U.S. AEC, *Siting of Fuel Reprocessing Plants and Waste Management Facilities* (compiled and edited by the staff of the Oak Ridge National Laboratory), ORNL-4451 (July 1971), p. 8–77.

The AEC has maintained that these calculations are not as pertinent to reactor accidents as implied; it claims that the comparison is invalid, since the calculated doses are strongly dependent on decay times.[86] The 150-day LWR decay time was chosen to be representative of current technology, whereas the 30-day LMFBR assumption was based on an objective of the development program.

The AEC, however, was not entirely correct.[87] In Table 24, the largest contributions to the lifetime doses to the body, bone, liver, and, to a lesser extent, the lung are from the plutonium and transplutonic elements. The differences in cooling times have little influence on comparisons in those columns. For equal energy generation, there is only about 25 percent less FBR fuel processed than LWR fuel. If one ignores the thyroid dose, where cooling time is the controlling factor; the FBR fuel release is still three to four times more hazardous. The increase in the hazard is principally a reflection of the increase in the content of plutonium and transplutonic elements.

The comparison here is also useful for other areas of the fuel cycle. If, for example, one considers sabotage or warfare, where power plants are prime targets, it seems reasonable to consider hypothetical accidents in which a major fraction of the fuel and fission product inventory is released. Kilogram for kilogram, the LMFBR fuel would constitute a greater hazard, due principally to the larger plutonium fraction. But here again, other factors such as plant design might be controlling.

ASPECTS OF A PLUTONIUM ECONOMY

Adequacy of Radiation Standards

In the standards for radiation protection established by the AEC to regulate occupational exposures for radioactive material (10 CFR 20), the maximum permissible concentration in the air of insoluble plutonium-239 is 4×10^{-11} per μ Ci/cc. The correspond-

---

[86]This statement was made in response to a similar analysis by Dr. Barry J. Smernoff, Hudson Institute, New York, at *LMFBR Demonstration Plant*, Hearings, p. 134.

[87]It is also misleading, in that the thirty-day cooling period for LMFBR spent fuel was used in the 1970 Analysis for economic justification of the LMFBR program.

ing maximum permissible lung burden is 0.016 μCi of plutonium.[88]
The ICRP established the maximum permissible lung burden
by equilibrating the exposure from the deposited radioactive
aerosol with that of an acceptable uniform dose of X rays. The difficulty with this procedure is that plutonium inhalation represents
a very special case of the low exposure problem, a case that is
peculiar to insoluble, aerosol-forming, long-lived alpha emitters.
As such, the ICRP recognizes that the maximum permissible lung
burden for plutonium may be greatly in error, specifically
". . . there is no clear evidence to show whether, with a given mean
absorbed dose, the biological risk associated with a nonhomogeneous distribution is greater or less than the risk resulting
from a more diffuse distribution of that dose in the lung."[89] As
Geesaman has noted, "they are effectively saying that there is no
guidance as to the risk for nonhomogeneous exposure in the lung,
hence the maximum permissible lung burden is meaningless for
plutonium particles, as are the maximum permissible air concentrations which derive from it."[90]

The AEC, on the other hand, takes the position that the lowest
dog exposure—3 nCi/g of blood-free lung—represents about 100
times this maximum permissible lung burden.[91] It claims, first,
that "extrapolation of the results of the [dog] studies to man supports the adequacy of the present occupational exposure limits";[92]
and second, ". . . the present standards are believed to afford pro-

---

[88]The AEC radiation standards (and guidelines) are based on recommendations
of national and international radiation protection organizations, i.e., ICRP and
National Council on Radiation Protection and Measurements (NCRP), and the regulations of the Federal Radiation Council (FRC). This maximum permissible commitment for insoluble plutonium-239 (together with others) was recommended by
the ICRP and NCRP in 1959. It has subsequently been reviewed and remains the
accepted limit [A. B. Long, *Nuclear News* (June 1971), p. 69]. It should be noted,
however, that the ICRP recommended the use of the maximum permissible concentrations for planning purposes to insure that the recommended maximum permissible doses would not be exceeded, and in this sense they serve as secondary ICRP
guidelines. Also, on the basis that bone was the critical organ, the ICRP recommended a maximum permissible body burden of 0.04 μCi (0.65 micrograms) of
plutonium-239 for occupationally exposed persons.

[89]ICRP Publication 9, *Radiation Protection* (Pergamon Press, 1966), p. 4.

[90]Donald P. Geesaman, "Plutonium and Public Health," p. 1530.

[91]U.S. AEC, *Plutonium Recovery Facility, Rocky Flats Plant, Colorado, Environmental Statement*, WASH 1507 (January 1972), p. 23. The blood-free lung of a standard man has a mass of 500 g.

[92]U.S. AEC, *Liquid Metal Fast Breeder Reactor Demonstration Plant Environmental Statement*, WASH 1509 (April 1972), p. 101.

tective conservatism. . . ."[93] This view is not supported by the analyses of Geesaman, Fish et al., and Long, as indicated in the previous section. The discussions of plutonium toxicity in the environmental impact statements prepared by the AEC make no reference to these studies or to the qualifying statements of the ICRP and NCRP. What are presented instead are wholly inadequate and unrepresentative descriptions of the human risk attendant on the exposure by plutonium aerosols, with essentially no discussion of the uncertainties involved.

There are no direct statements by radiation-standards setting organizations regarding an "acceptable" exposure associated with release of radioactivity in an accident. For purposes of evaluating sites for nuclear reactors, establishing site boundaries, and preparing safety analysis reports, the AEC has adopted specific criteria (10 CFR 100). These guidelines are based on the whole body and thyroid doses and are not applicable to a plutonium release, and therefore to the LMFBR, where bone, lung, or other organ doses from plutonium inhalation at the site boundary are shown to be controlling. In LMFBR safety analysis reports, the AEC staff (in lieu of official guidance) is now using 150 rem to the bone and 75 rem to the lung as being "equivalent" to 25 rem to the whole body and 300 rem to the thyroid [see Table 24(a)]. No equivalent liver dose is given, even though the more recent dog data suggest that the liver may be the critical organ.

While there do not appear to be any clear criteria for establishing the lung and bone dose limits used by the AEC, it has been suggested that

... in the case of chronic exposure, the maximum permissible dose (MPD) to the lungs and liver amounts to three times the MPD to the total body and one-half the MPD to the thyroid; consequently, if one were to extrapolate linearly from the whole-body criterion of 25 rems or the thyroid criterion of 300 rems, comparable figures would be 75 rems or 150 rems to lungs, liver, etc., depending on which criterion is chosen for reference. Although 75 rems might appear to be the conservative, hence the "best" choice, it is doubtful that the basic extrapolation is fundamentally sound. Consequently, lung dose and liver dose criteria should be established on their own merits where feasible.[94]

Based on the suggestion of Thompson et al., that there is a 50 percent lung tumor incidence in dogs for 5 nCi/g initial concentration

---

[93]U.S. AEC, *Plutonium Recovery Facility,* WASH 1507, p. 73.
[94]Fish et al., "Calculation of Doses," Ch. 7, p. 129.

in the lung, Gavankar estimated the total tumor risk (lung, bone, and liver) as a function of aerosol size.[95] Gavankar found that on the basis of organ doses calculated (using the model of the ICRP Task Force on Lung Dynamics), and the tumor risks extrapolated to humans from long-term animal inhalation experiments, the fifty-year accumulated doses to the lung, liver, and bone of 10 rem, 25 rem, and 75 rem, respectively, can be considered to be separately risk-equivalent to the 25-rem whole body irradiation.[96] On a total risk basis, Gavankar concluded that fifty-year accumulated doses of 7 rem to the lung, 3 rem to the bone, and 7 rem to the liver can be considered risk equivalent to the 25-rem whole-body exposure.[97] On the basis of Gavankar's work, the dose limits now used by the AEC staff (150 rem to bone and 75 rem to the lung), appear high by a factor of 50 and 10, respectively. Gavankar's numbers are based on the lung tumor risk in dogs suggested by Thompson et al.[98] If Geesaman's analysis is correct, that is, if the lung tumor risk is more a function of particle size and number, the lung dose limits now used by the AEC staff may be high by an additional one or more orders of magnitude.

Aside from the safety implication, the continued use of the higher bone and lung dose limits for establishing site boundaries could be viewed as favoritism toward fast reactors.

Health Hazards of the Plutonium Economy

Historically, the memberships of the ICRP, NCRP, and other radiation-standard setting organizations were derived largely from

[95]Gavankar found that the total tumor risk per person per μCi of inhaled $^{239}PuO_2$ decreased from 0.1 to 0.03 as the aerosol size increased from 0.05μ to 3.0μ AMAD. Gavankar, "Risks and Emergency Radiation Doses," p. 64. AMAD stands for activity median aerodynamic diameter. For the typical AMAD value of 0.5μ, the total tumor risk calculated by Gavankar was 0.05 per μCi per person, or about 3 × 10^{-3} per person per μg of $^{239}PuO_2$. See ibid., p. 70.

[96]Ibid., p. 75.

[97]Ibid., p. 69. Gavankar calculated that for monosized aerosols having activity median aerodynamic diameters ranging from 0.05 to 3.0μ, 10 nCi to 36 nCi [i.e., 0.2μg to 1μg] of inhaled $^{239}PuO_2$ is risk equivalent to 25 rem whole body radiation (ibid., p. 75). Twenty-five rem whole body dose is roughly four times the average fifty-year cumulative whole body dose from natural background radiation. On the basis of risk estimates in ICRP Publication 8, Gavankar used 40 × 10^{-6} per person per rad (rem) (10^{-3} per person per 25 rem whole-body radiation) as the total cancer (including leukemia) risk from whole-body exposure (ibid., p. 62).

[98]Thompson et al., "Some Speculative Extensions to Man of Animal Risk Data on Plutonium," p. 225.

the medical profession and related fields. Their primary interests have been assessing the health risk to an individual from radiation exposure. As a result, the AEC's regulations limiting the release of radioactivity to unrestricted areas, and their reactor siting criteria, were designed to limit the radiation exposure of groups or individuals at the site boundary. The AEC's regulations and guidelines are not based on an assessment of the total health risk to all people in the biosphere for all time, due to the cumulative release of radioactivity to the environment from a facility or industry. They do not accurately reflect the cumulative health risk to thousands of generations of persons, due to the release to the environment of the more hazardous radioactive isopes with very long half-lives; e.g., plutonium-239 with a half-life of 24,000 years and iodine-129 with a half-life of 17 million years. Likewise, the data in Table 24 are based on the first-year and fifty-year lifetime dose commitments to a twenty-year-old individual after a short-term exposure to a passing cloud of radioactive material. In this section, an attempt is made to place in perspective long-term risk of plutonium release from an LMFBR economy.

The 1970 Analysis, case 3, projects 4.5×10^6 Mw of nuclear generating capacity placed in operation over the next fifty years; 3×10^6 Mw of this would be LMFBR capacity. Each 1000-Mw LMFBR (AI design) would discharge over 1500 kg of plutonium annually during most of its lifetime of approximately thirty years. In effect, the projected generating capacity would result in the recycling of at least 100 million kg of plutonium[99] (the exact amount is unimportant to the discussion).

It is virtually impossible to estimate what fraction of this amount is lost to the environment, much less its chemical nature or particle size distribution. The fraction lost will surely be less than 10^{-2} to 10^{-3}, a range chosen to represent the capability of inventorying plutonium to safeguard against diversion, and surely greater than about 10^{-9}, a value representative of routine releases through air filters at fuel reprocessing and fabrication plants. The actual loss fraction is somewhere in between, with a corresponding uncertainty of about six orders of magnitude.

To carry through the calculation arbitrarily (for reference purposes only), assume a loss fraction of 10^{-6}. The resulting plutonium

---

[99]This is more than the total plutonium produced since some fraction of the total is cycled more than once.

released to the environment, from the projected fifty-year LMFBR commitment, would be 100 kg. The actual release could be two or three orders of magnitude higher or lower. Ignore all isotopes except plutonium-239. One hundred kilograms of plutonium (assuming 60 percent Pu-239) contains 4×10^3 curies of plutonium-239.[100]

As noted previously, the cancer risk per μCi body burden of plutonium-239 is very uncertain at this time. Ignore ingestion through the food chain, etc., and consider only inhalation, and, for reference purposes only, assume the cancer risk is 0.05 per person per μCi of plutonium-239 inhaled. The risk could be several orders of magnitude greater if the tumor risk is strongly dependent on the particle size distribution.

If all the plutonium-239 released to the environment were eventually deposited in human lungs, bone, liver, etc., at least once, using the reference loss fraction (10^{-6}) and tumor risk value above, it would produce on the order of 10^8 cancers. The number could be three or more orders of magnitude higher, or lower. Obviously, all the plutonium-239 will not be ingested by humans. What fraction will be resuspended and inhaled or simply ingested with food over the next several hundred thousand years is almost completely unknown. Is it 10^{-6} or 10^{-11}? One simply does not know. The combined uncertainty of the plutonium fraction lost to the environment, the fraction of this that is ultimately ingested, and the cancer risk from ingested plutonium is enormous. In effect, the cancer risk from the projected plutonium economy could be nil, or we may be talking in terms of hundreds, thousands, or even millions of cancers.

In an attempt to better quantify the fraction of plutonium in the environment that might be ultimately inhaled, assume arbitrarily that the reference 4×10^3 curies of plutonium-239 are uniformly spread over the contiguous United States (8×10^{12} m^2), resulting in 5×10^{-10} curies/m^2 of Pu-239. This may be a conservative assumption to the extent that commercial nuclear facilities are located in regions with population densities larger than the national average. The quantity of plutonium that gets resuspended

---

[100]By comparison, this is roughly 1 percent of the estimated 0.3 megacuries of plutonium-239 produced as a result of above-ground nuclear weapon tests through 1970. ICRP, "The Assessment of Internal Contamination Resulting from Recurrent or Prolonged Uptakes," No. 10A (April 1969), p. 54.

in the atmosphere is extremely uncertain. It depends on the particle size, meteorology, rate of percolation into the soil, and numerous environmental factors. Resuspension factors vary by a factor of a billion — anywhere from 10^{-3}/m (a dusty road) to 10^{-11}/m (a virgin forest).[101] They depend also on the depth distribution in the soil. Again for reference purposes only, assume the plutonium is in aerosol form and the average resuspension factor is 10^{-6}/m. The corresponding plutonium-239 concentration in the atmosphere near ground level would be 5×10^{-16} curies/m^3. The cancer risk from breathing this concentration is also very uncertain. Again, it depends on the particle size distribution, the dose-response model used, and other factors. Assuming a man inhales 20 m^3/day, and the cancer risk is 0.05 per person per μCi inhaled, the risk would be on the order of 10^{-7} per man per year. It could be many orders of magnitude more or less. Assuming a U.S. population stabilized at about 4×10^8 persons, and considering only the first ten years after release, an estimated 400 cancers would result from the inhalation of plutonium-239 following the release of the 100 kg of plutonium. The important point is that the uncertainties are enormous. The estimate could be higher or lower by several orders of magnitude depending on assumptions regarding the quantity of plutonium released, the particle size distribution, the resuspension factors as function of particle size, and the rate of percolation of plutonium in the soil. Aside from these, one must also consider the risk during the next ten years after release, and the next, and so on. Plutonium has a half-life of 24,000 years.

A more thorough analysis of the long-term plutonium hazard would undoubtedly place more realistic limits on the uncertainty of this health risk. At present it is simply not well quantified. The purpose here is to call attention to the problem and the uncertainties rather than provide an answer.

---

[101]Donald P. Geesaman, "Plutonium and Public Health," p. 1532. See also, R. L. Kathren, "Towards Interim Acceptable Surface Contamination Levels for Environmental PuO$_2$," Battelle Northwest Laboratory, BNWL-SA-1510 (April 1968) and Wright H. Langham, "The Problem of Large-Area Plutonium Contamination," U. S. Department of Health, Education, and Welfare, Public Health Service, Consumer Protection and Environmental Health Service, Environmental Control Administration, Seminar Paper No. 002 (1968). The units of the resuspension factor are g-m^{-3}/g-m^{-2}, or curies-m^{-3}/curies-m^{-2}, which reduces to m^{-1}.

UNAUTHORIZED USE OF FISSILE MATERIAL

One of the greatest hazards, or risks, associated with a civilian nuclear power economy arises from the possible diversion of plutonium and enriched uranium to unauthorized use. A properly designed nuclear weapon requires approximately 4 to 8 kilograms of plutonium-239 to give a yield of several kilotons of TNT.[102] A nuclear weapon crudely made from processed breeder reactor fuel, containing plutonium-240 at concentrations approaching 30 percent, might require twice as much plutonium. The critical mass of highly enriched uranium is over four to five times that of plutonium-239 and consequently roughly 20 kg or more of uranium—93 percent U-235—are required for a nuclear weapon of equivalent yield from this material.

There is enough public information readily available today to enable a resourceful group of persons with the necessary array of skills to fabricate such a device without damage to themselves, given the availability of highly enriched fissile material.

The Director of Physical Sciences of the Stanford Research Institute, after reviewing the availability of the technical information and the resources that would be needed to construct a nuclear device, concluded:

The processing of plutonium or enriched uranium is somewhat difficult, but if people wish to take reasonable risks with their health and don't worry about contaminating rooms or equipment, leaving the facilities they use for others to clean up, the equipment requirements would not be large. It seems that a few tens of thousand dollars worth of equipment properly installed in ventilated hoods or large gloved enclosures and operated by a small number of people would suffice to reduce plutonium to the metallic form and to cast it into shapes that could be used in weapons.[103]

Turning now to the question of availability of highly enriched fissile material, recall from the discussion of safeguards that: (1) weapon-grade plutonium is discharged from a 1000-Mw LWR at

---

[102]The exact amount depends on the design of the weapon and is a function of the desired yield, the degree to which the fissile material is compressed during the detonation of the weapon, and the type of neutron reflector material used to encase fissile material.

[103]E. M. Kinderman, "Economic and Political Factors in Special Nuclear Material Control or Is the Best Good Enough?" as cited in D. P. Geesaman, "Plutonium Diversion," paper presented at the Energy Panel on Radiological Issues Related to Nuclear Power Plants of the Assembly Science and Technology Council of the California Legislature (Sacramento, Calif., June 15, 1972), pp. 20-21.

a rate of 250 kg/yr (180 kg/yr fissile Pu); (2) plutonium will be discharged from 1000-Mw LMFBRs at a rate of 1500 to 1900 kg/yr (1100 to 1400 kg/yr fissile Pu), or roughly six to seven times the rate from LWRs fueled with uranium; (3) a 1000-Mw LWR using recycled plutonium will require roughly 440 kg/yr of plutonium (300 kg/yr fissile Pu) as makeup fuel in addition to the 1570 kg of Pu (830 kg/yr fissile Pu) which is recycled; and (4) the HTGR fuel cycle will have a fissile material inventory several times that in the LWR fuel cycle. Projections of LMFBR capacity alone would result ultimately in the recycling of over 60 million kg of fissile plutonium, over 500 thousand kg/yr by 2000. A central issue is whether safeguards will be sufficient to prevent the explosion, in a metropolitan area anywhere in the world, of a nuclear weapon constructed from about 15 kg of this fissile plutonium; that is, roughly one part in four million of the recycled LMFBR fuel. Should this event ever occur, it could easily offset any projected economic benefits of the LMFBR program. The implications of growth in nuclear power generation clearly go beyond economics. They also relate directly to the political problems concerning the spread of nuclear weapons.[104]

As noted previously, because of the large inventory of plutonium in the LMFBR fuel cycle, for the same energy generation, safeguarding should be more difficult than similar activities for LWR fuel. Spokesmen for the industry readily admit that past safeguard procedures have been inadequate. Theodore Taylor, president of International Research and Technology Corporation, an authority on safeguarding nuclear material, noted at a 1971 AAAS Symposium:

... the levels of physical security now applied to fissionable materials for civilian use, in the United States and other countries, are considerably lower than those overcome in many successful thefts of other valuables in the past. Many situations now exist where quantities of fissionable materials sufficient for several nuclear explosives are not protected by armed guards, major physical barriers, or intrusion alarms.[105]

---

[104]Some of the international implications of these problems have been discussed in detail by V. Gilinsky in "Fast Breeder Reactors and the Spread of Plutonium," RAND Corp., Memorandum RM-5148-PR (March 1967); and "Bombs and Electricity," *Environment*, Vol. 14, No. 7 (Sept. 1972).

[105]T. Taylor, "The Need for National and International Systems to Provide Physical Security for Fissionable Materials," as cited in Geesaman, "Plutonium Diversion," p. 44.

It is reputed that organized crime has thoroughly infiltrated the transportation industry and that no material is safe during transportation if organized crime decides it wants it.[106]

Several notable examples of the inability of the air industry to properly handle strategic nuclear material were cited by Samuel Edlow at the 1969 meeting of the Institute of Nuclear Materials Management. He concluded:

The high level of incompetency which has been achieved by surface and air carriers staggers the imagination. The inability of the air industry to properly handle the cargo handed to it for air carriage now approaches a national scandal.[107]

In February 1973, the AEC proposed extensive revisions to its regulations[108] to strengthen existing requirements for physical protection of fissile materials at nuclear facilities and in transit.

Because of the recent rash in airline hijackings, the AEC has limited the quantity of fissile material that can be shipped aboard passenger-carrying aircraft to 20 grams or 20 curies, whichever is less, of plutonium or uranium-232 and 350 grams of uranium-235.

Noting factors that lead to theft of vehicle commodities, the AEC proposed amendments designed to provide, while fissile material is in transit: (a) assurance that theft or diversion would require a significant armed attack; (b) assurance of prompt detection of an actual or attempted theft or diversion; (c) assurance of prompt alerting and timely response of armed guards or police; and (d) assurance against misrouting.

Despite these improvements, one cannot discount the rise in violent crime, militant operations by terrorist organizations, or even the traffic in drugs.

---

[106]The abstract of a report on safeguards in transportation, published in May 1970 by the Institute of Nuclear Materials Management, states that ". . .the transportation industry is characterized by its own press as 'rotting at its core,' law enforcement agencies advise that $1 billion dollars of merchandise is being hijacked or pilfered during transportation each year in the United States, and federal agencies acknowledge that organized crime has a strangle hold on the United States transportation industry. Into this milieu, professional managers of nuclear materials are currently shipping sufficient quantities of nuclear materials to produce nuclear weapons or to direct toward possible nuclear blackmail." See Geesaman, "Plutonium Diversion," p. 33.

[107]S. Edlow, "Safeguards during Transportation: A Shipper's View," as cited in Geesaman, "Plutonium Diversion," p. 14.

[108]10 CFR 73—Physical Protection of Special Nuclear Material; 10 CFR 50—Licensing of Production and Utilization Facilities; and 10 CFR 70—Special Nuclear Materials, Requirements for Physical Security.

The AEC and the industry anticipate small unavoidable losses of plutonium and enriched uranium—approximately 0.5 to 1 percent—during processing and fabricating reactor fuel.[109] These losses give a scale against which incremental diversion can be anticipated. For example, Craig Hosmer, before the 1970 Annual Meeting of the Institute of Materials Management, noted,

... If an SNM [strategic nuclear material] black market develops, the sales price to some country, individual, or organization desperately wanting to make nuclear explosives has been estimated as high as $100,000 per kilogram.

A gram is 1/1000th of a kilogram and 1/1000th of $100,000 is $100. Liberating a half gram of plutonium at a time from the local fast breeder reactor fuel element factory might be so small an amount as to be relatively undetectable even by the best black boxes and the sharpest eyed inspectors.[110]

Because of the potential value of plutonium, the AEC and the industry admit that it is likely that the vast traffic in plutonium will result in a worldwide black market.

Some people have argued that the traffic in plutonium is not new, that shipments have been made by the military for the last twenty-five years. However, the quantities involved appear to be small compared with the civilian shipments projected beyond about 1990. Also, the public was less informed about nuclear power than it is now. There was a mystic aura about nuclear energy that has largely vanished. Today, elementary nuclear theory has found its way into high school science books. Because of public concern, the need to demonstrate to the public that nuclear facilities can be operated safely, and simply to satisfy AEC licensing and National Environmental Policy Act (NEPA) requirements, plant designs as well as operating and shipping procedures are readily available to the public in the AEC document room, in libraries around the country, and from the companies involved. Then, there is always the possibility that, in order to dramatize the potential dangers of a plutonium economy, some competent scientist will publish a detailed treatise on the methodology of acquiring fissile material and constructing nuclear weapons. Should this occur, the lead time

---

[109]U.S. AEC, *Reactor Fuel Cycle Costs*, WASH 1099, Appendix A, pp. 129-157. Also, *Federal Register*, Vol. 38, No. 21 (Feb. 1, 1973), p. 3079.
[110]As cited in Geesaman, "Plutonium Diversion," p. 37.

and required expertise to construct a nuclear weapon would be considerably reduced.

It is argued that there are easier ways than stealing plutonium and fabricating nuclear weapons for terrorists to achieve their goals. This is undoubtedly the case, but to what extent should we rely on this view for public safety? In any event, plutonium can serve as an effective terrorist tool without fabricating it into a nuclear weapon. Due to its toxicity, it is only necessary to improvise an effective means of contaminating a large metropolitan area, e.g., via fire, explosives, air drop, etc. Only a few grams of plutonium spread over a metropolitan area could produce hundreds of cancers. The costs of decontamination and delays in reoccupation of the area would be enormous. There is no effective way of decontaminating the pavement, concrete, etc., short of digging it up.

It has also been argued that, given the amount of plutonium produced by LWRs, it is perhaps safest to invest it in breeders, rather than stockpiling it. Against this must be balanced the eventual multiplication of fast breeders and the possible surpluses of plutonium produced by breeders. Furthermore, a limited number of LWRs and HTGRs could be operated on a plutonium fuel cycle to burn the plutonium produced in conventional LWRs. Such an economy would have a 60 percent smaller plutonium inventory than an economy based on fast breeders, one-third the fissile inventory.

The concern over the problems of plutonium and highly enriched HTGR fuel comprise an argument for phasing out fission systems from the U.S. energy economy, and for providing the leadership to eliminate reactor systems on a worldwide basis. Should this become policy, it might be desirable to use a limited number of fission reactors to burn the present stocks of plutonium and thereby transform them into less hazardous substances. If the concern is sufficient to argue for the elimination of the existing generation of fission reactors, it seems illogical to adopt an LMFBR development strategy that exacerbates this problem rather than reduces it, particularly in light of the questionable economics of the LMFBR program.

As with severe nuclear accidents, there is little hope in quantifying the social cost of environmental releases of plutonium or the risk of plutonium diversion from an LMFBR economy. In the case of severe nuclear accidents, the AEC and the industry posit plausible sequences of events, develop models, and perform extensive design basis accident analyses. There are even some attempts to qualify the uncertainties in these analyses. With respect to the diversion of fissile material, which has a health risk possibly greater than the severe nuclear accident, there are no models of human behavior—no design basis accidents.

In the *LMFBR Demonstration Plant Environmental Statement,* the public is assured:

The AEC has . . . established a program to guard against possible thefts of plutonium and protect the national security. The AEC safeguards program is under continuing development and is oriented to cope with problems arising from the anticipated increase in power reactor traffic in plutonium. . . .

The safeguarding of nuclear materials is achieved through a balanced application of three fundamental control measures—physical protection, surveillance, and accountability. . . .

In summary, adequate procedures and equipment are available or under development to guard against diversion of plutonium from the . . . demonstration plant to unauthorized uses in all phases of the fuel cycle. . . .[111]

Similar statements appear in other AEC reports and congressional hearings. These statements could be applied equally to the safeguarding of money in banks. They do not reflect present inadequencies and the magnitude of the hazard, and they are simply inadequate for purposes of assuring the public that taking this risk is worth the purported benefits of the LMFBR program.

[111]U.S. AEC, *LMFBR Demonstration Plant Environmental Statement,* pp. 93-98.

III

Summary and Conclusions

III

Summary and Conclusions

Introduction to Part III

From our present institutional arrangements for developing new sources of energy, a significant imbalance has evolved with respect to the allocation of federal energy R&D funds. Federal energy R&D expenditures for fiscal 1973 will be about $622 million. About 42 percent ($260 million) is allocated to the LMFBR program; 15 percent to all other civilian nuclear power programs; 15 percent to coal R&D, one-third of which is for health and safety research; 10 percent to fusion energy, much of this for military applications; and 4 percent to petroleum and natural gas. About 1 percent is being spent for geothermal energy research and solar energy research with terrestrial applications. The funding for other civilian nuclear power programs includes only $5 million for the federal contribution to the high temperature gas-cooled reactor (HTGR) program and $1 million toward gas-cooled fast breeder reactor (GCFBR) research. During the previous four years (fiscal 1969-72), the federal R&D expenditures going to the LMFBR program increased from $133 million to $237 million, an increase from 37 percent to 45 percent of the total federal energy R&D funds. The Administration's fiscal 1974 budget includes $772 million for energy R&D; $323 million (42 percent) for the LMFBR program.

A basic question, though beyond the scope of this study, is, given what we know or can best estimate about the cost, environmental consequences, and uncertainties of each type of energy source, what would be (or is) the optimal energy R&D program? With respect to the LMFBR program, the central policy questions pertain to economics, health and environmental risks, and timing as they relate to alternative energy R&D investment strategies. For example, will safe, reliable, commercial-size LMFBRs be economical in the foreseeable future? If so, when? Will the economic advantages outweigh the health and environmental risks from unscheduled events following large-scale commercial utilization of LMFBRs? Is it the optimum U.S. R&D strategy to invest heavily in the commercial development of this reactor now, and at the expense of limiting funding for other attractive alternatives, some of which might have immediate impact on what has been termed the "energy crisis"? While answers to some of these questions are beyond the scope of this analysis, my thesis is that a different set of priorities with much lower allocation to the LMFBR program would probably constitute a better R&D strategy.

Questions pertaining to R&D priorities among the civilian nuclear energy programs have been studied and debated at length within the nuclear community, but have not been adequately studied by environmentalists and economists outside the AEC fold. From these studies and discussions have emerged a number of economic, environmental, resource conservation, and national security arguments for rapidly moving ahead with the LMFBR program, even at the expense of other alternatives. Below, the principal arguments are reviewed, and evaluated.

Economic Considerations

The economic arguments for rapidly moving ahead with the LMFBR program are based largely on studies dating from the 1960s. The latest results, based on 1970 input data, have been reported in hearings before the JCAE,[1] in the literature,[2] and in the AEC's 1970 Analysis,[3] released in May 1971. These results have been used to show a favorable program savings and benefit-cost ratio and have been used in justifying LMFBR program budget requests and the high priority given this program. An often repeated statement, based on results from the AEC's 1970 Analysis, is that deferring the LMFBR introduction date beyond 1986 reduces the discounted (at 7 percent) benefits of the program by an average of about $2 billion per year of delay. While this cost-benefit study is excellent in many respects, it is almost completely deficient with respect to an analysis of the uncertainties of the input data used in the cost-benefit model. The results of the AEC's cost-benefit model are extremely sensitive to changes in some of

[1]Hearings before the U.S. Congress, Joint Committee on Atomic Energy, on *AEC Authorizing Legislation–Fiscal Year 1972* (March 1971).

[2]M. J. Whitman, A. N. Tardiff, and P. L. Hofman, "U.S. Civilian Nuclear Power Cost-Benefit Analysis" (paper presented at the Fourth United Nations International Conference on the Peaceful Uses of Atomic Energy, Geneva, Switzerland, Sept. 6-16, 1971).

[3]U.S. Atomic Energy Commission, Division of Reactor Development and Technology, *Updated (1970) Cost-Benefit Analysis of the U.S. Breeder Reactor Program*, WASH 1184 (Jan. 1972).

the most important or critical input variables. Major future uncertainties relate to: (1) nuclear power plant capital costs; (2) fuel cycle costs; (3) performance characteristics of LMFBR designs; (4) electrical energy demand; and (5) uranium ore costs. The analysis I have made, considering the uncertainties in these and other variables, suggests that there is no basis for concluding either that there is a high probability that the LMFBR will be economical—if available in the late 1980s or early 1990s—or that a delay in the program, even for one or two decades, need necessarily result in an economic penalty. In fact, based on recent assessments of some of the more sensitive variables, the analysis suggests that LMFBR energy generating costs are unlikely to be competitive with generating costs using commercially available nuclear power plants for several decades after 1986, the AEC's target date of LMFBR commercial availability. The bases for these conclusions are summarized below.

CAPITAL COSTS

In 1967, the AEC was projecting that 1000-Mw LMFBRs would cost $150/kw (1967 prices); LWRs were about 10 percent lower in cost.[4] Total LMFBR energy costs were estimated to range from 3 to 4.5 mills/kwh, depending upon assumptions.[5] At the time, it was thought that breeder reactors could provide fuel cycle cost savings on the order of 1.0 mill/kwh or more, enough to offset any anticipated higher capital costs and to provide a "virtual limitless supply of low-cost energy." In 1968, the LMFBR Program Office was predicting:

To bring LMFBRs to a competitive status, fuel-cycle costs considerably lower than 1.75 mills/kwh [LWR fuel-cycle costs] must be achieved. How much lower depends on capital costs of LMFBRs. A reduction of LMFBR capital costs to $150-$200/kwe—a not unreasonable near-term goal—would require the fuel-cycle cost to be between 0.5 and 1.0 mill/kw-hr to yield competitive total power costs. . . . A fuel-cycle cost of 0.5 mills/kw-hr or lower should be possible, but fuel-cycle technology must be improved considerably to attain this cost.[6]

[4]U.S. AEC, *Potential Nuclear Power Growth Patterns,* WASH 1098 (1970), p. 2-27.
[5]U.S. AEC, An Assessment of the LMFBR, WASH 1100, unpublished, p. 21.
[6]U.S. AEC, *LMFBR Program Plan,* Vol. 8, *Fuel Recycle,* WASH 1108 (1968), p. 8-28.

Projected LWR capital costs used in the 1970 Analysis were never greater than about $250/kw, and the LMFBR-LWR capital cost differential used was $20/kw or less over the 1970-2020 period. These figures are in constant (1971) dollars. Today, with LWRs costing closer to $400/kw (1971 dollars), LMFBRs would not be competitive at costs about 15 percent over LWRs. The latest estimates by the same Oak Ridge National Laboratory staff that provided the capital cost curves used in the 1970 Analysis place the LMFBR-LWR and LMFBR-HTGR capital cost differentials roughly 50 percent to 100 percent greater than the differentials used in the 1970 Analysis. Without changing any other model assumptions, using these cost estimates, the 1970 Analysis would predict net benefits of the LMFBR program close to, if not less than, zero, and the model would probably predict that the LMFBR would not be competitive in 1986, even if it were commercially available. These estimates are based on a conservatively designed LMFBR. More advanced designs should lead to even greater cost differentials, although presumably their fuel cycle costs would be lower. There are reasons to believe that estimates of the capital cost differentials will be even higher in the future than they are today. The principal factors which are likely to lead to higher capital cost differentials are related to unanticipated LMFBR design problems, which, from experience with LWRs, we know can lead to costly solutions.

In the 1970 Analysis it was assumed that the normalized capital cost (dollars per kilowatt) of all power plants would decrease in time due to a classical learning effect and economics from increasing plant sizes. The AEC assumed "learning" rates such that the capital cost differentials between LWRs and fossil-fuel plants, and between LMFBRs and LWRs (and HTGRs), decrease in time. In fact they showed LWRs eventually costing more than LMFBRs, presumably to account for plutonium recycle in LWRs. Contrary to these expectations, since the turnkey and first few prototype LWRs were introduced into the commercial market, plant capital costs and the capital cost differential between fossil-fueled plants and LWRs have been increasing. There is evidence that this trend will continue for at least another decade and that the cost differential between LMFBRs and LWRs (and HTGRs) will similarly increase.

LMFBR PERFORMANCE CHARACTERISTICS

The AEC rightfully assumes an advancing LMFBR technology between 1986 and 2020. In the 1970 Analysis the first commercial LMFBRs in the four years following 1986 are of a relatively conservative design, but in the model for 1990 a very advanced design is to be introduced into the commercial market at no increase in its capital costs. This advanced design was based on a different safety philosophy. It was assumed that major accidents leading to complete voiding of liquid sodium coolant in the core and major meltdown of the fuel must be prevented by sophisticated accident detection and protection devices, or must be shown to be "incredible" by further development effort. Large blast shields to absorb great quantities of energy during a hypothetical fuel meltdown or large sodium voiding accident were not provided in the vessel structure design. Approximately 99 percent of the LMFBRs that the model predicts will be built prior to 2020 are of the advanced design. In other words, the 1970 Analysis results are based on an economy of LMFBRs having performance characteristics and low fuel cycle costs of this very advanced design. Recent studies suggest that this advanced design seems impractical in view of the need to accommodate swelling of the fuel rods. The difference between the energy-generating costs of the very advanced and the conservatively designed LMFBRs assumed in the 1970 Analysis could easily be 0.5 mills/kwh or more. It appears inconceivable that performance characteristics of the very advanced design will be available by 1990. With respect to the LMFBR demonstration plant, designs are moving in the direction of conservatism, under the assumption that it is better to achieve a safe, reliable, but uneconomical demonstration plant rather than take additional risks for higher performance. This philosophy in all likelihood will continue to prevail. Because of this and other safety considerations, some of the performance characteristics of the very advanced design may never be obtained.

LMFBR FUEL CYCLE COSTS AND URANIUM SUPPLY

It is generally believed that the first few LMFBRs will not be competitive, due to first-of-a-kind plant costs, and until the size of the fuel business increases to the point where economies of scale will substantially reduce fuel cycle costs. To bring LMFBRs to a competitive status, the AEC and the industry are banking on achieving fuel cycle costs considerably lower (0.5-1.0 mill/kwh) than commercially available light water reactors (LWRs) and high temperature gas reactors (HTGRs). The lower LMFBR fuel cycle costs would offset the anticipated higher capital cost. In part, because the LMFBR is introduced into the market at not more than $20/kw above LWRs and the HTGR, and because the very advanced LMFBR design is introduced in 1990 with no increase in capital cost, the AEC's cost-benefit model predicts that LMFBRs will be built as rapidly as possible for the first ten years—limited only by an arbitrary assumption that LMFBR capacity can not more than double in a two-year period. Hence, in the model the LMFBR fuel cycle rapidly benefits from economies of scale. Under these assumptions, the LMFBR looks very attractive, and utilities would be expected to "go breeder" just as they "went nuclear" in the 1960s. There are several factors which may prevent this.

With more realistic LMFBR capital costs and performance characteristics, the LMFBR will not look nearly as attractive as it does in the model and as it did in the past when nuclear plant capital costs were in the $150–$200/kw range. Also, there are serious uncertainties with regard to LMFBR reliability. Utilities may have in the HTGR an attractive alternative to the fast breeder—an alternative that is also less sensitive to uranium prices than the LWR, although not to the same extent as the LMFBR. There will be no geographical areas favorable to LMFBRs over LWRs or HTGRs, a factor that has enabled LWRs to compete with fossil-fueled plants. Finally, recent evidence suggests that low-cost domestic uranium is far more plentiful than the AEC was predicting a short time ago. According to the Nuclear Task Group of the National Petroleum Council's (NPC) Committee on U.S. Energy Outlook (the Task Group included representation by the AEC's Division of Production and Materials Management), "the domestic uranium reserves reported by the AEC have been discovered as a result of still incomplete exploration of less than 10 percent of the area favorable for finding uranium."[7] This conclusion was based largely on an assessment of ultimate domestic uranium resources, presented to the Nuclear Task Group by one of the larg-

[7]National Petroleum Council, "U.S. Energy Outlook, An Initial Appraisal, 1971-1985," Vol. Two, Summaries of Task Group Reports (Nov. 1971).

est domestic uranium producers in this country. It suggests that if the LMFBR program is delayed several decades, there is sufficient low-cost domestic uranium to fuel the nuclear industry without economic penalty. More plentiful foreign reserves and higher-cost domestic resources could provide additional backups in the unlikely event that domestic low-cost uranium resources have been overestimated. Should the United States be forced to rely heavily on foreign supplies to meet future uranium demands, or should it do so simply because foreign ore is less expensive, this would not significantly affect U.S. balance of payments. Importing one-half of the uranium requirements projected by the AEC for the year 2000, assuming no breeders, would amount to less than 2 percent of total imports for the same year. This does not consider the return of any capital due to U.S. investments in foreign uranium development. Since there are considerable foreign uranium resources in countries such as Canada and Australia, any national security argument with respect to uranium must be less strong than with respect to oil.

Properly viewed, uranium supply is simply another economic variable with uncertainty in the LMFBR economic assessment. Today, domestic uranium costs from $6 to $10 per pound of U_3O_8 (1972 dollars), depending on the delivery date. The foreign price is approximately one dollar less than the domestic price. It is conceivable that the average price in today's dollars would remain below $15 per pound for thirty years or so, even without the introduction of breeders. During the next fifty years it appears unlikely that uranium prices in today's dollars would go above $20 per pound, again without introduction of the LMFBR. The figure of $20 per pound would be conservative based on the NPC data, extensive strip mine reclamation costs, and radiation safety standards for underground mining that are more stringent than those existing today. Using the AEC's "probable" and "optimistic" uranium supply curves (these are 1969 estimates), the 1970 Analysis projects that the United States would be using $50 per pound uranium before 2020, unless breeders were introduced. To accept even the "optimistic" supply assumption, one must assume that there are virtually no low-cost domestic uranium resources beyond what are presently reported by the AEC in the proven reserve and estimated additional resource categories. This is clearly contrary to the view of the Nuclear Task Group of the NPC's Committee on U.S. Energy Outlook. At a constant $8 per pound of U_3O_8, the 1970 Analysis predicts LMFBR benefits to be less than the program costs, with the rest of the economic and technologic projections remaining unchanged from the AEC's most probable (1969) estimates.

In summary, there is serious doubt as to whether the AEC has adequately assessed the ultimate domestic (or foreign) uranium potential, or correctly assessed the technical and economic capability of the domestic uranium industry to meet the projected demand. Based on the uranium resource assessments of the NPC's Nuclear Task Group (which included AEC representation), there does not appear to be any necessity for making a commitment to the LMFBR in the immediate future as a hedge against higher uranium prices. A prudent energy policy might be to spend a greater effort in assessing uranium resources before giving priority to a capital-intensive LMFBR demonstration plant development effort.

The ground rules for estimating fuel cycle costs in the AEC cost-benefit study did not include estimates of the effect of possible future regulations on siting, safeguards, or effluent control. The fuel cycle cost estimates in the 1970 Analysis are based on an assumption that LMFBR spent fuel can be shipped to the processing plant after only thirty days of cooling. Due to high concentrations of volatile fission products, a spent-fuel shipping accident at this time could easily be ten times more severe than the 1957 Windscale accident. Population doses on the order of 0.5 rem, or more, could be expected. The decontamination and associated costs of such an accident could run into the tens of millions of dollars. Delaying the spent-fuel shipments could reduce the severity of such an accident by reducing the activity level of the volatile fission products by an order of magnitude. From a safety viewpoint, a prudent policy would require spent fuel to be cooled for 150 days or more before shipping. If longer cooling times, on the order of 150 days, are required, then the 1970 Analysis would understate the LMFBR fuel cycle cost by about 0.1 mill/kwh, and the breeder's fuel doubling time would increase by 10 to 20 percent. The longer cooling time and subsequent cost penalty may be realized because of the trade-off between the fuel inventory charge and the additional costs (over previous estimates) of the more stringent cask designs, shipping procedures, and fuel reprocessing requirements.

It is clear that the LMFBR fuel cycle subsequent to reprocessing spent fuel will be subject to stringent safeguards to protect the plutonium against theft. There is considerable uncertainty as to the cost of safeguarding plutonium and HTGR fuel, due in part to a lack of definitive studies. Whether safeguard costs are borne by the federal government or the industry, they are legitimate costs associated with the fuel cycles and should be included in cost-benefit analyses of the LMFBR and other nuclear power programs.

ELECTRICAL ENERGY DEMAND

The fifty-year electrical energy demand projections used in the 1970 Analysis are based on a simple extrapolation of a twenty-year forecast of the Federal Power Commission's 1970 National Power Survey (NPS). However, the electrical energy demand projection of the 1970 NPS is not very reliable beyond about ten years, due (1) to the inherent uncertainties characterizing all long-range energy forecasts, and (2) because it represents an aggregation of utility projections, which are inaccurate beyond about ten years due to the manner in which they are generated and because population and economic growth projections are not very accurate on a utility area basis. Other current long-range electrical energy demand projections, using independent forecasting techniques based on historical (national) trends in GNP growth, income and (gas and electricity) price elasticities, and per capita consumption, suggest that the 1970 Analysis projections overestimate future electrical energy demand. The true demand could easily be 25 percent, and possibly 50 percent below the "probable" projection in the 1970 Analysis for the year 2000. If the true demand is 25 percent less, then the projected discounted net benefits of the LMFBR program (assuming the rest of the economic and technologic projections remain unchanged from the AEC's most probable estimates in the 1970 Analysis) are reduced by one-half; if the actual demand is one-half the "probable" projection, the net benefits vanish, due to lower energy demand alone.

DISCOUNT RATE

The AEC used a 7 percent discount rate to compute present value benefits of the LMFBR program. With a 10 percent discount rate favored by many economists and now required by a 1972

Administration directive, the net benefits reported by the 1970 Analysis are reduced by 77 percent. Even using a 7 percent discount rate, less than 8 percent of the reported net benefits will have accrued by 2000. The risks in achieving an economically successful LMFBR industry before the turn of the century are extremely high, due in part to the uncertainties in economic factors and future technological developments that could influence the success of the LMFBR program during the next twenty-five years.

Economic Argument—Summing Up

Each of the more important input variables—nuclear plant capital and fuel cycle costs, reactor performance characteristics, electrical energy demand, and low-cost domestic uranium supplies—has been examined separately using more recent or, in some cases, simply more realistic, data, while the other input variables were held at the values considered by the AEC as most probable (as of late-1970). In each case, the estimated discounted net benefits of the LMFBR program are greatly reduced (in some cases, below zero) as compared with the 1970 Analysis estimate using the AEC's most probable values. If all of the more important input variables are examined together with the newer, or more realistic, data, the benefits would be even more negative. Taken together, the revised data imply that commercial-size LMFBRs will not be competitive for several decades beyond the AEC target commercial entry date of 1986.

One of the reasons for doing a cost-benefit analysis is to compare the various alternatives, e.g., no LMFBR, 1986 LMFBR entry date, delay the LMFBR, no GCFBR, and so forth. It is certainly possible to include in the analysis a quantitative assessment of the effect on manpower resources in the national laboratories, industries, etc., caused by dropping the LMFBR program, delaying the LMFBR and maintaining a skeleton work force, switching to the GCFBR, or working on other technologies. Likewise, the cost-benefit analysis should address the irreversible economic and environmental consequences of each of the alternatives, e.g., accidents involving plutonium releases and possible future spread of nuclear weapons made from plutonium. The AEC's cost-benefit studies consider none of these, and the *LMFBR Demonstration Plant Environment Statement* must be considered inadequate in this regard. On the basis of economics alone, the high priority given to the national LMFBR program is open to severe questioning. Investing heavily in this program at the expense of other attractive alternatives is not, in my judgment, a sound energy R&D strategy.

Environmental Considerations

The principal resource conservation and environmental arguments in support of the LMFBR program are: (1) it will provide a virtually inexhaustible fuel source resulting in a reduction in uranium ore demands and strip-mining requirements; (2) LMFBRs will have a higher thermal efficiency than LWRs in use today; (3) negligible amounts of radioactivity will be routinely released from LMFBRs to the environment, thereby virtually eliminating air pollution from electrical power plants.[8] These are reviewed separately below.

RESOURCE CONSERVATION

After the economic argument, perhaps the most often repeated arguments for the national program plan are related to the ability of breeders to increase the total amount of fissile material beyond naturally occurring uranium-235, which means more total energy can be produced from a given quantity of uranium. However, even if the breeder is delayed, the fraction of the uranium not converted to energy or plutonium fuel in nonbreeder reactors is still readily available for conversion to plutonium fuel and ultimately energy in breeders. Physically the same energy will be available regardless of the time breeders are introduced into the economy, assuming they are introduced at all. The energy represented by the

---

[8]To the extent that waste heat rejection results in air pollution, for example through the use of cooling towers, arguments (2) and (3) are related.

unconverted fraction of uranium is stored in the uranium tailings at the enrichment plants and the smaller fraction of uranium recovered from nonbreeder fuel reprocessing.

If the LMFBR program is postponed for one or more decades, the United States would simply continue stockpiling the depleted uranium, in the form of uranium tailings at the enrichment plant, as it is currently doing. When uranium ore prices become sufficiently high so that fast breeders are economical, then the United States could start breeding fuel (plutonium-239) from the uranium-238 in the enrichment tailings. In effect, postponing the market entry date of the LMFBR until it is economical does not necessarily influence the United States' or the world's ability to meet long-term energy requirements. With respect to uranium conservation, therefore, an early LMFBR entry date can *not* be viewed as a means of saving an exhaustible resource in the manner that fission, geothermal, and solar energy alternatives reduce the demand for coal or oil.

A corollary to the resource conservation argument is that, if the LMFBR is commercially successful, it will result in a reduction in future uranium ore demand in the short run, and absolutely, if alternative technologies replace fast breeders before the enrichment tailings are exhausted. Delaying the LMFBR entry twenty years, however, would result in the cumulative total of less than 50 square miles of additional uranium strip-mining during the next fifty years. By way of comparison, roughly 100 square miles of additional land are currently strip-mined for coal *annually*. The costs of completely reclaiming the open pit uranium mines plus all other environmental costs associated with uranium mining and milling operations should be less than about 0.1 mills/kwh added to LWR energy costs. This is about 1 percent of the estimated total generating cost using nuclear plants being ordered today. In any event, the costs of precluding environmental damage in mining and milling uranium appear to be of secondary importance compared with the health risks associated with severe nuclear accidents and the unauthorized use of fissile material.

THERMAL EFFICIENCY

While the LMFBR does have a higher projected thermal efficiency than today's LWRs (close to 40 percent as compared with the LWR's 32 percent), the projected LMFBR thermal efficiency is not appreciably different from that of today's large fossil-fuel plants or the high temperature gas-cooled reactor (HTGR), nor is it higher than the thermal efficiency projected for some of the other breeder concepts, such as the gas-cooled fast breeder reactor (GCFBR). Consequently, waste thermal energy for disposal will be about the same for LMFBRs as for fossil-fuel plants, HTGRs, and GCFBRs. If cooling towers are required to protect water quality, the waste heat will be discharged to the atmosphere. Depending on location, such discharges could have major impacts on urban heat islands regardless of the plant type.

At a specific power plant site, where waste heat rejection is a critical factor, the HTGR represents a good nuclear plant alternative to the LMFBR. Looking toward the future, to the development of closed-cycle gas turbines, the gas reactors, i.e., the HTGR and GCFBR, offer potential advantages over the other reactor concepts, with respect to waste heat rejection and conservation of fresh water. This would also be true looking even further into the future, through the development and application of magneto-hydrodynamic conversion to gas reactors. Both of these technologies would have substantially higher thermal efficiencies than the LMFBR.

AIR POLLUTION

With respect to air pollutants other than waste heat, there are two comparisons that are useful to make: (1) LMFBRs with other nuclear plants and (2) LMFBRs with fossil-fueled plants. With respect to the first, comparing only the nuclear plants and specifically *routine* releases at the reactor site, the proposed routine radioactive effluents from LMFBRs represent a significant improvement over *historical* releases from LWRs; a slight improvement over estimated releases from LWRs now being designed to meet proposed radioactive release standards, and HTGRs that do not remove the helium-3 from the coolant or bottle the volatile gases; but no significant improvement over LWRs built during the same time period as the LMFBRs and equipped with similar radioactive effluent control systems available to the LMFBRs; and finally no improvement over what is economically possible with HTGRs built during the same time period.

When the entire fuel cycles, including fuel reprocessing plants, are compared at a time shortly after the LMFBR is projected to be commercially available, it is impossible to say that any reactor type or types will have an overall advantage over others with respect to routine radioactive releases. This is because the contributions to routine radioactive releases at the reprocessing plant, due to processing the annual fuel discharged from a reactor, are greater than the routine release from the reactor itself. The principal differences in the man-rem dose per unit of electrical energy generated from one reactor fuel cycle to the next will depend as much, or more, on plant sizes, population densities, and meteorological conditions as on inherent design characteristics of the reactors.

With respect to the second comparison, the LMFBR, like other nuclear plants, will not discharge SO_2, nitrogen oxides, or particulates to the atmosphere, in contrast to fossil-fueled plants. Environmental costs of air pollutants from fossil-fueled plants are important to discussions of whether the United States should rely heavily on nuclear fission as an energy source; but these costs are central to LMFBR development strategy only to the extent to which LMFBRs would displace fossil-fueled plants in the market. Should the United States continue to rely on nuclear fission as a source of energy, there does not appear to be any evidence that LMFBRs will displace significant numbers of fossil-fueled plants in the market between now and about 2020. Further, any purported reduction in environmental costs associated with fossil-fueled plants resulting from LMFBR introduction in the foreseeable future does not appear significant compared with other possible costs, for example, the health risks associated with large-scale utilization of LMFBRs. A prudent energy R&D strategy would be to shift more of the R&D toward reducing fossil-fueled plant emissions, which in turn could result in short-term environmental benefits.

SAFETY ASPECTS

In order for LMFBRs to be attractive economically, they must be utilized on a large scale. But large-scale utilization of LMFBRs raises several serious problems and numerous unanswered questions related to safety.

LMFBR safety research abounds with uncertainties. For example, there are serious unresolved issues related to: (1) the adequacy of instrumentation to detect fuel pin failures, coolant channel blockages, and local fuel melting, on a timely basis; (2) the nature of molten-fuel–coolant interaction and the possibility of local accidents propagating through the reactor core; (3) the adequacy of mathematical models and computer codes to place realistic bounds on the explosive potential of a fast reactor nuclear excursion, and the amount of plutonium that could be released following such an accident; (4) the adequacy of models for assessing the biological significance of radiation doses following plutonium ingestion or inhalation; (5) following its release, the movement of plutonium in the environment over a period of from tens to hundreds of thousands of years and the potential health hazard of plutonium during this interval. Much valuable information in some of these areas will be gained from LMFBR safety research, including operational experience with the Fast Flux Test Facility, and it is important that the public be aware of the results and the risk-benefit issues that society must resolve.

Pigford[9] has shown that if the probability of a severe LWR accident is greater than about 10^{-7} per reactor year of operation, the health risk from a severe nuclear accident is greater than the risk from routine releases from the same plant. This would be true for other types of nuclear plants as well, including the LMFBR. Since one cannot now show that the accident probability is acceptably low, i.e., below about 10^{-6} per reactor per year, routine releases from nuclear plants are not central to the question of whether the U.S. energy policy should include reliance on fission plants, or if it should, then, whether the LMFBR should be introduced into the economy as now scheduled. The answer to the second question might be yes if there were strong economic, resource conservation, environmental, or national security arguments to support such a view. This analysis does not support such a view.

A second set of serious questions is related to unresolved safety questions that arise because large-scale utilization of LMFBRs must be accompanied by the support facilities needed to supply and recycle LMFBR fuel. For example, there are questions regarding

[9]Thomas H. Pigford, "Protection of the Public from Radioactivity Produced in Nuclear Power Reactors," *Nuclear Science*, Vol. NS-19, No. 1 (Feb. 1972).

trade-offs between the consolidation of nuclear power plants and their support facilities in large nuclear parks and the current trend toward separation of the power plants from those support facilities by large distances. Whether fast reactor spent fuels should be shipped from the power plant to the reprocessing plant after short cooling periods, as assumed in cost-benefit studies of the U.S. breeder program, can be questioned on safety grounds. There are questions regarding safety aspects of LMFBR fuel reprocessing plants themselves and the technology to limit radioactive releases from these plants under normal operating conditions.

Perhaps most important are questions regarding the problems, cost, and even feasibility of adequately safeguarding highly enriched nuclear fuels to prevent the unauthorized use of these materials for making nuclear weapons. Safeguarding highly enriched nuclear fuels is not a problem unique to LMFBRs. The plutonium produced in today's LWRs is highly enriched, as is the fuel used in HTGRs. Likewise, the GCFBR will have the same safeguard problems as posed by the LMFBR. Today, with less than thirty operating light-water reactors in the United States, it is suggested that present industry safeguard practices are inadequate, in the sense that they are unable to reduce to an acceptably small value the probability that nuclear fuel will be diverted for unauthorized use. These problems would be enhanced with the advent of LMFBRs. Plutonium will be discharged from LMFBRs at six to seven times the discharge rate from today's LWRs of equivalent size. An economy of LMFBRs would have roughly 2.5 times the plutonium (3 times the fissile plutonium) inventory of an equivalent-size economy of LWRs recycling plutonium.

The 1970 Analysis projections of LMFBR capacity alone would result ultimately in the recycling of over 60 million kg of fissile plutonium. The rate by the year 2000 would be 500,000 kg of plutonium per year. A central issue here is whether safeguards will be sufficient to prevent in a metropolitan area anywhere in the world the explosion of a nuclear weapon constructed from less than about 12 kg of fissile plutonium removed from the LMFBR fuel cycle, that is roughly one part in 4 million of the recycled LMFBR fuel. Thus far, no evidence has been presented which would provide firm grounds for believing this risk is necessarily negligible.

While inherent characteristics and more stringent safeguard procedures will make plutonium more difficult to steal, one cannot ignore the possibility. Is it reasonable to expect that large quantities of plutonium will not be stolen? Is it reasonable to expect that a terrorist organization will not fabricate a nuclear weapon from this material and utilize it? On the basis of these risks alone, it would appear that a prudent energy policy would be to delay commercial introduction of LMFBRs until there is strong overriding economic justification for the program.

Recent Events

The following events of recent years could significantly alter U.S. energy R&D priorities—the sale of six HTGRs; development of new information on the availability of domestic uranium; developments in fusion research; and promising developments in the closed-cycle gas turbine. These developments alone justify a reassessment of our present energy R&D strategy, one that carefully examines the environmental and economic advantages of the proposed LMFBR program and compares alternate energy strategies.

In light of the questionable economics and possible serious health risks surrounding the LMFBR program, it does not appear that the LMFBR program should be, in terms of federal expenditures, the highest priority energy research and development effort in the United States. Since in my opinion the cost-benefit studies of the U.S. breeder reactor program are not adequate to show an economic incentive to make the LMFBR available commercially in the late 1980s or 1990s, it would appear that a better strategy would be to accelerate development of fusion technology, and nonnuclear programs, e.g., coal, deep geothermal, and solar research. A better nuclear energy R&D strategy would be to give LWRs and the HTGR higher priorities in order to place these technologies on a stronger footing. What is suggested here is that the United States take a careful look at the additional benefits that might accrue over the next ten to thirty years if it accelerates: (1) LWR and HTGR safety research; (2) HTGR fuel cycle development; (3) closed-cycle gas turbine development; (4) high-level radioactive waste management studies; (5) nuclear material safeguard procedures and technology. With respect to breeder reactor development, more emphasis should be given to the GCFBR, which, while less

developed than the LMFBR, appears to have better economic, performance, and safety characteristics.

A corollary to the above strategy is to question whether the first
priority within the LMFBR program should be given to the very
capital-intensive demonstration plant development effort rather
than to further less-costly studies of some of the critical unresolved
environmental, safety, and economic issues pertinent to this program.

Wolfe et al.[10] have noted a number of benefits of a demonstration
plant program and a number of problems the demonstration plant,
or plants, by themselves will not solve. Some benefits of the
demonstration plant are, for example: (1) it forces basic design
choices; (2) it provides practical experience in manufacture, construction, and operation of equipment; (3) it forces managers to
focus on requirements of a new technology; and (4) it provides a
reactor system that addresses safety questions and carries the
design through the licensing process. However, the demonstration
plant will not be economic; the program will not determine the
optimum design choices; it will not demonstrate the ultimate performance of LMFBRs; and it will not result in a competitive
LMFBR system in one step.[11]

It is perhaps also worth noting that while demonstration plants
enjoy the combined support of the government, the utilities, and
the prospective vendors, all of which may be necessary for the final
commercial development phase of the technology, experience with
LWRs makes it clear that demonstration plants do not show that
commercial nuclear reactors can be operated with the requisite
degree of safety. In this regard it is noted that the LMFBR
demonstration plant program is not an experimental program to
determine the explosive potential of commercial LMFBRs, or to
verify mathematical models which are a principal basis for LMFBR
safety analysis. Furthermore, as Mr. Shaw has noted,[12] based on
LWR and HTGR experience, one should not be surprised if the

---

[10]Bertram Wolfe, A. S. Gibson, P. M. Murphy, and D. R. Sawle, "The Influence
of Component Development, Prototypes, and Construction Experience," *Nuclear
News*, Vol. 16 (Jan. 1973).

[11]Ibid., pp. 40-42.

[12]*Energy Research and Development*, Hearings before the Subcommittee on Science, Research, and Development of the Committee on Science and Astronautics,
U.S. House of Representatives, 92 Cong. 2 sess. (May 1972), p. 339.

utilities make commitments for larger LMFBRs before any operational experience is gained with LMFBR demonstration plants. Recent public hearings on the adequacy of emergency core-cooling systems in today's light-water reactors highlight the need for public awareness of nuclear plant safety issues at an early stage in the commercial development of new reactor types. Whether the demonstration plant merits the priority accorded it invites careful reconsideration.

APPENDIX A

Economic Structure
of the Model*

Figure A-1 is a diagrammatic representation of the economic structure used in the model. In the discussion that follows, the numbers in parentheses refer to the numbered streams on the diagram.

The large block at the left of the diagram represents all the electricity-generating companies or utilities. In the economic calculations performed in the model, these are considered as if they were one utility company. This company supplies electric power (1) to the consumers. A flow of cash (2) is received from the consumers in return. The company builds new electricity generating plants (3) and pays cash to the contractors (4); this is the capital investment in new facilities. It purchases fossil fuels (5) and pays cash in return (6). It also pays cash for operating expenditures, maintenance, taxes, and miscellaneous expenses (7). It obtains fresh nuclear fuel and other fuel cycle services from the nuclear fuel service companies (8). These services include U_3O_8 supply, conversion, enrichment, fuel assembly fabrication, transportation, chemical reprocessing of spent fuel, reconversion, and waste disposal. Cash is paid for these services at the time they are rendered (9).

As discussed later, the stockpiles of fissionable materials (Pu, ^{235}U, and ^{223}U) that have been recovered from irradiated fuels were assumed to remain in the ownership of the power companies. Transfers may therefore be made into and out of these stockpiles by the utilities (10) without any accompanying flows of cash. Fissionable material needed by the fuel cycle service companies for the manufacture of new fuel can also be obtained from the stockpile without payment of cash, since the material remains

---

*Extracted from U.S. Atomic Energy Commission, *Reactor Fuel Cycle Costs for Nuclear Power Evaluation*,, WASH 1099 (Dec. 1971).

FIGURE A-1. Systems Analysis Economic Model

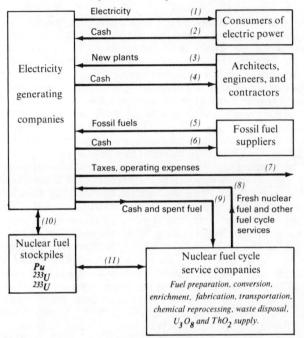

in the ownership of the utilities and is being fabricated for their account (11).

The electricity-generating companies have the option of selecting any plant-building program over the 50-year study period (1970-2020) that will enable them to meet the electrical demands of their customers. For any particular schedule of fossil and nuclear plant construction chosen, some resulting levelized cost of power must be paid to the generating companies by their customers. The levelized cost of power is defined as that constant number of mills per kilowatt hour which will yield a flow of cash to the generating companies sufficient to recover their investments, pay all operating and fuel cycle expenses, including taxes, and earn the required rate of return on investment. The discounted cash flow procedure used in the model determines the cost of power by determining the incomes necessary to satisfy the following equation:

Total present worth of cash incomes (stream 2)
        = Total present worth of cash outflows (streams 4, 6, 7, and 9).

For a given set of inputs the linear programming operation determines the plant-building program ("reactor mix") that minimizes the right-hand side of the equation above and hence minimizes the levelized cost of power for that case.

As mentioned earlier, all costs and prices were expressed in terms of 1967 dollars, with no allowance for escalation. The reason for doing the study in this way follows from the objective of minimization of total present-worthed costs. There is no logical basis for such a minimization unless it is done in terms of price levels at a specific point in time. Economically speaking, the study attempts to minimize the expenditure of real resources, and this requires that all prices be expressed in terms of the price levels existing at some point in time. The year 1967 was used because it is customary in studies of this type to use the price levels existing at the time the study is made. It would be proper, of course, to consider escalation when attempting to project future prices in terms of future dollars, but there was no attempt to make this kind of forecast.

It will be noted that Fig. A-1 does not show the investors in the electricity-generating corporation or the flows of cash between these investors and the corporation. Some explanation of this point may be in order. Dividends paid by the corporation to its investors are not cash expenditures in the sense used here and need not be considered in evaluating the cost of electricity. The investors, being the owners of the corporation, share in the profits or losses from all its transactions, regardless of the amount of dividends paid. Thus, for the purposes of this model, the investors and the corporation can be considered as a single entity. The present-worthing of the cash flows provides the necessary returns on investment which accrue to the benefit of the owners and from which dividends may be paid. For the calculation of the cost of electricity, however, the question of whether dividends are paid is irrelevant.

It will also be noted that no mention has been made of inventory charges on plutonium or other fissile materials. In the present-worthed cash flow method the only costs that need be considered are actual cash expenditures, that is, those costs that are actually paid out in cash by the power-generating company. As mentioned earlier, there is no direct cash payment for the privilege of holding fissile materials in inventory, in view of the assumption that these materials are owned by the company. Transfers made within the company, from one utility to another, have no external cash flow effect, because the money paid out by one utility is received by another. As for the indirect cash effects of storing fissile materials, it would be erroneous to assign an "inventory charge" to material stored for future use, except for the actual cash expense of building and maintaining the necessary storage facilities. If the power-generating company decides to store plutonium instead of using it immediately as fuel, the only financial penalty suffered is that some other cash expenditure must be incurred to generate the power that could have been generated by the plutonium. For example, U_3O_8 might have to be purchased, converted to UF_6, and enriched in a gaseous diffusion plant. The costs of these operations are collected as actual cash flows and thus become part of the power cost. By this procedure the model is able to weigh the alternatives of using plutonium immediately or storing it for the future.

Income taxes and property taxes were calculated within the SATF model and included in the overall discounted cost.

APPENDIX B

The Federal Water Resources Council's Proposed Standard for the Appropriate Discount Rate in Evaluating Government Investment Decisions*

D. THE DISCOUNT RATE

The discount rate will be established in accordance with the following concept:

The opportunity cost of all Federal investment activities, including water resource projects, is recognized to be the real rate of return on non-Federal investments. The best approximation to the conceptually correct rate is the average rate of return on private investment in physical assets, including all specific taxes on capital or the earnings of capital and excluding the rate of general inflation, weighted by the proportion of private investment in each major sector.

The difference between the interest rate paid on Federal borrowings and the opportunity cost rate in the private sector is due in part to the fact that private rates of return must be sufficient to pay taxes on earnings of capital. When investments are made by the Federal Government, these tax revenues are foregone. Use of the opportunity cost rate in evaluating Federal investments is necessary therefore to achieve equity from the standpoint of the Federal taxpayer who must finance Federal investments. The Federal Government should not displace funds in the private sector

---

*Extracted from Water Resources Council, *Proposed Principles and Standards for Planning Water and Related Land Resources*, 36 FR 245 (24144-24194), Washington, D.C., Dec. 21, 1971.

unless its return on investment is equal to or larger than that in the private sector.

1. *The opportunity cost of government investment.* Abstracting from income distribution considerations, the total value of the Nation's resources is maximized by expanding or contracting any specific activity to a level such that the marginal value of resources in that activity is equal to their marginal value in other feasible uses. Alternatively, the marginal value of resources in any activity is equated with the marginal cost of that activity, where cost represents the highest value forgone use of those resources in alternative activities. This general principle also applies to the Federal Government. For given total Federal outlays, the net benefit generated by the Federal Government is maximized by expanding or contracting individual Federal activities to a level for which the marginal value of resources is equal to the marginal cost of resources in all activities. If all Federal activities involved only a single time period, the prices of resources purchased by the Federal Government (including any specific excise taxes or subsidies to which other institutions are subject), would be a sufficient basis for estimating the cost of Federal activities. For those Federal activities that involve a distribution of costs over time, however, some estimate of the marginal value of resources in present uses relative to their value in future uses is necessary to estimate the cost of government activities, and this value is reflected by the selection of an appropriate interest rate for evaluating Federal investment activities. For any given Federal budget, the net benefit generated by the Government is maximized only if the marginal rate of return on all Federal activities is equal. However, the net benefit generated by Government is maximized only when the marginal rate of return on Federal investments is equal to the marginal rate of return on investments by other institutions in this Nation. Only this second condition assures a maximization of the net benefits of the Nation's investment activities and the appropriate division of investment activities between the Federal Government and other institutions.

The establishment of an interest rate for evaluation of Government investments is derived from this second condition. Once this rate is determined, individual Government investment activities should be expanded or contracted to a level such that the marginal rate of return equals this rate. The conceptually correct rate for Federal investments, assuming that the non-Federal sector will allocate additional investment funds among alternative uses in roughly the same manner as the present distribution, is the average of the marginal real rates of return in each part of the non-Federal sector, weighted by the proportion of present investment in each part.

2. *Estimating the discount rate for Government investments.* Estimating the appropriate real interest rate for Federal investments involves several problems: First, the critical assumption must be made that the different observed rates of return within the non-Federal sector represent equilibrium differences (reflecting different risks, taxes, and subsidies) or that the Federal Government does not systematically channel resources into a specific part of the non-Federal sector in its investment activities. If the

Federal Government could effectively channel resources into those parts of the non-Federal sector with the highest rates of return, the opportunity cost of Federal investments would be higher than the average of the marginal returns. Second, there are conceptual difficulties in estimating the marginal rate of return on investments in State and local governments, and no comprehensive estimate of this rate has been made. Third, the available data provide a basis for estimating only the average rate of return in the private sector. If the average rate of return is constant (as a function of the level of investment), this is not a problem as the average and marginal rates are equal and, in the long run, this appears to be a good approximation. In the short run, the rate of return on private investment displaced by additional government investment is probably higher than the average rate.

The best approximation to the conceptually correct rate that can be made is the average of the average rates of return on private investment, weighted by the proportion of investment in different parts of the private sector. This rate has been calculated in J. A. Stockfisch, "Measuring the Opportunity Cost of Government Investment," Institute for Defense Analyses, P-490, March 1969. Stockfisch first estimates the average rate of return on physical assets (exclusive of cash holdings), including the specific (corporate and property) taxes on capital, for the period from the Korean war to the Viet Nam war. He then weights these average rates by the proportion of investment in the different parts of the private sector during the later part of this period. Finally, he reduces this aggregate average rate by the average rate of inflation in the longer period. The resulting estimate of the real average rate of return in the private sector is 10.4 percent; for this concept, this estimation procedure is probably accurate within a ±1 percent range. Recognizing the two conceptual problems discussed above, inclusion of the rate of return on State and local government investments would somewhat lower this rate and a reduction in non-Federal investment displaced by additional Federal investment would lead to a marginal rate somewhat above the average. On net, it appears that the average of the marginal returns on physical investment in the non-Federal sector is around 10 percent, and additional evidence also suggests that the marginal return on investment in education is approximately equal to the rate of return on physical investment.

Moreover, there is strong reason to believe that the real rate of return in the non-Federal sector has been roughly constant over the entire period since the Korean war. The structural conditions that determine this rate are the long-run investment prospects in the U.S. economy and the levels of taxes on capital or the earnings on capital. The long-run investment prospects appear to be roughly constant. Although the corporate income tax has been reduced slightly since the Korean war, property taxes have been increased by a roughly equal magnitude. A significant redistribution of investment activities within the non-Federal sector would also change the average of the rates of return, but this has not been observed. This suggests that a frequent recalculation of the Stockfisch estimate need not be made unless there is evidence of a significant change in these structural conditions.

It is important to recognize that the stability of the real rate of return in the non-Federal sector is not inconsistent with the observed variance of the rates on marketed debt instruments. Changes in the yields on Government bonds and other debt instruments primarily reflect conditions— such as changes in the anticipated inflation, monetary policy, and the distribution between equity and debt financing—that are unrelated to the real rate of return on investment.

In summary, the conceptual and empirical issues are not fully resolved. The above discussion, however, suggests that the appropriate rate for evaluating Government investment decisions is approximately 10 percent and is substantially invariant to short-term changes in economic and money market conditions.

APPENDIX C

Reactor Power Coefficients*

A power coefficient is simply a mathematical term which describes the response of the reactor core to certain input stimuli. For example, if the reactor power is increased by withdrawing control rods which control the nuclear chain reaction, this normally causes the fuel to increase in temperature, and to expand physically. As the core expands from the higher temperature, its height grows slightly and its outside surface area becomes larger. This allows a greater number of neutrons to leak out of the core and to be lost from the system thus tending to reduce the number of neutrons which are fissioning and liberating energy. This in turn causes the reactor power increase to be reduced compared with what would have been the case if thermal expansion had not occurred. This entire effect is described as a negative thermal expansion power coefficient. It is negative because the total power increase is reduced compared to that implied by the control rod movement, and it is instantaneous or prompt because it occurs with the same velocity that neutron movement occurs. If the coefficient were positive instead of negative, the opposite effect would occur; namely, as power increase was fed into the reactor by withdrawing control rods this increase would be amplified beyond the movement implied by the control rods in a non-expansive core. For reasons having to do with the stability and safety of the reactor it is now known that it is desirable to have the combination of all the reactor power coefficients negative. One early fast reactor which had a prompt positive power coefficient was EBR-I (the net coefficient was negative, but a prompt portion was positive). This was a major factor contributing to a core meltdown in EBR-I.

*This discussion of reactor power coefficients, principally the sodium void coefficient and the Doppler coefficient, is extracted from A. S. Gibson, "The Fast Breeder Reactor," General Electric Company, Breeder Reactor Department, 1971. [footnotes omitted]

During early development of the fast reactor it became apparent that two particular reactor characteristics were desirable. One of these characteristics is a long fuel lifetime and the other is the negative power coefficient just discussed. A long fuel lifetime, which results from leaving the fuel in the reactor for an extended period, can yield a low fuel cost. Most of the early fast reactor designs included uranium fuel in the form of metal. Under irradiation this metal is gradually damaged until it must be removed from the reactor. However, by changing the form of the uranium or plutonium metal to uranium or plutonium oxide, it was found that the lifetime of the fuel could be extended substantially (10,000 to 20,000 MW days/ton for metal fuel compared with 100,000 MW days/ton burnup for oxide fuel). [Difficulties in achieving the high burnup with oxide fuel are discussed in the text.]

Metal fuel expands as its temperature increases in response to a power increase, and this results in a prompt negative power coefficient. Oxide or ceramic fuel also expands with increasing temperature, but because of the way in which the fuel is fabricated, this expansion is less predictable than that of the metal fuel. Fortunately, it was found that using ceramic fuel not only improved the fuel lifetime characteristics, but also introduced a prompt negative power coefficient which was as predictable as the expansion coefficient in metal fuel. This particular coefficient is known as the Doppler coefficient. Since the ceramic fuel is a high temperature material, in order for the fuel to undergo damage it must reach very high temperatures. It is the change in temperature from the operating point to some higher temperature which produces the Doppler effect. The effect is caused by the heating up of the atoms of uranium in the fuel, thus causing them them to move faster. Neutrons which are passing through the fuel tend to be captured by some of the uranium-238 atoms at what is known as a "resonant" energy. The increased velocity of the uranium atoms increases the number of these atoms which are at the resonant capture energy relative to the passing neutrons. These U-238 atoms therefore stop some of the neutrons which otherwise would have continued their travel until they were captured in the fission process, and this tends to reduce reactivity and power. Again a negative reactivity or negative power coefficient results.

Other reactivity coefficients arise from changes in the average fuel concentration in the core such as can arise from the bowing of fuel elements or subassemblies induced by radial and axial temperature gradients. Axial fuel movement from thermal expansion, particularly in the course of a transient power excursion, can also lead to significant reactivity feedback.[1]

Discovery of the Doppler effect in fast reactors was an extremely important development. By using ceramic fuel it was found that the fuel lifetime

[1]C. N. Kelber et al., Safety Problems of Liquid-Metal-Cooled Fast Breeder Reactors, Argonne National Laboratory, ANL-7657 (Feb. 1970).

could be extended and at the same time a mechanism was found to exist which would instantaneously reduce the effect of inadvertently adding large amounts of reactivity which could cause the reactor to become "prompt critical" or uncontrolled. In a typical large sodium cooled fast breeder reactor, for example, it is possible to imagine a very improbable event in which one of the control rods is instantaneously removed while the reactor is running at full power. If we further imagine that none of the many automatic safety devices function so as to insert the other safety rods, then the fuel temperature will rise slightly and hesitate at a value which is below the point at which damage to the fuel would occur. This hesitation for 1 second or so allows corrective action to be taken. The major factor in this hypothetical accident which prevents the reactor from becoming uncontrolled is the Doppler effect. Similarly, if a hypothetical and extremely unlikely meltdown and secondary criticality accident is assumed to occur, a fast reactor with a typical Doppler coefficient ($-TdK/dT = 0.003$ or larger) would have an energy release for doing damage 5 times smaller than a reactor which had no Doppler effect.

One of the power coefficients in a sodium cooled fast breeder reactor which is not negative is the sodium void coefficient. If the sodium were to boil it could be expelled from the coolant channels. Depending upon the geometry of the fast reactor core and the manner in which the sodium is removed, this can result in a positive reactivity effect. This occurs because sodium tends to slow neutrons down and reduce the number of *fast* neutrons available for fissioning. Therefore, when sodium is removed from the core by boiling, not as many neutrons are slowed down and more fast neutrons are available for the fission process. An offsetting effect is that removal of sodium also tends to allow more neutrons to leak from the core (because of less scattering) and this results in a decrease in the total number of neutrons. The net result of these two competing effects is dependent upon the geometric pattern of the sodium being removed from the core. Under the proper circumstances, the net effect can be to increase the number of neutrons available for fission with a consequent reactivity increase and an increase in the power level of the reactor. As previously observed, the sodium operates very much below the boiling point in the reactor and this reduces the likelihood of boiling. Furthermore, instruments are present to detect conditions which might cause boiling and the reactor can be shut down if anomalies appear. Finally, in order for the boiling to introduce large amounts of positive reactivity it must be generated in a uniform manner starting in the center of the core and progressing gradually outward as a sphere. Experiments and analyses have shown that, in fact, boiling cannot occur in this manner but would develop in a manner which is non-coherent and does not produce as much positive reactivity as would otherwise be the case.

From the foregoing discussion of the characteristics of fast breeder reactors, it is clear that some of these characteristics have a salutary effect on the safety of the reactor and others have a deleterious effect. The intelligent designer selects parameters and design features so as to amplify the desirable characteristics, and so as to deemphasize or to properly cope with the undesirable characteristics. By this means the designer can achieve a system which responds in a conservative manner with considerable design safety margin for both normal and abnormal operating conditions.

By designing to have a safety margin for abnormal operating conditions, such as might occur in an accident, the designer does not expect to be able to identify exactly how an accident will occur. Indeed, if the exact sequence of events of an accident could be foreseen, then the designer could incorporate features to prevent these events from occurring. Instead, the designer considers a sufficiently broad range of unlikely events that he is able to identify an envelope of safe and unsafe conditions. He can then choose design features and parameters so that the unsafe conditions have a very low probability of harming humans.

APPENDIX D

Foreign Uranium Resources

At present the United States prohibits the enrichment of foreign uranium for use in U.S. reactors. At one time the AEC set mid-1973 as the provisional target date for permitting the first imports.[1] It now appears that the AEC will not remove the import restriction until the latter part of the decade to allow the U.S. uranium industry to gain a stronger competing position.[2]

A working party of twenty-five experts from fourteen countries estimated in 1970 that on a worldwide basis the uranium supply and price outlook was stable for the next ten years.[3] Recently the price of uranium on the non-U.S. free-world market has been approaching, if not surpassing, all-time lows.[4]

The free world resources of uranium, as reported by the Nuclear Task Group of the National Petroleum Council, is shown in Table D-1. The Task Group noted:

Six countries—the United States, Canada, South Africa, South West Africa, Australia and France (together with its former colonies of Niger, Gabon and the Central African Republic)—have 94 percent of the reasonably assured resources and 96 percent of the estimated additional resources at $10 a pound of U_3O_8. These countries also have 93 percent

[1]"Stockpile Disposition," *Nuclear Industry,* 18, Part I (Oct.-Nov., 1971), p. 12. [No author indicated.]

[2]"Late News," *Electrical World* (Nov. 1, 1971), p. 19. [No author indicated.]

[3]"Nuclear Briefs," *Electrical World* (May 4, 1970), p. 59. [No author indicated.]

[4]"Price Deterioration Lurks in Background at Uranium Session,"*Nuclear Industry,* 18 (Sept. 1971), p. 11. [No author indicated.]

243

of the total reasonably assured and estimated additional resources up to
$15 per pound of U_3O_8.

It should be noted that the likely rate of production of uranium reserves
is limited in some areas by such factors as size and distribution of deposits
(Canada) and association with other types of mining operations (South
Africa). Considering the problems and proposed operational rates, it is
estimated that not over 800,000 tons of presently delineated reasonably
assured reserves (U_3O_8 at $10 or less per pound) would be produced over
the 15-year period. However, the required additional U_3O_8 will be avail-

TABLE D-1. Free-World Resources of Uranium in 1970

(U_3O_8 in thousands of short tons)

Location	Reasonably assured[a]	Estimated additional[a]	Total resources
	Price to $10 per pound		
Canada	232	230	462
South Africa	200	15	215
France, Niger, Gabon, C.A.R.[b]	95	81	176
Other[c]	63	49	112
United States[d]	390	680	1070
Southwest Africa, Australia[e]	100	200	300
Subtotal	1080	1255	2335
	Price $10–$15 per pound[f]		
Canada	130	170	300
South Africa	65	35	100
France, Niger, Gabon, C.A.R.[b]	22	35	57
Other	43	70	113
United States	190	360	550
Subtotal	450	670	1120
Total	1530	1925	3455

SOURCE: National Petroleum Council, "U.S. Energy Outlook, an Initial
Appraisal, 1971–1985," Vol. 2, Summaries of Task Group Reports (Nov. 1971).
These estimates were based in part on data from "Uranium: Resources, Production
and Demand," (Sept. 1970), a Joint Report by the European Nuclear Energy Agency
and the International Atomic Energy Agency to the Organisation for Economic Cooperation and Development.

[a]See Glossary for definition.
[b]Central African Republic.
[c]Argentina, Australia, Brazil, Italy, Japan, Mexico, Portugal, and Spain.
[d]According to U.S. AEC estimates of Jan. 1, 1971, some 90,000 tons of U_3O_8
may occur as a by-product of phosphate and copper production through year 2000;
25,000 might be available by 1985.
[e]The task group decided it would be desirable to recognize recent reported discoveries in Southwest Africa and Australia. In the absence of specific data, the
task group arbitrarily added 100,000 reasonably assured and 200,000 estimated
additional for these discoveries.
[f]Excludes reasonably assured of 350,000 tons and estimated additional of 50,000
tons for Sweden considered to be essentially unavailable because of production limitation and stated Swedish policy of meeting only a "certain part" of Swedish
requirements.

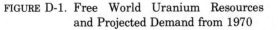

FIGURE D-1. Free World Uranium Resources
and Projected Demand from 1970

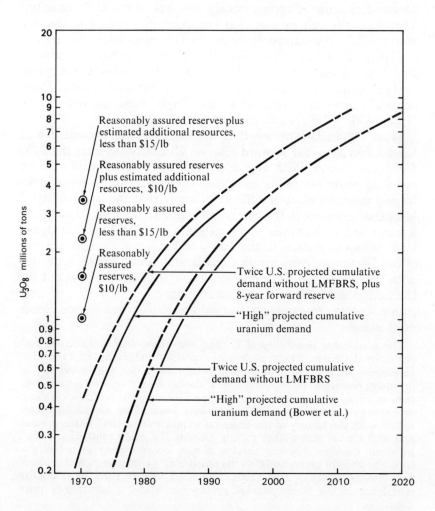

SOURCE: National Petroleum Council, "U.S. Energy Outlook: An Initial Appraisal, 1971-1985," Vol. 2 (Nov. 1971); and L.W. Boxer, W. Häussermann, J. Cameron, and J.T. Roberts, "Uranium Resources, Production and Demand" (paper presented at the Fourth United Nations International Conference on Peaceful Uses of Atomic Energy, Geneva, Sept. 6-16, 1971).

able from additional deposits delineated as reasonably assured reserves by continuing exploration and development.[5]

Nuclear generating capacity in the rest of the free world is assumed to grow at approximately the rate of the U.S. capacity.[6] Therefore, one can assume that the uranium demand in the free world will be approximately twice the U.S. demand. In Figure D-1 the lower dashed curve represents twice the U.S. projected cumulative demand without the LMFBR. The upper dashed curve represents this same demand plus an eight-year forward reserve. These demand curves are higher than the "high" demand predicted by Boxer et al., which is also shown in the figure.

From Figure D-1 we see that the free world at present has at least a fourteen-year forward reserve, almost twice what the AEC feels is necessary. With over 90 percent of the free world's known uranium resources in six countries, and the rest of its resources largely unexplored, it is difficult to argue that the availability of low-grade uranium in the free world is not substantial. In addition, a major find in Australia in recent years has added another significant uranium district to the free world reserve. Seventy percent of the foreign reserves are in Canada and South Africa, countries with limited power requirements. The Canadians have asked the United States to lift the uranium embargo.

In discussing free world geological and exploration factors, Boxer et al. state:

The favourable possibility of finding such [low-cost] uranium is supported by the views of most geological experts. It is believed that considerable areas of the world, geologically favourable for the occurrence of uranium, remain to be explored and, if the necessary exploration expenditure is committed, there are good possibilities that sufficient low-cost uranium can be found to satisfy the future needs. This conclusion is consistent with the history of the uranium industry from 1945 to the present and with that of many other metals. Despite the many conflicting factors involved, the discovery and proving of new low-cost reserves is likely to be fairly directly proportional to the amount of exploration which is done. The amount of exploration funds committed will, in turn, be related to confidence in the future market requirements and a satisfactory price level.[7]

[5]National Petroleum Council, "U.S. Energy Outlook, An Initial Appraisal, 1971-1985," Vol. Two, Summaries of Task Group Reports (Nov. 1971), pp. 143-54.

[6]L. W. Boxer, W. Haussermann, J. Cameron, and J. T. Roberts, "Uranium Resources, Production and Demand" (paper presented at the Fourth United Nations International Conference on Peaceful Uses of Atomic Energy, Geneva, Sept. 6-16, 1971).

[7]Ibid.

APPENDIX E

The Cost of Proving Uranium Reserves

The following is a discussion of the relationship among gross sales, expenditures for exploration and development, and the cost of proving reserves in the uranium industry. Similar analyses have been used by the EEI Reactor Assessment Panel[1] and others to examine whether the uranium mining industry can meet forward reserve requirements.

Given the AEC's 1970 projection of uranium demand in the absence of the LMFBR, and in order to maintain an eight-year forward reserve, the average relationship between uranium prices (P), the fraction of gross revenues represented by expenditures for exploration and development (f), and the cost of proving reserves (q) would be approximated by the curves in Figure E-1. The two curves in the figure are simply reciprocals of one another, and are found by solving $fPR(t) = qR(t+8)$, where $R(t)$ is the rate of production in year t given by the derivative of the AEC's 1970 projected demand curve (see Figure 13, solid line).[2]

At present, it costs by AEC estimates approximately $0.90/lb to

[1]Edison Electric Institute, *Report of the EEI Reactor Assessment Panel,* Publication No. 70-30 (New York, 1970).

[2]This analysis is performed on the uranium demand projection (Case 1) from the 1970 Analysis. If the demand curve is revised to reflect the more recent AEC projections through 1985 [*Nuclear Power, 1973-2000,* U.S. AEC, WASH 1139 (72), December 1, 1972], the relationship between f, p, and q would change; however, the thesis of the argument presented here would not change.

247

FIGURE E-1. Relationship Between Uranium Price, Revenues, and Exploration Costs

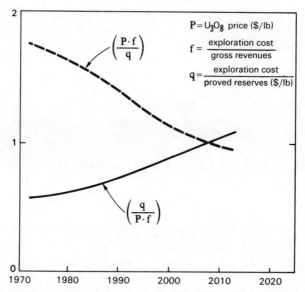

NOTE: This relationship between uranium prices (P), fraction of gross revenues allocated for exploration (f), and yield of proved reserves per dollar (q) must be met on the average in order to maintain an eight-year forward reserve without the LMFBR.

prove reserves.[3] This includes the cost of land acquisition, exploration drilling, and development drilling. About 20 percent of gross revenue from the sale of U_3O_8 (at \$6/lb to \$8/lb) has been represented by expenditures for exploration and development in recent years; in the past, this figure has sometimes been around 10 percent.

What appears to concern the EEI Reactor Assessment Panel, and others, is the following. In the event that the cost of proving reserves increases, due for instance to scarcity of supply, increases in drilling costs, necessity for drilling to deeper depths, etc., it is argued that the industry may be unwilling to commit the additional percentages of expected income to develop reserves rapidly

---

[3]Wilfrid Johnson, "Status of the Uranium Producing Industry," *Mining Congress Journal* (Feb. 1972).

enough to meet the forward reserve commitment. In other words, the belief here is that we are in trouble if q, the cost of proving reserves, increases more rapidly than the solid line, $q/(P \cdot f)$, in Figure E-1. This would have to be offset by similar increases in $(f \cdot P)$; otherwise we would fall behind in our reserve position.

APPENDIX F

Electrical Energy Demand

FORECASTS BASED ON GROSS NATIONAL PRODUCT[1]

Every power company periodically makes the kinds of forecasts described here as part of its over-all planning. From time to time these forecasts are reviewed and changed to meet changing conditions.

In 1959 an exhaustive forecast was made of the total electric utility industry. This forecast was made two ways: by a task force with knowledge of its local conditions and by the staff of the Edison Electric Institute.

In order to supply the information for the forecast by regions, the task force made estimates of the peak loads and energy requirements in its respective regions. The Edison Electric Institute assembled all the regional forecasts and summarized the industry's forecast based on local conditions. The staff of the Institute then made a forecast based on a number of correlations. Kilowatt-hour sales on a national basis are influenced by the level of business activity, the growth of the economy, and population. In analyzing historical trends in kilowatt-hour sales it was found that positive relationships existed between kilowatt-hour sales in the various customer classifications and components of the gross national product in constant dollars, and the Federal Reserve Board Index of Industrial Production. By a series of correlations it was found that long-term estimates of kilowatt-hour sales could be derived with a reasonable degree of confidence from estimates of growth in the national economy as measured by GNP in constant dollars. Residential sales showed a definite correlation with disposable personal income; commercial sales correlated with personal consumption expenditures for services; and industrial sales correlated with the FRB Index of Industrial Production (Charts 6.14, 6.15, 6.16 [not shown]). All these, in turn, could be correlated with GNP in con-

---

[1]Extracted from Edwin Vennard, *The Electric Power Business* (New York: McGraw-Hill Book Co., 2nd ed., 1970), pp. 144-46. Vennard is the former managing director of Edison Electric Institute.

250

stant dollars. Two such estimates were made. One assumed the GNP (in constant dollars) would continue to grow at the 3.57 percent average annual rate of the twelve years 1946-1958, and the other assumed an annual average increase in the GNP of 3 percent per year, which was the average rate of growth in GNP (in constant 1954 dollars) over the preceding fifty years.

The aggregate kilowatt-hour generation as estimated by the task force coincided with the projection of kilowatt-hours based on the average rate of growth in GNP between 1946-1958 of 3.57 percent per year compounded. Generation was estimated from total sales by adding an estimated amount for losses in transmission, company use, and so on. The projection was based on a 3.57 percent rate of growth in GNP. To project to the year 2000 involved a great deal of speculation. Studies by EEI indicate that in the year 2000 total output will range between 8 trillion and 10 trillion kilowatt-hours, depending on the rate of growth of the national economy and the rate at which new energy uses are introduced, especially electric space heating.

Every year the forecast is checked against the actual kilowatt-hour production for that year. The cumulative error has been so slight that it has been found unnecessary to change the forecast from that made in 1959. Through 1968 the cumulative error was 0.182 percent—slightly less than two-tenths of one percent. That is, the actual production through 1968 was within about two-tenths of one percent of the production forecast nine years ago. On this basis the cumulative error for 1980 should be within the range of 1 percent, plus or minus.

FORECAST BASED ON A GOMPERTZ CURVE FITTED TO ELECTRICAL ENERGY DEMAND PER CAPITA

The Gompertz curve describes a trend in which the growth increments of the logarithms are declining by a constant percentage. It is frequently valid for situations in which there are saturation effects. The equation for the Gompertz curve is:[2]

$$y = ka^{b^t} \tag{1}$$

The Edison Electric Institute (EEI) in the late 1960s used this equation to fit the annual per capita electrical energy demand. Their results, curve (a) plotted in Figure F-1,[3] correspond closely to the Gompertz curve having

[2]F. E. Croxton, D. J. Cowder, and S. Klein, *Applied General Statistics,* 3rd ed. (Prentice-Hall, 1967).

[3]Edwin Vennard, *The Electric Power Business* (New York: McGraw-Hill, 2nd. ed, 1970).

FIGURE F-1. Gompertz Curves of Projected Electrical
Energy Demand Per Capita

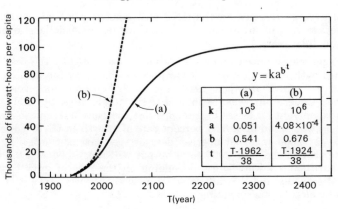

NOTE: Gompertz curve (a) is fitted to historical U.S. electrical energy
demand per capita. Curve (b) is a similar curve with asymptotic limit
of 10^6 kwh.

$$k = 10^5 \qquad\qquad b = 0.541$$
$$a = 0.051 \qquad\qquad t = \frac{T - 1962}{38} \qquad (2)$$

where T is the calendar year.[4] This projection forecasts an electrical demand in the year 2000 equal to approximately 20,000 kwh
per capita.

The per capita demand can be related to the total U.S. electrical
energy demand using current population projections. Two Census
Bureau projections, based on July 1, 1969, data, are shown in
Figure F-2. At the time of this projection, most demographers considered the Series B and E projections as representing reasonable
limits within which the future U.S population would grow.
Roughly speaking the Series B and E projections correspond
respectively to three- and two-children family norms. With evidence that society may be responding to the zero population growth
movement, many demographers now feel the U.S. population will
follow more closely the E Series rather than the B Series

[4]Milton Searl, private communication.

FIGURE F-2. Current and Projected U.S. Population

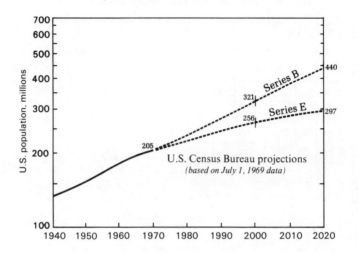

projection.[5] Had the annual U.S. electrical energy demands using the EEI Gompertz fit (eqs. 1 and 2) and the Census Bureau's Series B been plotted in Figure 16, the projection would lie just below Searl's curve for 4 percent GNP growth. The corresponding curve using Series E would lie between Searl's projections for 3 percent and 3.5 percent real GNP growth rates. In the year 2000 neither population projection yields a demand as high as the low demand curve used by the AEC. Referring back to Figure 17, it is seen that if this EEI projection, based on the historical trend in per capita electrical energy demand, is correct, the discounted net benefits of an early commitment to the LMFBR program effectively vanish based on energy demand alone.

Looking at the same data in reverse, one can ask what per capita electrical energy demand growth would be needed in order to meet

[5]The fertility rate—complete cohort fertility (average number of births per woman upon completion of childbearing)—has dropped from well over 3.6 as recently as 1961 to below the replacement level of 2.11 (2.11 children per family would cause zero population growth after about 70 years). In the first nine months of 1972 the fertility rate was 2.08, or even 2.04, depending on the method of estimation. [*New York Times*, December 18, 1972, pp. 1, 56]. The Bureau of Census in its 1972 projections abandoned Series B. Its 1972 projections of total population for 2000 range from 251 million (Series F) to 300 million (Series C); for 2020 the corresponding estimates are 265 million and 392 million. Series F and C correspond to fertility rates of 1.8 and 2.8, respectively.

FIGURE F-3. Annual U.S. Electrical Use Per Capita,
and Curves Fit to These Data, 1947-70

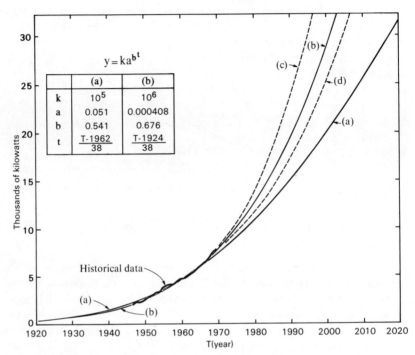

NOTE: Curves (a) and (b) are the Gompertz curves shown in Figure F-1;
curves (c) and (d) are described in the text.

the AEC energy demand projections. Again, this depends on which
census projections we use. In Figure F-3 the curve (c) is the per
capita demand which would be required to meet AEC/FPC "probable" U.S. electrical energy demand curve (in Figure 16) if the
Series E census projection is correct. Curve (d) in Figure F-3 is
the per capita demand required to meet the AEC's lower total electrical energy demand (Figure 16) and the higher, Series B, census
projection. The curves for the two other cases of interest, Series
E population trend with the AEC's lower energy demand curve and
Series B population trend with the AEC's probable energy demand,
lie between the (c) and (d) curves in Figure F-3. They are not
shown because they would simply add more confusion to the
already cluttered figure.

These data suggest that the per capita energy demand will have to increase much more rapidly than one would expect based on the EEI's Gompertz fit to the historical data.

The Gompertz projection has several major weaknesses. It is based on the regression fit to the data. Unlike the electrical demand versus GNP regression, the Gompertz regression uses time (calendar year) as the independent variable. It is more likely that the technology of generating, transmitting, and distributing electricity, costs, per capita income, and a host of other variables are the controlling factors which influence per capita electrical energy demand. It is difficult to believe that the interaction of these factors will continue in a manner which will enable us to predict per capita consumption over a fifty-year period from the trend in the historical data. But even if one discounts this fact, as seen from curve (a) in Figure F-1, the available historical data (1880–1970) only covers a small segment of the significant portion of the curve (1900–2200). In effect this means that the variance of the asymptote k (in eq. 1) will be large when the Gompertz curve is fit to the historical data. This implies that a good fit to the historical data can be obtained by fixing k at some larger value. In Figure F-3, curve (b) was obtained by setting k at 10^6 and solving for the Gompertz curve which intersected the other Gompertz solution, curve (a), at 1924 and 1962. As seen from curve (b) in Figure F-3, this Gompertz solution also provides a good fit to the historical data. It, however, forecasts a much larger per capita electrical energy between now and the year 2020. This curve also forecasts the necessary per capita electrical energy demand needed to meet the AEC/FPC projections, i.e., curve (b) in Figure 16 is straddled by curves (c) and (d).

Although k equal to 10^6 corresponds to a per capita electrical energy demand by the year 2300 that is 1000 times the present demand, a value that is difficult to believe, this analysis does suggest that: (1) reasonable errors in the asymptotic value of the per capita energy demand can have a significant effect on the projected demand during the next few decades, and (2) the Gompertz projections are not very reliable for forecasting energy demand.

FORECAST OF RICHARD SALTER

Richard G. Salter of RAND recently projected the U.S. electrical energy demand in the year 2000. He estimates that there is a high probability that the U.S. electrical energy consumption in 2000 will be less than 4.5 trillion kwh.[6] Salter notes that this estimate does not attempt to mobilize either the full depth of expertise available in the contributing disciplines or a comprehensive set of historical data.[7] Nevertheless, he considers the results meaningful. While Salter notes that his estimate is about one-half the values published elsewhere, it is his opinion that the other published forecasts do not adequately account for the saturation phenomena involved.[8]

[6]Richard G. Salter, "A Probabilistic Forecasting Methodology Applied to Electrical Energy Consumption," RAND No. R-993-NSF (draft, Feb. 1972), p. 19.
[7]Ibid., p. 1.
[8]Ibid., p. 25.

APPENDIX G

The LMFBR Demonstration Plant

EXCERPTS FROM STATEMENT BY RICHARD E. WEBB[1]

Explosion potential

The "Environmental Statement" (WASH-1509, April 1972) issued by the Atomic Energy Commission for the LMFBR Demo states that the substantiation of the claim that the reactor will be safe must await the issuance of the Preliminary Safety Analysis Report (PSAR) when the construction permit application is filed with the AEC. (See E.S., p. 37, 107). But it is obvious from reading the Environmental Statement that the AEC and the Joint Committee on Atomic Energy have prejudged the question of safety. For example, Congress has already authorized the LMFBR Demo and appropriated the money for it. (E.S., p. 1) Furthermore, the AEC asserted in the Environmental Statement that the provisions in the reactor containment structure for "blast and missile protection within the inner barrier provide substantial margins against major potential energy releases for *all* classes of accidents". (E.S. p. 54; emphasis added) The AEC added: "While it is impossible to postulate with precision the detailed course of accidents, including their likelihood and possible environmental

---

[1]"Liquid Metal Fast Breeder Reactor (LMFBR) Demonstration Plant," Hearings before the Joint Committee on Atomic Energy of the U.S. Congress, 92 Cong. 2 sess. (Sept. 7, 8, 12, 1972), pp. 179-187. Portions of Webb's statement pertaining to the unconstitutionality of the LMFBR program and the difficulty of obtaining technical reports are not reproduced here. Webb had extensive training in nuclear reactor operations before receiving his Ph.D. in Nuclear Engineering at Ohio State University. His dissertation concerned the explosive potential of LMFBRs. He is one of the leading critics of the LMFBR program, and his concern stems from his analysis of the safety aspects of the program.

257

consequences, *it is possible to place bounds on such accidents*". (E.S., p. 119; emphasis added)

These statements have no scientific foundation. Based on my knowledge of the state of the science of LMFBR explosion calculations, there is no chance that the aforesaid PSAR will substantiate such conclusions. Therefore, the construction of the LMFBR Demo should not be undertaken until after the necessary theoretical and experimental research is conducted, if such research demonstrates safety. The alternative is for Congress to recall the authorization and appropriation for the LMFBR Demo, wait for the issuance of the PSR, and its review by the AEC and the Public, then hold public hearings on the safety of the LMFBR Demo.

. . . .

The calculational methods for determining the maximum explosion possible in an LMFBR have not been developed to include all possibilities, and their combinations, for autocatalytic phenomena during and after an initial nuclear runaway. That is, there are conceivable mechanisms by which "reactivity" can or might be rapidly "inserted" due to the motion of fuel material resulting from an initial core explosion or meltdown event. (Recall that in fast reactors, a core meltdown presents a mechanism by which reactivity can increase semi-rapidly and trigger disruptive or explosive power pulses.)[2] In other words, an initial event, or series of events, might cause the reactor to feed itself a massive dose of "reactivity" which would amplify the initial runaway, or cause a very severe secondary runaway; either of which might lead to a disastrous explosion.

When the calculational methods are developed to include all possible autocatalytic effects, they would still need experimental confirmation. Moreover, the present calculational methods have not been confirmed experimentally for power reactor designs. For example, it has been claimed by Hirakawa and Klickman[3] that the KIWI-TNT power excursion experiment (TNT stands for Transient Nuclear Tests) has confirmed the MARS fast reactor excursion computer code. (The basic theory in MARS is the Bethe-Tait theory, which is partially used in the more advanced explosion codes such as VENUS. This theory provides the reactivity feedback mechanism that ends or "shuts down" the power excursion, and thereby, limits the explosion force.) However, though the *post facto* MARS calculation of energy yield agreed fairly well with the KIWI-TNT measurement, the power pulse height (peak power), pulse shape, and pulse width as calculated by the MARS code are completely different that the KIWI-TNT experimental results. I used a simple thermal expansion model, which excludes the basic theory in MARS that was thought to be tested (i.e., the Bethe-Tait theory), and calculated all four of the above

    [2]LMFBR Demostration Plant Environmental Statement, WASH-1509, United States Atomic Energy Commission, April 1972, p. 118.
    [3]N. Hirakawa and A. E. Klickman, "An Analysis of the KIWI-TNT Experiment with MARS Code", *Journal of Nuclear Science and Technology*, Volume 7, No. 2, pp. 1-6, January 1970.

items in excellent agreement with the experimental results.[4] This strongly indicates that the inherent shutdown reactivity mechanism of the KIWI-TNT experiment was not the Bethe-Tait mechanism, but one due to the simple thermal expansion of the KIWI core; and that the agreement between the MARS value of energy releases and experimental measurement was concidental. In support of my conclusion, Jankus stated that the "Bethe-Tait assumption is definitely unjustified" for the KIWI-TNT excursion.[5] Furthermore, KIWI was not a fast reactor. Therefore, the KIWI-TNT explosion test has not been shown to be a confirmation of LMFBR explosion theories.

The SEFOR power excursion tests, which were performed to confirm the mitigating action of the Doppler effect for fast reactors, cannot be considered as proving out the LMFBR *explosion* calculational methods because the SEFOR excursions were not designed to lead to an explosion.[6] The tests involved (1) relatively mild rates of programmed reactivity insertion, (and then the total reactivity inserted was limited to a small amount); (2) designed Doppler feedback magnitudes that were much greater than typical 1000 MWe LMFBR design values; and (3) automatic termination of the power transient by control rod scram (probably preprogrammed) to ensure against unexpected secondary excursions. Because of the strong Doppler and the limited amount of total reactivity that was inserted, the strongest power excursion tested was easily stopped with only about a 10% rise in the fuel temperature, which means that the SEFOR tests approached no threshold for meltdown or explosion. Normally in LMFBR accident calculations one assumes that the initial reactivity insertion is not limited, but is unrelenting. Thus, in a real accident situation the Doppler effect alone would not be sufficient to terminate the power excursion, and the core would continue to generate energy until there is an explosive or disruptive "disassembly" of the core that finally stops the power excursion and shuts down the reactor, if one could still call the reactor destroyed a "reactor". (Just how severe the explosion is and whether it is aggravated by autocatalytic effects is my main concern.)

Therefore, although the SEFOR tests were very useful in demonstrating the Doppler mitigating mechanism, and were evidently successful in that regard,[6] they provide no confirmation of explosion calculational methods. This is just as well, since there is a report which indicates that SEFOR was not designed to contain severe explosions.[7] With one-half ton of Plutonium in the SEFOR reactor, it appears that the AEC simply took a chance with the public safety by purposely causing power excursions, which one tries normally to prevent in power reactors, to test a safety

[4]R. E. Webb, "Critical Review of the KIWI-TNT Power Excursion as Calculated by the MARS Fast Reactor Excursion Code", Draft paper, unpublished.
[5]V. Z. Jankus, "Calculation of the Energy Yield in the KIWI Transient Nuclear Test, KIWI-TNT", ANL-7310, p. 366.
[6]SEFOR Reports: GEAP-13598, 10010-24, 29, 30 and 31. See Ref. 2 and 10 for discussion of SEFOR in regards to LMFBR safety, Ref. 2, pp. 19-20.
[7]R. E. Shaver and N. G. Wittenbrock, "Review of Reactor Safety Analyses of Fast and Liquid Metal Cooled Reactors", BNWL-477, UC-80, Reactor Technology, November 1967, pp. 21, 35.

effect (Doppler feedback) that was not beforehand demonstrated in a fast-reactor power excursion. (SEFOR is now being decommissioned now that the tests are finished.) Whereas, prudence would suggest that such tests involving so much Plutonium should have been conducted only after a thorough research into autocatalytic reactivity effects was completed to establish the maximum possible accident, and with a containment designed to contain the maximum possible accident. Then, prudence would suggest that such a test reactor would be placed deeply underground just in case something was overlooked. (The EBR-I, BORAX-I, and SPERT-I reactors all suffered accidents because the power excursions were undercalculated.)[8] But instead, SEFOR was built above ground and may have been without explosion containment. Similarly, the LMFBR Demo would be an experiment with unknowns, involving 1.3 tons of Plutonium, and fission product Strontium-90 and cesium-137 and the like. That is, the LMFBR Demo is simply a chance that will be taken with the health and safety of the Public if allowed to be built without a firm ground of scientific research to establish the containment design.

I mentioned so far the lack of experimental confirmation of existing calculational methods, as well as the inadequacy of the calculational methods from the standpoint of autocatalytic reactivity effects. The improved, calculational methods for predicting the LMFBR explosion potential, once developed, would still require experimental confirmation, just as was done to some extent for the Doppler effect in the SEFOR tests. To be sure fast reactor explosion tests were proposed by Nims at the 1963 Argonne National Laboratory Conference on "Breeding, Economics and Safety in Large Fast Power Reactors".[9] Nims considered the straightforward approach to simply building a prototype reactor, causing the core to meltdown, and observing the resulting explosion. Such tests would have to be repeated in a variety of ways in an effort to cover all possible or conceivable ways in which the core might meltdown. Nims indicated that the costs for such a series of tests would be prohibitive, since a series of costly reactors would have to be built, just to be destroyed. As an alternative he proposed a series of partial core meltdown experiments, short of explosion, to learn the manner in which the core would meltdown; and then with a more confident understanding of core meltdown acquired by such tests, full scale reactor meltdown tests would be designed and performed to determine the severity of the explosions associated with the prior established core meltdown patterns.

Nims argued that this alternate scheme may provide the desired information regarding LMFBR explosion potential at acceptable costs. I would add that the development of improved calculational methods regarding autocatalytic effects, that I contend is necessary, would be of help in designing such explosion experiments. (Of course, there is the possibility that such improved calculational methods might predict with confidence

[8]T. J. Thompson and J. G. Beckerley, "The Technology of Nuclear Reactor Safety", Volume 1, p. 616.
[9]J. B. Nims, "Fast Reactor Meltdown Experiments," *Proceedings of the Conference on Breeding, Economics and Safety in Large Fast Power Reactors*, October 1963, ANL-6792 (December 1963), pp. 203-231.

that the explosion potential of LMFBRs is simply too great to ever consider building LMFBRs at all). The LMFBR Program Plan (Volume 10, Safety) provides for studies of the necessity for such explosion testing.[10] (The Plan has adopted the alternate scheme investigated by Nims as that which is to be considered, without mentioning the more direct method of testing prototype reactors.) I have seen no results of such studies. Presumably, they are still being conducted. But regardless of their outcome, until improved theoretical methods are developed and tested by reactor explosion experiments, claims that the LMFBR containment structure is designed to contain "all classes of accidents" and that "it is possible to place bounds on such accidents" will continue to be groundless. Accordingly, if the United States is to pursue LMFBR development, we should discard the plans for a demonstration power reactor in favor of further research, terminating in explosion testing, unless the theoretical research proves that LMFBRs are inherently unsafe, so that we can be assured of confining the Plutonium and other radioactivity in the event of the worst possible LMFBR accident.

....

Additional Comments

Having given the Joint Committee my basic comments, I would like to offer several additional comments concerning the safety of the LMFBR Demo. These comments should not be construed as a report of an exhaustive evaluation on my part of the accident potential of the LMFBR Demo.

On page 39 of the E.S. the AEC asserts that a major objective of the LMFBR Demo project "will be to demonstrate . . . [the] safety . . . of the LMFBR power plant in a utility environment". As discussed earlier, prudence dictates that a demonstration of safety should be carried out scientifically and in such a way that the safety of the public and environment is assured *prior* to an operational demonstration of the LMFBR. That is, further theoretical research, experimental confirmation using test containers designed to contain the predicted, worst possible explosions, and then underground citing of the tests to provide protection against unforeseen effects is the approach that should be taken for demonstrating the safety of the LMFBR. However, as is now planned, the public and the environment must suffer the damage if safety is *not* demonstrated during the operation of the LMFBR Demo.

Furthermore, the 300–500 MWe LMFBR Demo *cannot* demonstrate the safety of the 1000 MWe LMFBR that the AEC plans for the 1980s. (See pages 8–9 of E.S.) This is because the larger the LMFBR is, the more hazardous are some of the safety related characteristics. For example, in a 1000 MWe LMFBR more Plutonium fissile material will be present in the core, which aggravates the core-compaction-induced power excursion (nuclear runaway) accident and the potential for associated autocatalytic

---

[10]LMFBR Program Plan, WASH-1110, Volume 10, Safety, pp. 10-213—10-23.5.

reactivity effects. Also, the larger the reactor core is, the greater is the autocatalytic reactivity effect due to reactor coolant (sodium) boiling,[12] an effect which can transform a relatively mild power excursion into a severe reactivity or nuclear runaway accident. (See pp. 112–113 of the E.S. for a brief discussion of this sodium boiling or voiding effect on reactivity.) Therefore, the LMFBR Demo will *not* demonstrate the safety of the larger 1000 MWe plant, even if the LMFBR Demo reactor core is purposely caused to suffer either the worst credible accident, or the worst possible accident.

To be sure the 1000 MWe size is not the upper limit on the size of the LMFBRs that are being contemplated in the LMFBR Research and Development Program. It is common knowledge that the bigger the LMFBR is, the more profitable it is expected to be. With this incentive Argonne National Laboratory and Westinghouse Electric Corp. performed a feasibility study[13] of a 3,880 MWe (10,000 MWt) LMFBR, which would contain, not .93 to 1.3 tons of Plutonium as will the LMFBR Demo, but 11.6 tons of Plutonium. This study concluded: "The 10,000 MWt sodium-cooled fast breeder is feasible within the context of the ground rules of this study"; and "Successful development of fast breeders of nominal 1,000-MWe size will provide the technological base for very large fast breeders with no significant further R & D program required". Therefore, we must assume that the LMFBR Demo will not only be an alleged demonstration of safety for the 1000 MWe LMFBR, but for the 3,880 MWe plant as well. But as asserted earlier, the safety of any size LMFBR has not been scientifically established; and moreover, testing one size does not establish the safety of larger sizes. For justification of the LMFBR safety, the public basically has only, therefore, the statement of the AEC on p. 6 of the E.S. concerning the stages of research, development, and engineering which the LMFBR concept has passed: "This work has led to the conviction that safe commercial size plants are technically feasible and economically promising". But the People have not elevated the "convictions" of the nuclear community or the AEC to the status as the supreme Law of the Land.

The E.S. (p. 39) states that the "safety of the LMFBR will be insured" by, among other things, (1) "duplicate and independent shutdown systems"; and (2) "a plant protection system that senses any abnormalities and automatically shuts down the plant". Item No. 1 is not reassuring, since no explicit assurance is given that each of the separate shutdown systems can individually and alone render safe all abnormal conditions where a fast shutdown would be needed to prevent serious explosion. Furthermore, the concept of "duplicate" systems does not imply systems of *diverse* design. The late AEC Commissioner Theos Thompson at the 1965 Argonne National Laboratory Conference on "Safety, Fuels, and Core Design in Large Fast Power Reactors" persuasively advocated not only redundant *scram* (fast acting) shutdown systems, but "diversity" in the

---

[12]G. H. Golden, "Elementary Neutronics Consideration LMFBR Design", ANL-7532, March, 1969.
[13]K. A. Hub, et al., "Feasibility Study of Nuclear Steam Supply System Using 10,000-MW, Sodium-Cooled Breeder Reactor", ANL-7183, September 1966, p. 25.

design of the scram systems.[14] It has been said that the boundary line between a maximum credible accident, and the more severe hypothetical accidents, is whether or not a reactor is scrammed during a serious core malfunction.[15] Therefore, the safety of the LMFBR Demo will depend in part on its scram systems. And inasmuch as Dr. Thompson argued *against* the concept of "duplicate" scram systems, the AEC's assertion, that the safety of the LMFBR Demo will be insured by such a concept, is in dispute. In this regard, I am reminded of the EBR-I core meltdown incident, which, incidentally, was caused by an autocatalytic power excursion.[16] During the excursion the control rods were scrammed, but that action failed to control the power excursion. The back-up scram system was then called on to stop the excursion. (If the back-up system would have been activated one-half second later than it was, a super prompt critical power excursion would have ensued, for which no bounds on the explosive energy release have yet been scientifically established). This back-up system consisted of dropping the reflector blanket away from the core, which was a different design concept than the control rod scram system that was first activated during the EBR-I incident. This fact supports the principle of *diversity* advocated by Theos Thompson.

The provision for the "plant protection system that senses any abnormalities and automatically shuts down the plant" strikes me as wishful thinking. Of course, we would have to await the specific design of such systems to evaluate how close to the ideal such systems can be designed for. However, there is always the possibility of unforeseen problems, human errors, carelessness, deliberate violations of design and operating procedures, and the like. In this regard I am reminded of the FBR-I core meltdown and Fermi partial core meltdown incidents. In the former the reactor operator failed to scram the control rods when he should have, and the attending scientist, who knew better the significance of the unfolding core behavior, promptly pushed the scram button himself. (See footnote 16.) During the Fermi meltdown incident, the control rod system was not scrammed when the fuel melting first occurred. Indeed the control rods were withdrawn further after the start of melting. Even after the Fermi Operator noticed that the control rod positions were abnormal, and after the core temperature readings were "found to be too high", the control rods were withdrawn still further, rather than scrammed. It wasn't until eleven minutes after a radiation leakage alarm sounded before a scram was initiated.[17] These incidents emphasize the possibility of plant protection systems not functioning as planned.

The "third level of safety" described by the AEC for the LMFBR Demo "concerns the postulated failure of protective safety systems simultane-

[14]"Discussion of Papers Among Panel", *Proceedings of the Conference on Safety, Fuels and Core Design in Large Fast Power Reactors*, October, 1965, ANL-7120, pp. 269-270.
[15]*Ibid.*, p. 268.
[16]R. O. Brittain, "Analysis of the EBR-1 Core Meltdown," page 2156, *Proceedings of the International Conference on the Peaceful Uses of Atomic Energy*, Geneva, 1958; and Reference 8 noted above, p. 628.
[17]Inferred from: R. L. Scott, Jr., "Fuel Melting Incident at the Fermi Reactor on October 5, 1966", *Nuclear Safety*, Volume 12, No. 2, March–April, 1971, pp. 123-134.

ously with the accident they are intended to control. The consequences of such hypothetical accidents must be evaluated and understood. Furthermore, if a practical means can be found to provide an additional measure of safety to mitigate the accident or accommodate the consequences, that also may be considered". (E.S., p. 106)

This description of the way in which severe accidents will occur is misleading, since it implies that two independent adverse happenings must occur simultaneously, i.e., at the same point in time without any connection. In truth severe accidents can occur because of prior, undetected failures of safety devices which won't function when an accident situation does develop. Or, conceivably, an accident could cause the safety system to fail.[19]

I do agree with the AEC that the consequences of such hypothetical accidents must be evaluated and understood. But I could not agree that only those means practical for accommodating the consequences need be considered. (Indeed, the AEC states they *may* be considered.) Rather, if no practical means can be found to accommodate all possible accidents, the LMFBR Demo should not be built. Here is another example of how subjective judgments of AEC officials are used to justify claims of safety.

The Environmental Statement includes the AEC's response to the comments from the Scientists' Institute for Public Information (SIPI). Of special importance is the AEC's response to Dr. Edward Teller's article in *Nuclear News* (August 1967), which SIPI requested. Teller's article is critical of the LMFBR from a hazards standpoint. The article expresses concern for the possibility of secondary criticality accidents following a core meltdown, which is the same concern I am addressing in this statement. The AEC's response is unintelligible:

"This problem has been recognized, and technical efforts toward its solution include the development of means to assure that meltdown will not occur, and means to prevent reassembly into a critical mass if it were to occur". (E.S., p. A-130).

Is the AEC asserting in their response that recriticality following a meltdown is impossible? If so, it would be in conflict with its statement on page 118 where the possibility for such an accident, and associated "release of explosive energy", was admitted. The fact is, such accidents are possible, and their probability of occurring is mostly a matter of speculation. In short, the AEC did not respond to Teller's concern, except to say that he "overstates the criticality hazard" by not recognizing the dilution of the Plutonium with other core materials. (However, this dilution does not preclude criticality.) It would be helpful if the Joint Committee would request and obtain Dr. Teller's answer to this reference to dilution, and to the rest of the AEC's response as well.

Furthermore, in refuting Dr. Teller's concern, the AEC asserts "that fast

[18]George R. Gallagher, "Failure of N Reactor Primary Scram System", *Nuclear Safety*, Volume 12, No. 6, November-December, 1971, pp. 608-614.
[19]W. H. Zinn, see reference No. 14 noted above, p. 268.

reactor behavior [during a mishap] is also well understood". (E.S., p. A-129). On the contrary, under accident conditions, it is not well understood. In this regard I believe the AEC distorted Teller's article. In summarizing his article, the AEC neglected to mention that Teller stated:

"I have listened to hundreds of analyses of what course a nuclear accident can take. Although I believe it is possible to analyze the immediate consequences of an accident, *I do not believe it is possible to analyze and foresee the secondary consequences*". (Emphasis added)

Similarly, an authority of fast reactor design, K. P. Cohen, of General Electric Company, stated at the before mentioned Argonne Conference in 1965 on LMFBR safety, fuels and core design:

"[W]e don't know very much about what the meltdown accident is going to be, and though one can indeed make calculations about it, one would be naive to really believe them".[20]

As I asserted earlier, the LMFBR Demo hypothetical accident predictions will be based only on *calculations*. Without the recommended improvements in these calculational methods along with experimental confirmation, we really would be naive to believe them. Sha and Waltar gave a recent status of the state of development of the calculational methods for analyzing core meltdown and explosion, and admitted that a "substantial amount of effort is yet required".[21]

---

[20]K. P. Cohen, see reference No. 14, noted above, p. 271.
[21]W. T. Sha and A. E. Waltar, "An Integrated Model for Analyzing Disruptive Accidents in Fast Reactors", *Nuclear Science and Engineering*, Volume 44, No. 2, May 1971, pp. 135-156.

EXCERPTS FROM AEC STAFF REVIEW OF WEBB'S STATEMENT[2]

2. *Safety Issues Pertinent to the LMFBR Demonstration Plant*

The Division of Reactor Development and Technology has under way extensive base technology and development programs for the purpose of providing engineering and safety understanding and thus assuring the success of the LMFBR program objectives, including the Demonstration Plant. Volume 10 of the LMFBR Program[1] covers all questions relating to the LMFBR Safety program and in particular such questions as raised by Dr. Webb, which fall in the category of hypothetical accidents and their consequences. In the area of hypothetical accidents, the safety program has as its objective the understanding of phenomena related to hypothetical events and their consequences through the conduct of extensive in-pile

---

[1]WASH-1101–1110. LMFBR Program Plan, August 1968. (It is presently being updated.)

---

[2]"LMFBR Demonstration Plant," Hearings before JCAE, pp. 188-189. Portions of this statement pertaining to Webb's remarks regarding the unconstitutionality of the LMFBR program and the difficulty of obtaining technical documents are not reproduced here.

and out-of-pile testing as well as analytical programs which complement the experiments. This understanding will provide realistic bounds and estimates of risk so as to permit both favorable engineering selection and assessment of risk relative to alternatives and to benefits anticipated. The LMFBR base and development program will encompass a full consideration of accident situations. Finally, the construction and the operation of the LMFBR Demonstration Plant will be subject to the Commission's regulatory requirements; as required by law, a permit or license will not issue if the Commission believes such issuance could be inimical to the health and safety of the public. The Commission's regulatory review will, among other things, be based on the state of the technology at that time, and on the specific features of the design being considered. Some examples of work under way in the areas of most concern to Dr. Webb are:

a. In the area of calculational methods for determining the magnitude of disassembly accidents, Argonne National Laboratory has developed the two-dimensional VENUS reactor disassembly code. This code takes into consideration autocatalytic reactivity effects such as fuel motion. The main conclusion from this work so far is that it takes only a moderate pressure and a very small amount of material movement to cause the disassembly of a nuclear reactor. Thus, during a hypothetical nuclear excursion, the maximum energy and thus the generated pressures are limited by the early occurrence of disassembly. This work has been conducted by using the FFTF parameters and characteristics. As can be seen from the referenced LMFBR Program Plan, work in this area is continuing. Because of the close coupling of potential safety problems to a particular design, a specific design (the demonstration plant for example) will be used to bring into sharp focus the LMFBR safety program, including work in the area of disassembly accidents of concern to Dr. Webb.

b. The in-pile meltdown tests performed to date in the TREAT reactor indicate that the mechanical damage potential is less than that which is thermodynamically possible by two or more orders of magnitude.

Dr. Webb uses the EBR-I incident as a strong justification for his argument of the autocatalytic nature of fuel element melting. It has been established that the meltdown of the EBR-I fuel was due to fuel element bowing which because of the fuel's structural design caused a positive coefficient of reactivity. It is this effect that caused the short period transient in the EBR-I experiment and eventually led to the meltdown. The post-mortem examination of EBR-I indicated that uranium was expelled from the core. More than half of the uranium which was originally at the core center had been pushed out by melting to a position near the edge of the core. Therefore, the EBR-I meltdown incident demonstrated that this phenomenon contributed to the shutdown of the reactor instead of leading the reactor into a "runaway" condition as asserted by Dr. Webb. In fact, the importance of fuel motion as a shutdown mechanism is also evident from recent analyses (ANL's SAS and HEDL's MELT Accident Analysis Codes) and the results from the in-pile testing in the TREAT reactor.

. . . .

COMMENT ON AEC REPLY TO WEBB

Webb has prepared for layman's comprehension a detailed rebuttal to the AEC's comments.[3] Although it is too long to be reproduced here, the following brief points are worth noting.

Contrary to the AEC's statement above, its LMFBR Program Plan does *not* "cover all questions relating to the LMFBR safety program and in particular such questions as raised by Dr. Webb." The Plan avoids a definite commitment to full-scale, core meltdown/nuclear runaway tests which Webb contends are necessary in order to verify the LMFBR accident analysis codes—the computer methods used in predicting the LMFBR explosion potential.[4]

The AEC states ". . . the maximum energy and thus the generated pressure are limited by the early occurrence of disassembly," and ". . . The in-pile meltdown tests performed to date in the TREAT reactor indicate that the mechanical damage potential is less than that which is thermodynamically possible by two or more orders of magnitude."[5] These experiments have no relation to full-scale, core-destruct tests, which are necessary to verify the accident analysis codes.[6] Also, with respect to the first quote, i.e., early occurrence of disassembly, this response appears to be based on a study by Waltar et al.[7] and the belief that the location in the reactor core where fuel faults first appear (above, below, or near the core midplane) and the sequence and time histories of their development can be predicted with a high degree of centainty. With respect to the second quote, concerning the TREAT tests (p. 268), again, because of their limited extent, there are simply too many uncertainties to reach any definitive conclusion about the efficiency for converting the thermal energy of the fuel to mechanical energy. Furthermore, the properties of sodium in the subcooled liquid state have heretofore been approximated because of a lack

---

[3]Richard E. Webb, *The Explosion Hazard of the Liquid Metal Cooled Fast Breeder Reactor (LMFBR) and the Unconstitutionality of the AEC's Civilian Nuclear Power Program,* July 1973.

[4]Ibid., pp. 17-18.

[5]"LMFBR Demonstration Plant," Hearings before the JCAE, p. 189.

[6]Richard E. Webb, *The Explosion Hazard of the LMFBR,* p. 18.

[7]A. E. Waltar, W.L. Partain, and B. E. Simpson, "Effects of Molten Fuel Movement during a Fast Reactor Overpower Transient" (paper presented at the Annual Meeting of the American Nuclear Society, Las Vegas, Nev., June 18-22, 1972). See also Hanford Engineering Development Laboratory, "Fast Flux Test Facility Design Safety Assessment," HEDL-TME 72-92 (July 1972), Ch. 3, Section 3.2.3, p. 3.2-2.

of experimental data. This procedure may also lead to significant errors in the calculations of pressure pulses and mechanical work during the time the sodium is in the single-phase liquid state [e.g., during a fuel-coolant interaction involving the whole core].[8]

[8]C. A. Erdmann, P. L. Garner, and A. B. Reynolds, "Use of Saturated Liquid Sodium Properties in Fuel-Coolant Interaction Analysis" (paper presented at the International Conference on Nuclear Solutions to World Energy Problems, sponsored by the American Nuclear Society, Washington, D.C., Nov. 12-17, 1972).

Glossary

Breeding ratio: *See* Conversion ratio.

Cladding: Tubing—generally either stainless steel or zirconium alloy (zircalloy)—in which reactor fuel pellets are encased to form fuel rods. Today, almost all light water reactors use zircalloy cladding, whereas LMFBR designs use stainless steel.

Control rods: Mechanical devices used to control the reactor's reactivity and maneuver the power level.

Conversion ratio: This ratio can be defined in a variety of ways. For example, on a point-in-time basis,
$$CR = \frac{\text{rate of formation of fissile material}}{\text{rate of consumption of fissile material}}$$
It can also be computed over the total life of the reactor, or the life of each core, as: mass of nonfissile material converted to fissile material/mass of fissile material burned or simply the ratio of fuel bred to fuel burned. A conversion ratio greater than one is referred to as the breeding ratio.

Core voiding: Loss of liquid coolant from the reactor core, generally through vaporization.

Delayed neutrons: Neutrons released after the initial fission from fission products as they undergo radioactive decay. Delayed neutrons make up 0.3% to 0.7% of the total, and are released on the average of 10 to 20 seconds after the prompt neutrons.

Design basis accident: Hypothetical accident used as a basis for designing reactor containment and engineering safeguards which must function under emergency conditions.

Doppler Coefficient: A power coefficient (see definition below) in which the input stimulus is a change in the fuel temperature. See Appendix C.

Doubling time: Time required for a reactor or reactor system to double its original inventory of fissile material.

Estimated additional resources: Uranium surmised to occur in unexplored extensions of known deposits or in undiscovered deposits in known uranium districts and which is expected to be discoverable and economically exploitable in the given price range.

MT: Metric ton—1,000 kilograms.

Mwd: Megawatt days (thermal units).

Mwe: Megawatts (electrical units).

Mw(t): Megawatts (thermal units).

Nuclear runaway or power excursion: An extremely rapid rise (to extreme peak levels) and fall in the reactor power, resulting in an explosive burst of energy before the "nuclear excursion" is terminated.

Oxide-fueled: Fueled with a mixture of PuO_2 and UO_2, often written as $(U,Pu) O_2$.

Power coefficient or reactivity coefficient: A mathematical term describing the response of the reactor—the reactivity and the power level—to certain input stimuli. If the coefficient is positive, an increase in power from any cause would be amplified by the input stimulus in question; if negative, the stimulus would tend to counter the power increase.

Power density: Power per unit volume.

Prompt critical: The condition where a reactor or fission assembly is critical due to prompt neutrons alone. The reaction rate in such an assembly increases very, very rapidly. Prompt criticality is the threshold for an explosive nuclear runaway.

Prompt criticality: See prompt critical.

Prompt neutrons: Neutrons released at the time of fission.

Proved reserves: Same as reasonably assured resources or reserves.

Reactivity: The fraction of neutrons born in a reactor which are in excess of those required to hold the neutron population constant. This reactor parameter is controlled to change the power level while avoiding a nuclear runaway. When the reactivity is zero the power level stays constant and the reactor is said to be "critical," a desired condition for normal steady fullpower operation. The reactivity is positive and the power level increases for a supercritical reactor, and the reactivity is negative and the power level decreases for a subcritical reactor. Mechanisms by which the reactivity is increased in an LMFBR accident situation include fuel compaction, control rod withdrawal and sodium coolant expulsion, or voiding from the interior of the core. Mechanisms by which reactivity is decreased include core expansion, fuel temperature rise (Doppler Effect) and control rod insertion.

Reasonably assured resources: Uranium which occurs in known ore deposits of such grade, quantity, and configuration that it can, within the given price range, be profitably recovered with currently proven mining and processing technology. Equivalent to reasonably assured reserves, proved reserves or simply reserves in the mining sense.

Rem: The unit of dose equivalent; i.e., one rem is equivalent, in biological damage of a specific sort, to one rad of X rays at a given energy. A rad is a unit of absorbed dose equal to 100 ergs per gram.

Scf: Standard cubic feet.

Separative work unit: A measure of the effort expended to separate a quantity of uranium into two components: one with a higher percentage of U-235 (the product) and one with a lower percentage (the tails).

Sodium void coefficient or simply void coefficient: A power coefficient (see definition above) in which the stimulus is the removal of liquid sodium coolant. The average sodium void coefficient over the core of a large LMFBR is generally positive.